Family Love
in the
Diaspora

METROPOLITAN COLLEGE OF NY
LIBRARY, 12TH FLOOR
431 CANAL STREET
NEW YORK, NY 10013

Memory and Narrative Series
Mary Chamberlain and Selma Leydesdorff, series editors

Trauma: Life Stories of Survivors
Kim Lacy Rogers and Selma Leydesdorff, editors
(with Graham Dawson)

Commemorating War: The Politics of Memory
Timothy G. Ashplant, Graham Dawson, and Michael Roper, editors

*Environmental Consciousness:
The Roots of a New Political Agenda*
Stephen Hussey and Paul Thompson, editors

*Memory and Memorials:
From the French Revolution to World War One*
Mathew Campbell, Jacqueline M. Labbe,
and Sally Shuttleworth, editors

*The Stasi Files Unveiled:
Guilt and Compliance in a Unified Germany*
Barbara Miller

*The Uses of Narrative:
Explorations in Sociology, Psychology, and Cultural Studies*
Molly Andrews, Shelley Day Sclater, Corinne Squire, and Amal Treacher, editors

Narrative and Genre: Contests and Types of Communication
Mary Chamberlain and Paul Thompson, editors

*The Clash of Economic Cultures:
Japanese Bankers in the City of London*
Junko Sakai

Narratives of Exile and Return
Mary Chamberlain

Family Love in the Diaspora
Mary Chamberlain

Migration and the Anglo-Caribbean Experience

Family Love in the Diaspora

Mary Chamberlain

Memory and Narrative Series

Ian Randle Publishers
Kingston (Jamaica)

Transaction Publishers
New Brunswick (U.S.A.) and London (U.K.)

Second paperback printing 2009

Copyright © 2006 by Transaction Publishers, New Brunswick, New Jersey.

First published in the United States and other parts of the world by Transaction Publishers, 35 Berrue Circle, Piscataway, NJ 08854.

First published in the Caribbean and Latin America by Ian Randle Publishers, 11 Cunningham Avenue, Box 686, Kingston 6, Jamaica.
ISBN: 976-637-266-7   www.ianrandlepublishers.com

All rights reserved under International and Pan-American Copyright Conventions. No part of this book may be reproduced or transmitted in any form or by any means, electronic or mechanical, including photocopy, recording, or any information storage and retrieval system, without prior permission in writing from the publisher. All inquiries should be addressed to Transaction Publishers, Rutgers—The State University, 35 Berrue Circle, Piscataway, New Jersey 08854-8042. www.transactionpub.com

This book is printed on acid-free paper that meets the American National Standard for Permanence of Paper for Printed Library Materials.

Library of Congress Catalog Number: 2008035581
ISBN: 978-0-7658-0307-8 (cloth); 978-1-4128-0855-2 (paper)
Printed in the United States of America

Library of Congress Cataloging-in-Publication

Chamberlain, Mary, 1947-
   Family love in the diaspora : migration and the Anglo-Caribbean experience / Mary Chamberlain.
     p. cm.
   Includes bibliographical references and index.
   ISBN 978-1-4128-0855-2 (alk. paper)
    1. Blacks--Caribbean Area--Migrations. 2. Blacks--Great Britain--Migrations. 3. Families, Black--Caribbean Area--History. 4. Families, Black--Caribbean Area--Social conditions. 5. Families, Black--Great Britain--History. 6. Families, Black--Great Britain--Social conditions. I. Title.

F2191.B55C43 2006b
306.85089'969729041--dc22

2008035581

Contents

Acknowledgments	vii
Abbreviations	xiii
Prologue	xv

Part 1: Introduction and Perspectives
1. Families and Oral History	3
2. Historical Perspectives on African-Caribbean Families	19

Part 2: Narratives of the Family
3. "Praisesongs" of the Family	45
4. Continuities and Change	63
5. Transnational Narratives and National Belongings	89

Part 3: Families through the Narratives of...
6. The Wider Household: Grandparents and Other Kin	119
7. Small Worlds: Families and Children	141
8. Brothers and Sisters, Uncles and Aunts	167

Part 4. Comparison and Conclusion
9. Indo-Caribbean Families in Britain and the Caribbean	185
10. Conclusion	213
Bibliography	225
Index	241

METROPOLITAN COLLEGE OF NY
LIBRARY, 12TH FLOOR
431 CANAL STREET
NEW YORK, NY 10013

Acknowledgments

I owe many, many people a sincere thank you for their help in this book. First, and most importantly, the members of the following Caribbean families who gave freely and generously of their time and memories to be interviewed; without them, this book would not be possible.

Rosalyn Ali, Valda Allen, Ashley, Del and Louise Alleyne, Mrs. and Silvia Andrews, Penny Anthony, Rosita Arthur, Elena, Marcia and Kevin Beckford, Vernon Benjamin, Hilda and Elfrida Bennett, Michelle Boreland, Heather and Oneta Bridge, Darrel Brown, Mr. and Mrs. and William Butcher, Jenetta Callender, Pearl Campbell, Enrique Chandler, Lemuel and Phyllis Chase, Norma Chung, Maud Colmity, Beverley Croasdale, Charles, Eddy and Samantha Cummins, Granville Dale, Mr. and Mrs. and Linda Dean, Daphne Doublin, Mr. and Mrs. Drayton, Eris Felix, Donaise and Yvette Foxe, Olive Gardner, Frank and Meg Goodman, Clove Graham, Vasel, Glen and Anne-Marie Greaves, Iris Greenidge, Mr. and Mrs. Greer, George and Mrs. Griffiths, Mr. and Mrs. and Gareth Hainsley, Jean, Patrick and Jermain Hamilton James, Hamland, Sharon and Mrs. Hanomansingh, Virginia and Cynthia Harewood, Mr. and Mrs. Dawn, Alex and Nathan Harrison, Aletta Holmes, Deltima and Leon Hutchinson, Michael Innis, Nancy Jacobs, Latisha, Flora and Frank James, Prunella and Albert and Mrs. Khalawan, Daniel, Becky and Sheila Khan, Dorothy, Elaine and Muriel King, Lilian, Jason and Carolyn Lawrence, Augustus Lewis, Frank Lindsay, Anne-Marie Lucas and Denise Lucas, Keston, Lennox and Nicki Malwah, Sheila Martindale, Audrey McCracken, Maria Odeleye, Anne King and Josie Okoko, Beverley, Joy and Clive Palmer, Claudette Patterson, Della Perez Thomas, Diane Perez Marshall, Mrs. Persaud, Lorna Phillips, Karen Powell, Monica Pryce Ross, Suresh Rambaran, Helena Ramirez, Heramti RaMraj, Myrtle Reddie, Mr. and Mark Rollock, Shirlene, Melanie, Lionel, Tyrone and Mrs. Rudder, Kwame and Margaret Sacki, Cossyle Sanders,

Hermina, Steven and Brenton Scales, Germane Selman, John Sessahi, Selina Shepherd, Ricky Singh, Damien Small, Raphael Smith, Irene Sobors, Vernon, Clifford and Vasco Stephenson, Iris and John Stewart, Mavis Stewart, Simon and Yinka Swanson, Mr. and Mrs. Thompson, Leroy and Lisa Tyrell, Campbell Vaughan, Barbara White, Anna Lea, Arnold, Arthur, Clovis and Donald Williams, Frank and Noel Wilson, Mavis Wisdom, and Princess Yard.

Second, I would like to acknowledge the support of the ESRC whose initial grant to Harry Goulbourne and myself for Living Arrangements, Family Structure and Social Change of Caribbeans in Britain (Award number L315253009), within the ESRC Research Programme on Household and Population Change (under the directorship of Professor Susan McRae) enabled the research to be carried out. In this, particular thanks are due to Dr. Dwaine Plaza, our research fellow, who carried out the interviews in Britain, Jamaica and Barbados. His charm, good humour and intelligence contributed in no small measure to his skills and success, and he was always a pleasure to have as a member of the School of Humanities at Oxford Brookes University. Considerable thanks must be given to Dr. David Owen, also part of the original research team, who willingly and unfailingly provided us with statistical data, and drew for us a range of profiles of Caribbeans and Caribbean families in Britain and the Caribbean. His work provided the framework for this research. Special thanks are also due to Harry Goulbourne for his contribution to running the project, organizing its seminars and co-writing the final report, submitted to the ESRC in 1998. Our coedited book (Harry Goulbourne and Mary Chamberlain, *Caribbean Families in Britain and the Transatlantic World*, 2001) contains some of our findings from the research. A full list of publications arising from the research can be found on the ESRC/Regard website (www.esrc.ac.uk/regard).

This book is the result of revisiting this original data and represents a way of continuing the interpretation beyond the initial conclusions of the final report. It is, however, my work rather than a collaborative effort by the research team, and they have had no authorial input into it. I would like to acknowledge the AHRB, which awarded me research leave to complete this book, Oxford Brookes University, which provided me with matching leave, and the School of Arts and Humanities at Oxford Brookes, for a further term's research leave. Without this time, I would not have been able to complete the book.

I also owe a huge debt of gratitude to Constance Sutton and Kate Hodgkin, who took the time to read the completed manuscript and to comment with wisdom, insight, and generosity, and to Irving Horowitz at Transaction Publishers, for his very helpful and astute editorial advice and assistance.

I took on board many of their comments and criticisms but they are in no way responsible for any of the book's failings and shortcomings. I would like to give especial thanks to Constance Sutton, who has been a guide, mentor, and inspiration for many of my ideas on Caribbean families and on the Caribbean, and has been a very special friend for some years now. It is always a pleasure to be with her. Kate Hodgkin, at short notice, similarly excelled way beyond the call of duty and provided a very thorough and thoughtful reading of the manuscript, before recommending it for the Memory and Narrative series. I am enormously grateful to her. Similarly, Selma Leydesdorff provided valuable editorial as well as administrative input in the final submission of the manuscript. I would also like to thank Paul Thompson for his support and intellectual stimulation over the thirty three years of friendship and collaboration.

This book has been a long time gestating, from the initial research carried out between 1995 and 1998. In the course of the original project, and subsequently, versions of some of the chapters have been presented as research papers or talks at: Fourth International Metropolis Conference, Georgetown University; Oxford Brookes University; Elsa Goveia Memorial Lecture, University of the West Indies, Barbados; "*Narrating Selves and Others: Feminist Theory in Practice*" University of Antwerp/University of Nijmegen; the Commonwealth History Seminar, University of Oxford; the Race, Culture and Society Seminar, University of Oxford; the Social Science seminar at the University of Swansea; the Centre for Caribbean Studies, University of Warwick; the Autobiography and the Social Self seminar at the University of Lancaster; "*Uncertain Directions in a Fluid Society: Evaluating Social Mobility towards 2000,*" University of Essex; the ESRC Research Group for the Study of Care, Values and the Future of Welfare, University of Leeds; the Max Planck Institute for Demographic Research, Rostock; Les migrations caraïbéennes vers les métropoles: identité, citoyenneté, modèles d'intégration. Colloque à la Maison des Sciences de l'Homme, Paris; the European Social Science History Conference, The Hague, Netherlands; the Annual Conference of the Association of Caribbean Historians, in Trinidad and Barbados; the Narratives of Belonging Conference, University of London, Goldsmiths College; the Caribbean Diaspora Conference, South Bank University; the ESRC Household and Population Change End of Programme Conference, London; International Conference on Caribbean Families in the Atlantic World, Cheltenham & Gloucester CHE; and the Society for Caribbean Studies Conference, University of Hull. Colleagues at every venue provided invaluable comments and criticisms and I am enormously grateful to them for this. As a result, some early versions of a number of chapters have appeared in the following journals and edited collections. Part of chapter three appeared as "*Praise Songs of the Family: Lineage and Kinship in the Caribbean Diaspora*" in History Workshop 50 (2000); a version of chapter five was published as "*Language, Identity and Caribbean Families: Transnational Narratives*" in Jean Besson and Karen Fog Olwig (eds.) Narratives of Belonging (2004); an early version of part of chapter six appeared as "*Re-Thinking Caribbean Families: Extending the Links*" in Community, Work and Family, 6:1 (2003); similarly, some of the material from chapter seven was published as "*Small Worlds: Children and Empire*" in the Journal of Family History, 27:2 (2002). Finally, an early version of chapter eight, "*Brothers and Sisters, Uncles and Aunts*" was published in Elizabeth Silva and Carol Smart, The New Family? (1998). Jean Besson, Anna Davin, Ramon Grosfoguel, Selma Leydesdorff, Karen Fog Olwig, Stein Ringen, and Paul Thompson were among those who commented on these earlier versions, providing useful advice and criticism, which was much appreciated. Many thanks are due to them and to Rob Pope for his useful insights into narrative.

There are also many other people whose friendship, over many years, has been central to my life and to the intellectual climate in which it has been lived and who have, wittingly and unwittingly, contributed to the making of this book. I would therefore like to thank Sally Alexander, Alissandra Cummins, Anna Davin, Catherine and Stuart Hall, Gad Heuman, Keith Laurence, Selma Leydesdorff, Woodville Marshall, Connie Sutton, Bill Schwarz and Paul Thompson (and their respective partners), and many others with whom I have spent some memorable days and evenings. Special thanks are also due to Alissandra Cummins and Keith Laurence, for their wonderful hospitality when I have stayed with them in Barbados and Trinidad, respectively, conducting research, and to Rajni Ramlakan, who helped me to navigate my way round Trinidad while conducting interviews for the project, and who introduced me to some memorable roadside food.

Finally, I would like to thank my family for unquestioning love and support, my daughters Rosie, Kate, and Alice, my husband Stein, who transformed my life in the course of this project, and my little grandson Aaron, and new granddaughter Lola who just make me want to laugh. They all bring joy into my life and I am proud of them all.

Abbreviations

CO: Colonial Office papers, National Archive, London

BDA: Barbados, Department of Archives

For abbreviations in the notes that refer to interview tapes and transcripts, see the bibliography, under primary resources—interviews.

Prologue

The following obituaries appeared in the *Sun* (Barbados) in May 2004. Typical of their genre, and as an illustration of family and kinship, only the names, places, and work venues have been changed.

SCANTLEBURY—Ethel Eudine, aged 90 years, late of Easy Hall, St. John. Wife of the late John "Alsa" Scantlebury; mother of Randolph Toppin and Ophelia Clarke (USA), Seymour Scantlebury and Heather Gollop (of UK), Elinda Scantlebury (of Saudi Arabia), Byron and Orrendelle Scantlebury (of Canada), Richard Scantlebury, Leroy Scantlebury (of Health Ministry), Venilla Callender (of Data Processing Department), Cirleine Scantlebury and the late Everton Toppin; grandmother of Richard Toppin, Delcina Kellman, Dr. Decourtney Scantlebury (World Renowned Pianist), Merton King and Doriel Scantlebury (of UWI), Celestine Kellman and 27 others; great grandmother of 51; sister of Vernita Wiltshire (of Ruby, St. Philip), Eureta Goddard (of Easy Hall, St. John), Errol, Kirkland, Dorothy and Mervene Beckles (of USA), the late Joseph Belgrave, Violet Edgehill, Cynthia Greaves and Wesley Grant; aunt of Ulric Spooner, Herman Spencer and Carlyle Sobers; relative of the Toppin, Kellman, Spencer and Sobers families; friend of the many…

Ivy Adelle Jordan—Aged 85, affectionately called "Ta" of Parish Land, St. Philip, and formerly of Boston, Mass. USA, was called to her Maker on Wednesday, May 19, 2004. Adored mother of Jacqueline Griffith, Loleta and Raymond Jordan, Owen Jordan (Probation Department), James Jordan (UK), Morris, Olvin, Monica, Celia, Roy and Ruby Jordan (all of USA); cherished sister of Roy Large (UK). Dear grandmother of Hermina Jordan-Kennedy, Rosalind, Karen and Linda Jordan (all of USA), Hugh and Hudson Jordan (both of UK), Marion Burke, Pastor Selwyn Jordan (Church of God in Christ, Haggatt Hall, St. Michael), Sherley, Marjorie Dahlia, Othneil and Sonia Jordan and many others too numerous to mention; Friend of Reneta Williams and many others.

Part 1

Introduction and Perspectives

1
Families and Oral History

"Over the inner thoughts of the slaves and their relations one with another the shadow of fear ever hung, so that we get glimpses here and there, and also with them, eloquent omissions and silences. Mother and child are sung, but seldom father; fugitive and weary wanderer call for pity and affection, but there is little of wooing and the wedding; the rocks and the mountains are well known, but home is unknown."[1]

Shaped by slavery, dispersed through migration, African-Caribbean families have long confused church and civil authorities and figured as the scapegoat for social ills in the Caribbean and its diaspora. DuBois' haunting words introduce these essays on African-Caribbean families that attempt to rethink the meanings and forms that such families have assumed for family members in the Caribbean and Britain.

The book is based on life story interviews across three generations of forty-five families who originated in the former British West Indies,[2] centering on the axes of Caribbean peoples to Britain from the former British colonies of Jamaica, Trinidad and Tobago, and Barbados. The mechanisms and success of the incorporation of African-Caribbean peoples into their "host" societies has depended on the reception climate and environment,[3] and has played out differently in Europe and North America. In terms of family life, however, the experience of Anglophone African-Caribbean families in Britain echoes that of Canada and the United States, and shares similarities with other African-Caribbean families in the Francophone and Dutch Caribbean and in their diasporas in France and the Netherlands.[4] The focus of this book, on the Anglophone Caribbean, may be narrow and British, but the resonances, like the families themselves, are broad and global.

***

The predominant belief that guided colonial social policy in the British West Indies throughout the nineteenth and into the twentieth century assumed that black families lacked morals, structure, and men, a void that could explain poverty and lack of citizenship. African-Caribbean families appeared as the mirror opposite of the "ideal" family advocated by the white, colonial authorities.[5] Varieties of conjugal unions, high illegitimacy rates, female-headed households, female employment, child fostering, and an inclusive embrace of all kin (and fictive kin) as family members stood in marked contrast to the (apparently) stable unions of Christian marriages, predicated on the autonomy and exclusiveness of family life, on the subservience of women and children to the authority of the male, and on the prominence given to the male line in inheritance and family identification. African-Caribbean families, and Caribbean family life, were marked out as abnormal and, as R. T. Smith observed, "elaborate theories have been developed to explain why the nuclear family [in the Caribbean] should exist and what forces have inhibited its proper development. Most of these theories assumed that the lower classes have 'deviant' families and then attempt to explain why."[6]

As we shall see in chapter two the notion of deviancy has a long pedigree, inextricably caught up in the prejudices of slave society, the prescriptions of colonial rule, and the presumptions of an academic community that long attributed cultural absence and social negativity to observations and analyses of African-Caribbean families. Migration to Britain provided it with a new twist by catapulting the "traditional" Caribbean family into the divisive and disruptive modern, Western world in which—unlike other "traditional" communities—there were no customs or cultures on which to draw and from which to derive strength and sustenance. Despite some sensitive work by Driver and Barrow[7] that indicated the vitality of families and the strength of culture on family life through migration, it was widely (and authoritatively) assumed that African-Caribbean families were deficient. "It is no cause for surprise," observed Lord Scarman, in his report on the Brixton riots of 1981, "that the impact of British social conditions on the matriarchal extended family structure of the West Indian immigrants has proved to be severe. Mothers, who in the West Indies formed the focus of family, became in many cases wage earners who were absent from the family home."[8]

The 1991 U.K. census data highlighted what appeared to be this deviation by the African-Caribbean community from the "British" norm, revealing in particular high levels of single-parent mother-headed households. It was assumed that this was evidence of a breakdown in the transmission of family values and authority between the generations, aggravated (in one view) by undue influences from the more libertarian sectors of the white community toward single parenthood and state dependency.[9] Far from West Indians becoming "like us," as the early race relations ethic wished and assumed, African-Caribbean peoples in Britain had refused to conform to the categories set by politicians or academics. African-Caribbean families had "broken down" in the course of their sojourn in Britain. "The shocking truth about the breakdown of black family life in Britain can be revealed today." So ran a lead story by the journalist Jon Salmon in the *Sunday Express* in 1995:

> Research shows that among the West Indian community the sanctity of the family is in "meltdown." Latest unpublished Government Statistics obtained by the *Sunday Express* reveal that almost six in ten black mothers are bringing up children on their own, urged on by our benefits system. ...In the black community the traditional family is collapsing at a faster rate than among any other group, costing the State at least £130 million a year.[10]

***

These essays take a different perspective. They are an oral history of migrant African-Caribbean families, presenting the varieties, organization and dynamics of family life through the memories and narratives of three or more generations of family members in the Caribbean and the United Kingdom. They tell a very different story, and one rarely recorded through the words of the participants. It is a story of survival and resistance, of solidarity and reciprocity. It is a story of emotional attachments and family support that extends vertically through lineages, horizontally through kinship networks, and transnationally across the oceans. Above all, it is a story of families that evolved, against the odds of slavery and poverty, to form a distinct creole form,[11] through which much of the social history of the English-speaking Caribbean is refracted.

Contemporary patterns of marriage and family life emerged during slavery, as Barry Higman[12] has shown and, developing *in opposition* to slavery, evolved into a recognizable creole marriage system, drawing on both African and European values and practices. Far from representing an inchoate social system, the extensiveness and inclusiveness of African-Caribbean families is one of the major drivers of Caribbean social organization. The complex structures that characterize Caribbean creole families are based on a communitarian philosophy of society, in which lineage and kinship are foregrounded as structuring practices, through and in which the individual and his/her sense of self is inextricably bound. Social organization was premised on metaphors of family and models of family life in the Caribbean and its diaspora, and contributed toward defining a sense of identity and nationhood.

Overt acknowledgment of the importance of families in the structuring of West Indian society and nationhood has, for the most part, been slow and reluctant. Its first articulation can be traced to the aftermath of the 1937 riots in the West Indies. While those riots drew official attention to the poverty of the region, and to the families who lived within it, they also crystallized demands for change, converting the postemancipation quest for freedom into recognition that emancipation could not be achieved without political self determination and independence. In the process, they heralded a new confidence not only in the idea and development of nation, but in Caribbean culture and society.

Until then, West Indians had lived within a dual perspective: a sanitized sanctioned perception of colonies blessed to be under the benign rule of Britain, and her superior governance, culture, and social organization, and an unofficial, unsanctioned perception that British rule in practice meant poverty, hardship, and discrimination, and a denigration of the culture, social organization and family life of the region. The 1937 riots provided permission—in the Halbwachian sense[13]—to think and articulate this duality, and to begin to acknowledge, and later valorize, in literature and poetry, the families, village life, communitarian values, culture, and popular culture of the vast majority of black West Indians. As the Barbadian novelist and writer, George Lamming, whose novel *In the Castle of My Skin* was one of the first to celebrate families as the mainstay of Barbadian life, explained:

> It is not often recognized that the major thrust of Caribbean literature in English rose from the soil of labor resistance in the 1930s. The expansion of social justice initiated by the labor struggle had a direct effect on liberating the imagination and restoring the confidence of men and women in the essential humanity of their simple lives. In the cultural history of the region, there is a direct connection between labor and literature.[14]

The sense of pride with which West Indians recalled their childhoods and the family and neighborhoods that structured them, and the sense of achievement with which West Indians described their extensive family networks, often dispersed through migration, may be seen as bedrocks of social pride, and a confident assertion of social relations. That many of these recollections were located and filtered through the struggles for independence from the 1920s to the 1960s is important, for their articulation was an affirmation and celebration of difference, an alternative and, sometimes, subversive worldview. They thus became a contributory element in the creation of West Indian nationhood and remain key to contemporary identities in the diaspora.

The centrality of families to the social history of the Caribbean is argued in the following chapters. The paucity of conventional sources on family history means that life stories and oral histories have become an important source, as well as offering the possibility of observing families from the inside. What people say about their lives and life choices provides rich empirical data into the hidden and sometimes secret histories of those disenfranchised from the historical record by class, race or gender. In addition, it can provide not only what Clifford Geertz described as "thick description"[15] but also insights into the structures, realities and mentalities that shape the past and the present.[16] As a first port of call, therefore, life stories can offer the everyday detail of material life and the social relationships that underpin and weave through it. They offer insights into the imaginative structures that provide it with coherence and relevance[17] and into the sensibilities and subjectivities of the narrator.

The emphasis on structuralism and positivism, at least in the second half of the twentieth century, has tended to demote the personal account as statistically irrelevant and objectively unverifiable even though, paradoxically, such demotion goes against the grain of what should constitute sociology: an interest in the subject and his/her relation to society and its history, the "varieties of individuality" and "the modes of epochal change."[18] More recently, however, there has been a revival of interest in the personal account, as Ken Plummer suggests in his powerful plea for the value of life stories as the means of:

> getting close to living human beings, accurately yet imaginatively picking up the way they express their understandings of the world around them, perhaps providing an analysis of such expressions, presenting them in interesting ways, and being self-critically aware of the immense difficulties such tasks bring.[19]

Although critics of qualitative methods may doubt the veracity of a single account, or the ability of a (relatively) numerically small sample to exemplify larger group behavior (for qualitative methods lack what Lévi-Strauss termed the "anonymity of numbers"),[20] a qualitative approach to a subject as complex and as intimate as the family can exemplify its beliefs, mores, and activities. Moreover, the value of a qualitative approach lies in its choice of informants as articulators of the group, not as representative of a statistical norm. The critical question is not therefore statistical but, as Ron Grele observed, sociological or historical—who defines the "group" under scrutiny.[21]

In terms of family and household, life stories may reveal detail on membership, organization, functions, and on change within the life cycle or course of the individual and of the family. Where one is situated within the life cycle will inflect views on youth, or old age, or child-rearing, and on the family in general, and thus life stories can remind us of the movement and flexibility within families, and lead away from an essentialist position on all families (and *the* Caribbean family in particular). It can also provide information from perspectives often ignored or undocumented—of children, for instance, or the elderly, or reveal emotions or feelings, or uncover the inner dynamics of family life, particularly when two or more generations of the same family are interviewed. Above all, it can hint at the meanings that families and family practices have for their members, and the intimate worlds that these meanings inhabit, articulate, and replicate. It is this latter point that these essays seek most to illustrate.

The use of life story methods, premised as they are on memory, individuality, and subjectivity, raises both epistemological and ontological questions. We take the concept of "life story" as a given, but it relies on a very particular concept of the self rooted in Western modernity, in which, as Anthony Giddens put it, "the self ...[is]...reflexively understood by the person in terms of his or her biography."[22] There has been a considerable interest recently in the relationship between identity and biography, and its development in the West.[23] The large and highly sophisticated literature in both the humanities and the social and behavioral sciences theorizes on the formations, and representations, of the self. These representations may themselves be informed by narrative conventions without which no memory would be possible and no story could be understood,[24] though the emphasis given to narrative convention differs between disciplines.

This, however, presupposes the universality of what Adriana Cavarera calls the "narratable self."[25] Indeed, the quest of modernity (as reflected in the European Romantic tradition) has been to elevate the individual, and to identify the self with, or in terms of, memory, such that Cavarero, for instance, can argue that

> we are all familiar with the narrative work of memory, which, in a totally involuntary way, continues to tell us our own personal story. Every human being...is aware of being a *narratable self* - immersed in the spontaneous auto-narration of memory...the narratable self is at once the transcendental subject and the elusive object of all the autobiographical exercises of memory.[26]

But who is an individual, a self, is by no means universally understood, any more than the rhetorical devices of stories or narratives are universally recognized, or necessarily linear. Thus, who is recalling may have a very different sense of self, may be remembering from a different epistemological base, through different narrative conventions, and different narrative functions. They may, in other words, be fashioning themselves according to a different cultural dynamic. Interviewing—particularly cross culturally—demands, therefore, sensitivity and an awareness that the interview itself may be imposing a pattern and a practice alien to the informant's own.[27]

In the narratives of the African-Caribbean, two features stand out that suggest a very different epistemological base. First, the language of self conveys different concepts and approaches. The sense of self conveyed in African-Caribbean life stories is one in which, on the one hand, descent and rebirth consistently blur the boundaries of selfhood ("I am a grandmother child," "I am from my mother") and, on the other, an intrinsic existentialism, epitomized by phrases such as "when I first knew myself coming up" and "when I born and I got the sense." The concept of self, and its narration, and the concept of biography may have different meanings and purposes in which some identification with the group and ancestry takes precedence over the metaphysics of the self. This may well be one element that can be traced to an African philosophy and ancestry.[28] Orlando Patterson, suggesting the vibrancy of African traditions in Caribbean slave culture, and citing Radcliffe Brown, points out that "[t]here is a widespread custom of privileged familiarity between grandparents and grandchildren" in Africa based on the "structural principle" that "one generation is replaced in the course of time by the generation of their grand*parent*."[29]

The implications of this on individual memory are significant. In many ways, all memories extend beyond the individual, as personal memories necessarily incorporate the retold memories of others—of themselves, of other family members, and of friends and acquaintances. Public and official memories similarly become absorbed into the personal repertoire, not always voluntarily, or with beneficial effects.[30] Equally, as already suggested, how memories are framed and articulated is structured by the range of narratives and genres available, which will vary from culture to culture, faith to faith, ritual to ritual.[31] Examining memories in relation to these narrative structures and genres may, therefore, reveal more than the "purely" personal and open ways in which culture not only makes possible the articulation of memory, but (in some cases of pain and trauma) its soothing and resolution or, conversely, its celebration of shared values. Equally, memories of individuals may be recounted in terms of prototypical behavior, which may function as both an individual and collective biography: one individual may stand as the embodiment of all.[32]

While oral history and life stories are well-established research tools, their use in exploring *family* histories is less well known. Interviewing across generations made it possible to build a profile of family life and behavior that, in some cases, extended beyond three generations. Family groups, however, form a unique sub-culture in which, in many cases, a family ethos or dynamic can be detected. Such an ethos could account for behavior patterns repeated over generations, for values reinforced over generations, and for the language or descriptors employed by family members over generations.[33]

Families, obviously, cannot be isolated from their environment. No life story can be told without reference to the broader milieu as it interacts with the individual and the family—through work, play and education, health, death, and consumption, and a host of other major and minor interventions. The meanings ascribed to the roles that family members perform, the definitions of family, and the expectations derived from that are embedded in society and culture. Life stories can, therefore, reveal the specificities of social and cultural practice, and guard against assuming that one model of social or cultural organization can (or should) explain all. Families are not merely the stage upon which dramas of class, race, or gender are played out. They are also conduits for the wider community, reflecting and endorsing (and sometimes, of course, rejecting) dominant values and norms. Families may endorse local values; they may also be used as a point of resistance against other, imposed values, such as those of a colonial authority or, more recently, the "host" society of migrant populations. Indeed, in any local enquiry (of which the individual life story is the most localized) there is always an element of a wider world, and in the case of the Caribbean a very wide world indeed. The transnational dimension of African-Caribbean families, both historically (for African-Caribbean families are above all creolised families, interculturated with and by a range of global influences) and contemporaneously, reveals insights on the global *gestalt* of the family, on the economic and emotional strategies for family survival that were sometimes played out across a very large geographic area. The informational content of life stories may provide detail on a global canvas, and on the continuing dialogue between the two.

Interviewing across generations made it possible to build a profile of family life and behaviour that, in some cases, extended beyond three generations. In addition, by asking the oldest generation about their parents and grandparents, the family memory was extended across time and expanded across five (or more) generations. Again, the longevity of the collective family memory was able to provide considerable information and detail, and to offer the possibility of comparison across time within and between families. Thus transgenerational life stories enabled the investigation of family organization and living arrangements and the suggestion of family models that were transmitted, or transformed by settlement and regeneration in Britain and elsewhere. At the same time, the emphasis on family history and traditions enabled exploration of the migration experiences of previous generations, the assessment of the relationship between the two, and its influence on household adaptation, and the examination of the factors that had an impact on re- and return migration, and the influence on family members in the Caribbean and those left in Britain.

Generational transmission implies—indeed, privileges—a hierarchy of, at the very least, age and a linear process whereby the young inherit from the old. But the old often modify their behavior, attitudes, and expectations in the light of the pressures from, or experiences of, young people. Indeed, in terms of Caribbean families in Britain, it was precisely the experiences of their young people in the schools and on the streets that led many of their parents to revise their views on the British educational system, the police, and other authority figures. Similarly, the influence of siblings, peers, and other family members in forming the personality is an important element in family life and any study of family life must therefore take into account the multiplicity of relationships and perspectives.

Families are located not only within specific social circumstances, but also in historical periods, both in Britain and the Caribbean. While the chronology may coincide, the historical watersheds and what Raymond Williams describes as the "structure of feeling"[34] may be very different between the Caribbean and Britain. Necessarily, therefore, the nature of memory itself needs to be considered in the analysis of life stories. While the interview is in essence a dialogue between the interviewer and interviewee, it also contains a dialogue between the past and the present. The process of remembering is a dialectical process, incorporating current questions and preoccupations, as well as the act of remembering, into the memory. It is laced with the hopes, dreams, and regrets from the past that entangle themselves with current recollection, leading sometimes to forgetting, denial, and even fabulation. The fact that people do remember, and remember differently at different times in their lives and in different contexts, highlights the complexity of meaning and the transformations that take place in interpretation and reconciliation. Above all, it suggests that memory itself has a history, and that that history can provide a clue to how an individual sees him- or her- (or them-) self(ves), and forms an identity.[35]

For migrant communities this becomes particularly complex, tied up with space—with concepts of home and belonging—as well as time. Where home is, one's relationship to it, where one belongs necessarily changes over the life cycle and in the case of migrants their relationship to the "home" of their origin is constantly changing—receding or advancing—according to the number of visits, the number of family who remain (alive), the contact kept, the practicality of return, the dream of return, the pull of children elsewhere. In that sense, home itself changes and may never, in reality, be "there," except in memory or the imagination. The children of migrants may also inherit a spatial dimension to their memory, or fabricate one to supplement an identity. In the case of the English-speaking Caribbean, that the major migrations to Britain took place at a time of decolonization when the historical watersheds of the Caribbean were often at variance with those of Britain, injected a political dimension into family memories, a priority to establish and reinforce the special qualities that defined and contextualized family life in the Caribbean.

***

The focus here, then, is on a range of relationships conveyed through the narratives of the informants, narratives that weave in and out of historical moments. Reclaiming the link between citizenship and family, they show how one element in the development of twentieth century Caribbean national confidence was early socialization into the fundamental, but thoroughly creolized, institution of the family. They also dissect the family into its constituent relationships, arguing that family dynamics and a family ethos are transmitted and transformed across the generations, permitting social change and adaptation, as well as continuities, and that the replications and repetitions of family memory within and across families, and the language used to articulate them, encode prescriptions for ideal behaviour and "living good."

The book is structured along these lines. Chapter 2 provides a historical profile of African-Caribbean families, tracing their formations and influences, in tandem with the commentaries of contemporaries and colonial authorities. Part 2, "Narratives of the Family," examines the language used by families to describe themselves and offer clues into their dynamics and priorities. Thus chapter 3 looks at the languages of repetitions in accounts of childhood and the self, and argues that repetitions can be analyzed through the imaginative structures or cultural templates that have informed them, revealing, in the process, the social priorities, values, and influences embedded within. Chapter 4 introduces three case studies of African-Caribbean families and shows how difficult it is to generalize or typologize family life, for all three families display, at different times, evidence of the complexity of cultural influences that have contributed to the evolution of family life in the Caribbean and abroad. Chapter 5 continues the analysis by examining the languages used by families in their accounts of relations with family members dispersed around the world arguing, again, that repetitions in these accounts encode family values that have sustained kinship ties across generations and oceans.

Part 3 moves the focus away from the languages and narratives of family, to look at family life across the generations through the lens of family members. It is a lens that highlights the importance of consanguineal, rather than conjugal, links to African-Caribbean families, which proved so crucial to nineteenth- and twentieth-century migration. Chapter 6, therefore, looks at the role of grandparents and other foster or surrogate parents in the rearing of children in the Caribbean. While grandmothers are usually identified as key in fostering, the chapter also points to the importance of grandfathers, and the role played by the paternal family in the support of children. Chapter 7 examines families through the eyes of children and their childhoods. It suggests that social attitudes to children can be read as barometers of values and social progress; thus the communal care of children as experienced in the rural Caribbean was premised on values of mutual respect. Nevertheless, there was potential for slippage between values and practices, particularly in the cases of children separated from their parents as a result of migration. Chapter 8 looks at family life through siblings—brothers and sisters, uncles and aunts. Despite the profound influence siblings have on the development of the personality, and in family dynamics, studies of siblings in the sociology or history of families are relatively rare. Yet in migrant families in particular, siblings play a central and continuing role in the support and nurture of family members.

While chapters 3 to 8 explore the contemporary dynamics of African-Caribbean families at home and abroad, Part 4 introduces some comparison and conclusions. Chapter 9 looks at Indo-Caribbean families, and suggests ways in which these families have also been part of the creolization process of the Caribbean. While in many ways very different from their African-Caribbean counterparts, nevertheless their evolution, like their histories, shares certain characteristics. Chapter 10 concludes by returning to the original theme of dysfunctionality by looking at some of the contemporary anxieties in Britain (and elsewhere) relating to African-Caribbean families and, in particular, to the profiles of its young, male members.

***

The peculiarity of the Caribbean, the singularity of African-Caribbean families, and the consistency of the criticism toward them, makes it impossible to disentangle commentary from historical context. Attitudes first formulated under the regime of slavery continue to echo to the present. As a result, as Constance Sutton has stated.

> As a result, as the anthropologist Constance Sutton has stated, There is no other ethnic group I know of whose family culture has so consistently been regarded as problematic by the state and formal religions; whose family life is seen as the source of the problems they confront. It is amazing when one steps back and think about this. African-Caribbean family forms, which some view as embedded in pre-modern cultural traditions that possess their own logic, are considered different and difficult to integrate into "modernizing' projects."[36]

These essays are an attempt, therefore, to unravel some of the cultural and historical logic that drives Caribbean families at home and abroad.

Notes

1. W.E.B. Dubois, *The Souls of Black Folks* (New York: Signet 1995 [1903]), 272.
2. Data collected during earlier research on Caribbean families in Britain that used a quota sample of three generations of forty-five families who originated in Jamaica, Barbados, Trinidad, and Tobago, but who had settled or lived in the United Kingdom. Harry Goulbourne and Mary Chamberlain, *Living Arrangements, Family Structure and Social Change of Caribbeans in Britain,* funded by the ESRC (L315253009. Final Report 1998). A "snowball" technique was used to fill the quota and ensure that it was representative of gender, class, age, and (particularly for Trinidad) race. In the Caribbean, the parents (or parent-substitute) of the UK based informants were interviewed. An open-ended interview guide was used, which was broadly the same for all generations, thus ensuring common parameters for comparison and correlation. The guide followed the life cycle of the informants, and the life cycle of the family, and included questions on parents, grandparents, siblings, kin and other family, childhood, education, neighbourhood, employment, migration, racism, discrimination, housing, children, and grandchildren. Informants were also asked questions on family lineage and were invited to reflect on such issues as the "ideal" family, on hopes, aspirations, regrets and identity. In this way, the research was able to investigate family models and dynamics, the nature and process of family development, and the transmission and transformation of family values over time, to look at migration from both ends of the generational spectrum, and to explore emotional and social adjustments. The interviews were conducted by Dr. Dwaine Plaza, the research fellow on the project, with the exception of interviews in Trinidad conducted by Mary Chamberlain.
3. Ramon Grosfoguel, "Modes of Incorporation: Colonial Caribbean Migrants in Western Europe and the United States" in *Caribbean Migration. Globalised Identities*, ed. Mary Chamberlain (London: Routledge, 1998); Nancy Foner, "Towards a Comparative Perspective on Caribbean Migration" in *Caribbean Migration. Globalised Identities* (1998).
4. For the Francophone Caribbean see Yves Charbit, *Famille et Nuptialité dans la Caraïbe* (Paris: Institut National d'Études Démographiques. Presses Universitaires de France, 1987); for Haiti, Nina Glick Schiller and Georges Fouron, *Georges Woke Up Laughing: Long Distance Nationalism and the Search for Home* (Durham: Duke University Press, 2001); for the Netherlands, Helma Lutz, "The Legacy of Migration: Immigrant Mothers and Daughters and the Process of Intergenerational Transmission" in *Caribbean Migration. Globalised Identiites*, ed. Mary Chamberlain (London: Routledge, 1998).

5. Jean Besson, *Martha Brae's Two Histories. European Expansion and Caribbean Culture-Building in Jamaica* (Chapel Hill and London: University of North Carolina Press 2002).
6. R. T. Smith, *Kinship and Class in the West Indies. A Genealogical Study of Jamaica and Guyana* (Cambridge: Cambridge University Press, 1988), 4.
7. G. Driver, "West Indian Families: An Anthropological Perspective" in *Families in Britain*, eds. R. N. Rapoport, M. P. Fogarty, and R. Rapoport, (London: Routledge and Kegan Paul, 1982); Jocelyn Barrow, "West Indian Families: An Insider's Perspective" in *Families in Britain* (1982).
8. *Lord Scarman's Report on the Brixton Disorders* Command 8427, 1981. Scarman continued: "Some idea of the destructive changes wrought in family lives by their new circumstances can be got from a few statistics. The percentage of children in care and of single-parent families in the black community is noticeably higher than one would expect in relation to the proportion of black people in the community as a whole. Fifty per cent of single-parent families in the Borough of Lambeth in 1978 were non-white. The two wards where the April disorders were centred—Tulse Hill and Herne Hill—contain some 22 percent of all the single-parent households in Lambeth and 2.1 per cent of the 0-18 age group in those wards are in care. Of the 185 children in care in those two wards on 10 September 1980, 112 (61 percent) were black." Research shows, however, that black children are more likely to be taken into care earlier than their white counterparts, and to remain there longer. See Ravinda Barn, "Caribbean Families and the Child Welfare System in Britain" in *Caribbean Families in Britain and the Atlantic World*, eds. Harry Goulbourne and Mary Chamberlain (London: Macmillan, 2001).
9. Geoffrey Dench, *From Extended Family to State Dependency* (London: Middlesex University CCS, 1992); Geoffrey Dench, *The Place of Men in Changing Family Cultures* (London: Institute of Community Studies, 1996).
10. Sunday Express, 13 August 1995,1.
11. There is debate about the nature of "creole" but a broad consensus suggests that it refers to the cultures and societies that evolved in the Caribbean and former Spanish and French regions of the United States. For the West Indies see Edward Kamau Brathwaite, *The Development of Creole Society in Jamaica 1770-1820* (Oxford: Clarendon Press, 1971); Fernando Ortiz, *Cuban Counterpoint. Tobacco and Sugar* (Durham and London: Duke University Press, 1995 [1940]); Verene A. Shepherd and Glen L. Richards, *Questioning Creole. Creolisation Discourses in Caribbean Culture* (Kingston: Ian Randle Publishers, Oxford: James Currey Publishers, 2002).
12. Barry Higman, *Slave Population and Economy in Jamaica 1807-1834* (Cambridge: Cambridge University Press 1976); Barry Higman *Slave Populations of the British Caribbean 1807-1834* (Kingston: The Press, The University of the West Indies 1995 [1984]).
13. Maurice Halbwachs, *On Collective Memory* (New York: Harper and Row, 1980).
14. George Lamming, cited in Glyne Griffith, "Deconstructing Nationalism: Henry Swanzy, Caribbean Voices and the Development of West Indian Literature," *Small Axe* 10 (2001).
15. Clifford Geertz, *The Interpretation of Cultures* (New York: Basic Books, 1973), 5.
16. See John and Jean Comaroff, *Ethnography and the Historical Imagination* (Boulder: Westview Press, 1992).
17. Alissandro Portelli, "What Makes Oral History Different?" in *The Oral History Reader*, ed. R. Perks and A. Thomson (London: Routledge 1998).

18. C. Wright Mills, *The Sociological Imagination* (Harmondsworth: Penguin 1970 [1959]), 247.
19. Ken Plummer *Documents of Life 2* (London: Sage, 2001), 2.
20. Claude Lévi-Strauss, *Structural Anthropology* (London: Allen Lane, 1968 [1963]).
21. Ron Grele, *Envelopes of Sound: The Art of Oral History* (Chicago: Precedent Publishing, 1985).
22. Anthony Giddens, *Modernity and Self-Identity. Self and Society in the Late Modern Age* (Cambridge: Polity Press 1991), 52.
23. See Prue Chamberlayne, Joanna Bornat, and Tom Wengraf, *The Turn to Biographical Methods in Social Science* (London: Routledge, 2000).
24. Anthony Giddens, *Modernity and Self-Identity*; Adriana Cavarero, *Relating Narratives* (London: Routledge 2000); Tess Cosslett, Celia Lury, Penny Summerfield (eds.), *Feminism and Autobiography* (London: Routledge, 2000), Ken Plummer *Documents of Life 2*. Marie-Françoise Chanfrault-Duchet, 2000, "Textualisation of the Self and Gender Identity in the Life Story" in *Feminism and Autobioghraphy;* Maurice Halbwachs, *On Collective Memory* (New York: Harper and Row, 1980).
25. Adriana Cavarero, *Relating Narratives.*
26. Cavarero *Relating*, 33-34. See also Carolyn Steedman, "Enforced Narratives: Stories of Another Self" in Cosslett et al., *Feminism.*
27. See Yvette Kopijn, "The Oral History Interview in a Cross-Cultural Setting" in *Narrative and Genre*, eds. M. Chamberlain and P. Thompson, Routledge Studies in Memory and Narrative (London: Routledge, 1998).
28. Paget Henry, *Caliban's Reason. Introducing Afro-Caribbean Philosophy* (London: Routledge, 2000).
29. Orlando Patterson, *The Sociology of Slavery* (London: MacGibbon and Kee, 1967), 170.
30. For a fuller discussion of public memory see Katharine Hodgkin and Susannah Radstone (eds.), *Contested Pasts. The Politics of Memory* (London: Routledge, 2003); Timothy Ashplant, Graham Dawson, and Michael Roper (eds.) *The Politics of Memory: Commemorating War* (New Brunswick and London: Transaction Publishers, 2004); Barbara Miller, *Guilt and Compliance in a Unified Germany: The Stasi Files Unveiled*, (New Brunswick and London: Transaction Publishers, 2004).
31. For a brilliant exposition of this see Tayba Hassan Al Khalifa Sharif, *Resistance and Remembering: History-Telling of the Iraqi Shi'ite Arab Refugee Women and their Families in the Netherlands*, unpublished PhD thesis (University of Amsterdam, 2003).
32. See Gloria Wekker, "One Finger Does Not Drink Okra Soup: Afro-Surinamese Women and Critical Agency" in *Feminist Genealogies, Colonial Legacies, Democratic Futures*, eds. M. Jacqui Alexander and C. Talpade Mohanty (London/New York: Routledge 1997).
33. John Byng-Hall, "The Power of Family Myths" in *The Myths We Live By,* eds. R. Samuel and P. Thompson (London: Routledge 1990); Daniel Bertaux and Paul Thompson (eds.), *Between Generations. Family Models, Myths and Memories,* International Yearbook of Oral History and Life Stories Volume II, (Oxford: Oxford University Press, 1993). See also Gillian Gorell Barnes, Paul Thompson, Gwyn Daniel, and Natasha Burchardt, *Growing Up in Step Families* (Oxford: Clarendon Press, 1998).
34. Raymond Williams, *The Long Revolution* (London: Penguin 1975 [1961]), 64-68.

35. Louisa Passerini, *Fascism in Popular Memory: The Cultural Experience of the Turin Working Class,* tr. Robert Lumley and Jude Bloomfeld (Cambridge: Cambridge University Press, 1987); Louisa Passerini *Autobiography of a Generation*, tr. Lisa Erdberg (Hanover: University Press of New England, 1996); Alissandro Portelli "Uchronic Dreams: Working Class Memory and Possible Worlds" in *The Myths We Live By;* Alissandro Portelli, "The Massacre at the Fosse Ardeatine: History, Myth, Ritual and Symbol" in *Contested Pasts.*
36. Constance Sutton, private email 24 June 2004.

2

Historical Perspectives on African-Caribbean Families

"It wasn't unusual to find people would live together for years and years, on their deathbed, would marry. And these have a good laugh, 'Oh, guess what! Mr. and Mrs. So and So are getting married!' These were people of highly respected families. And, because they wanted to go to Heaven, they would have to marry before they died. And my parents were not married. But that doesn't mean to say that we were deprived as a family, of anything. The closeness and the sharing, the total lifestyle, barring the wedding, was there. And my parents married much later in life. And I'll tell you something, my mother had a white wedding! They could never, you see, you had to live there to understand...my mother, my father looked resplendent, and Mother was in her white dress, and her veil, because that was how you married. ...Strangely enough we were taught about having bastard children, but somehow it didn't seem to relate to the fact that we were bastards really, you might say. But we were born within, without wedlock, but within a confined, caring relationship. We were taught about having children outside, and so we couldn't really relate that to my mum and dad. That was really quite funny."[1]

From the early years of the seventeenth century, an estimated fifteen million Africans arrived in the New World, the majority of them destined to work as enslaved labor in the British West Indies.[2] In addition, smaller numbers of Europeans came in the same period as indentured servants, plantation owners, workers, merchants, professionals, and political prisoners. By the early years of the eighteenth century, Africans far outnumbered the surviving native peoples and the white colonizers.

The Africans were plucked from their routines of culture and kin, and thrust into the logic of the plantation regime. This logic, as Sidney Mintz argued, transformed not only the pattern of production and the organization of labor, but the social and family life of the labourer. The Caribbean peoples were the first *modern* people.

> People who come from different places and who are not *in* their own culture can become modern, in part because institutional recourse to a standard common tradition is

not immediately available. Soon after the Conquest, Caribbean people began coming from somewhere else. Most of them had to come with imperfect institutions, and in the company of others culturally unlike themselves. Most came without kinfolk. That was also modernizing, because the minimal cells of tradition-perpetuation are familial.[3]

The situation was new in the history of European conquest, and the Caribbean emerged as a region that confused, confounded and resisted conforming to existing explanations.[4] "A region of open frontiers" is how R. T. Smith has described the Caribbean,

> [of] shifting populations, vast cultural heterogeneity, complex economic relations and unstable political authority. Caribbean history has been turbulent, bringing together peoples from every part of the globe in a swirling vortex of greed, lust and striving reminiscent of the destructive hurricanes that sweep through the region each year.[5]

The consolidation of slavery in the seventeenth century as a routine source of labor required, however, legal and moral justification.[6] By the eighteenth century, Africans had come to be characterized by licentiousness, brutishness, and stupidity, a characterization that legitimated the harsh penal code, and exonerated their enslavement. "They are void of genius," wrote the eighteenth century Jamaican planter and historian Edward Long, "and seem almost incapable of making any progress in civility or science."[7] Listing their weaknesses and faults, and comparing their sexual behaviour and temperament to "monkies or baboons" he concluded that Africa "is the parent of every thing that is monstrous in nature."[8]

Long was by no means alone in his views. For him, such observations were self-evident, and replicated by other eighteenth- and nineteenth-century observers, such as Bryan Edwards, or the Reverend George Wilson Bridges. In the view of Long, and other pro-slavery advocates, slavery performed a civilising function by introducing Africans to industry, discipline and Christianity.[9] The process of civilizing the African generated, however, another very real anxiety: sexual organization. Slavery created slave society, in which all—white, black, free, enslaved—were implicated.[10] It was a society organized around positions of super- and sub-ordination, premised on racial division. "They (the slaves) were held (by the whites) in contempt, as a totally distinct race, unworthy of a place among the common herd of mankind." Remarked the stipendiary magistrate, John Colthurst, in 1837 adding with prescient insight:

> These feelings of the whites were so strongly impressed upon the slaves themselves, that it is little wonder *they* were fully convinced they were of a very inferior race of beings. Hundreds of circumstances prove this. If it was not the case extensively, how

was it possible that a few whites could keep such overwhelming numbers in slavery and subjection?[11]

The shortage of white women that characterized the early years of the West Indian colonies, and the restrictions on marriage imposed on the white indentured servants, resulted, almost from the beginning, in sexual relations between the races and between slaves and slave owners. Miscegenation was a living challenge to the assumptions of racial super- and sub-ordination upon which these societies were premised. While white men were excused and, for the most part, forgiven their peccadilloes, the male slaves were depicted in terms of unbridled promiscuity. "Concubinage and venery without restraint," railed *A Jamaican Planter* in 1815, "A multiplicity of mistresses, whom they call wives, prevails, nocturnal rambles, or excursions, to visit those on the adjoining plantations, drunkenness and other excesses."[12]

But Long, Bridges, and Edwards, inveterate observers as they were, were also quick to point out that the "continued depression of the negro character" cannot be blamed on the slaves alone, for "Empty churches, the unhallowed burial of the dead in fields and gardens, the criminal delay of baptism; the discouragement of marriage, and the profanation of the Sabbath, are models which the slaves can hardly be expect to improve."[13] Long was more specific. White creoles, "with a strong natural propensity to the other sex...are not always the most chaste and faithful of husbands"[14] Although he regarded this situation as an improvement from an earlier one "where the name of a *family man* was held in the utmost derision."[15] (emphasis original), he condemned the dissolute life styles led by these men "cohabiting with Negresses and Mulattas, free or slaves...not one in twenty can be persuaded that there is either sin, or shame in cohabiting with his slave."[16]

"Tuesday, 3rd December 1751," wrote the Jamaican planter Thomas Thistlewood in his diary, "Last night *cum* Jenny III in *me. Lect.* Wednesday 4th. Jenny continue with me *ad noctibus*'...Saturday, 21st. *cum* Susannah...Friday, 1st March: p.m. *Cum* Phibbah...and, in the evening, *Cum* Susannah in the curing-house, *stans*."[17] "The overseer [was] a civil, vulgar, Scotch officer, on half-pay," observed Lady Maria Nugent, the wife of the Governor of Jamaica, on her visit to Hope estate,

> The overseer's *chère amie*, and no man here is without one, is a tall black woman, well made, with a very flat nose, thick lips, and a skin of ebony, highly polished and shining.

> She shewed me her three yellow children, and said, with some ostentation, she should soon have another. The marked attention of the other women, plainly proved her to be the favourite Sultana of this vulgar, ugly, Scotch Sultan, who is about fifty, clumsy, ill made and dirty. He had a dingy, sallow-brown complexion, and only two yellow discolored tusks, by way of teeth.[18]

Indeed, as Special Magistrate John Anderson concluded in 1836 "The lazar spot of bastardy is stamped upon the bulk of the population."[19]

While white men, however much they contravened the norms of respectable sexual behaviour, remained beyond condemnation and punishment (the climate, it was argued, rendered white men incapable of sexual self control; white women transgressing were less charitably treated), promiscuous sexual mores had emerged by the end of the eighteenth century as the essential, deviant, defining characteristic of black West Indians.

***

Until the late eighteenth century, slave marriages were neither promoted nor recognized by civil and church authorities. Slave families were similarly disregarded. Yet, as Barry Higman has shown, slaves did form families, although their characteristics and composition depended on a range of variables: new and old colonies, nature and size of the plantation and plantation work, occupation, location (urban or rural), African, creole, black or colored.[20] Even in these years, certain features of the interior life of African-Caribbean families stand out. While Edward Long, William Dickson,[21] and other contemporaries remarked on the common practice of multiple liaisons, Long noted also the importance of filial obedience and lineage:

> Murder is with most of them esteemed the highest impiety. Filial disobedience, and insulting the ashes of the dead, are placed next. ...The greatest affront that can possibly be offered a creole Negroe, is to curse his father, mother, or any of his progenitors.[22]

From the end of the eighteenth century, Christian marriage began to be encouraged by more enlightened planters who saw it as a way to improve fertility and deflect criticism from abolitionists. As part of the ameliorative measures imposed at the end of the eighteenth century, mothers were rewarded for giving birth, couples were rewarded for fidelity and, where possible, marriages were encouraged. In Jamaica, William Sells insisted that marriage was promoted by planters and had increased such that "in the last fourteen years, 3,596 legal marriages have been celebrated in the island of Jamaica."[23] In Barbados, however, the plans for marriage were not so ambitious and only eleven marriages were recorded as having taken place between 1808 and 1838. In St. Vincent, Sir Charles Brisbane, the Governor noted that if marriage did take place, it was not "till after middle life, when constancy and attachment become very common between the father and mother of a family."[24]

By the early years of the nineteenth century, a pattern of family formation could be discerned that followed particular chronological and kinship rules, characterised by three key elements:

> *A dynamic complex marriage system*, based on multiple conjugal forms and sequential unions or serial polygamy; *ego-focused bilateral kinship networks*, recognizing relatives for each individual on both parental sides; and *ancestor-orientated nonunilineal or cognatic descent lines*, traced from a common ancestor of either gender through both males and females.[25] (original emphasis)

Marriage followed a particular pattern as younger slaves enjoyed what is now termed "visiting relations" with their partner, from whom children may or may not have resulted. While these visiting relations did not involve (and often could not involve) co-residence, they were far from being casual sexual relations. The second phase was that of cohabitation, practiced by older slaves and often leading to the final stage, of marriage "after middle life." "Having occasion one day to ask a colored woman of the better class," observed the special magistrate John Anderson in 1839, during the Apprenticeship period, "...if her son was born in *Wedlock?* She exclaimed 'No, in Barbadoes. Where's Wedlock?'"[26] (Original emphasis). Despite some encouragement for slaves and ex-slaves to marry prior to having children, for the most part, they did not conform. Christian marriage, when it occurred, was accepted not as the prerequisite to family formation, but its opposite: as confirmation and celebration of a couple's loyalty and fertility.

The practice of accepting as kin friends made in the middle passage ensured exogamy. "It is interesting to know," commented William Sells, in what was otherwise a cautious and calculated defence of the civilizing impact of slavery, "that they [slaves] do not only object to sexual intercourse between relatives, but commonly disallow of it between those who have been shipmates in the same vessel from Africa; as they form an attachment for each other resembling that of a brother and sister, which is prohibitory of further intimacy."[27] At the same time, multiple liaisons further encouraged exogamous unions and resulted in a wide kinship network. Kinship relations began to emerge as a model for social behaviour. The deference demanded by, and accorded to, older family members was equally required in the community. "It was customary for persons of their parents' generation to be addressed with the prefix 'Ta' or 'Ma' (Father or Mother) or in other cases, 'Uncle, Aunty, Tatta, Mama, Sister, Boda,' even where no obvious blood relation existed." [28] "Monk" Lewis, the Jamaican planter and writer, observed that

> [a]mong the Negroes it is almost tantamount to an affront to address by the name without affixing some term of relationship such as 'grannie' or 'uncle' or 'cousin'. My Cornwall boy, George, told me one day that 'Uncle Sully' wanted to speak to 'mass.' "Why, is Sully your uncle George?" "No massa; me only call him so for honour."[29]

In similar vein, Joseph Sturge and Thomas Harvey, on their tour of the West Indies in 1837, quoted a local magistrate in Barbados who observed that "they [the former slaves] attach great importance to being addressed in respectful language and always use it in their common intercourse with each other." [30]

The advertisements for runaway slaves offer testimony to the importance of kinship networks, their role in slave resistance and their value in providing sanctuary and help.

Reward of $5 for Amelia:

> suppose to be harboured by her father or his connections. This man has a sister or some family connections near Canewood-Moore estate, and no doubt his daughter meets with a welcome reception there

Reward of a Joe for Polly Grace (and three children):

> 'suppose to be harboured by her sister living in Mason Hall, and by her husband, James Gill, living in the vicinity of Constitution' [31]

The elaborate rituals involved in burial and the importance of the burial site,[32] all testify to the centrality of ancestors in the family cosmology, and in defining who constituted kin. In similar vein, Long's observation—replicated by others—of the slaves' love of the place of their natality reflects the link with ancestors and the link with family. Deportation—and therefore separation from family—was considered by the slaves as the worst form of punishment. It is no surprise, therefore, that some of the rebel slaves implicated in the 1816 slave revolt in Barbados who were deported first to Honduras and then, in 1819, to Sierra Leone, wrote (in 1841) from Sierra Leone to Queen Victoria, begging to be returned to Barbados "the place of our nativity."[33]

***

Emancipation, for the abolitionists and their supporters, offered the promise of reform and conversion. The former slave, in the view of many, such as John Colthurst, was capable, with Christian instruction,

> To become what all now wish him to be: a man fearing God and honouring the king; respectful to his superiors but not mean; honest, sober, and industrious; discharging his duties creditably as Husband and Father of a family.[34]

The issue of family life proved, however, intractable in the eyes of the authorities. According to evidence presented to the 1842 Select Committee on the West Indian colonies, any increase in the marriage rate, and religious attendance needed to be treated with caution for, "of the few marriages which do take place, the majority is contracted between old people who for long periods have cohabited together"[35] The 1844 Census in the West Indies confirmed that although marriages in Monserrat[36] had increased from twenty-one in 1833 to 111 in 1843, the number of illegitimate children born in 1843 was 196, well over half (58 percent) of the 336 born that year,[37] suggesting, again, that marriage was a custom practiced by older, rather than younger, couples. At the same time, the evidence to the Select Committee also pointed to the high levels of "concubinage" and cohabitation (confusingly, for the Committee members, combined with a profession of Christianity). In Barbados, the evidence suggested, "they still practise the custom of polygamy, therefore they have various homes, inasmuch as they have various wives."[38] In St. Christopher, applying the Marriage Act presented insurmountable problems

> because we found there were double, and even, in some cases, treble marriages. The negroes...would separate and form fresh connexions and get married again, and in some cases we found they had been married three times. We did not in that case understand which marriage we should legalise; if we legalised the first marriage we might destroy existing connexions, and if we legalise the last marriage we might destroy the legitimacy of the first children.[39]

Many couples resisted marriage altogether. John Colthurst found that of the sixty-four estates in his district in Barbados as stipendiary magistrate, only five (which were regularly visited by a black clergyman) had "a greater number of lawfully married couples."[40] Family life may have been reconstituted in the post-Emancipation period, but it did not conform to the ideal espoused by missionaries and recognized by the authorities. Sir Robert Schomburgk's observations of an improvement in the rate of marriage immediately following Emancipation in Barbados referred, again, primarily to couples in long-term relationships. Among younger people, "There is still a much greater unreserved intercourse than those who take an interest in the moral and religious state of the colony would wish to see."[41] As a result, "In England every fifteenth child is illegitimate, in Belgium the fifteenth, in Sweden the fourteenth, in Prussia the thirteenth, in France the thirteenth, in Austria the ninth, in Bavaria the fourth; in Barbados the illegitimate children exceed those born in wedlock.[42]

Emancipation offered the longed-for opportunity to reunite families separated in slavery, and families undoubtedly took advantage of this. "People badly want to unite with the family" recalled Samuel Smith, who was born in 1877 in Antigua, "particularly the womenkind. I hear that the women was furious and desperate to find their people."[43] "There were people who had connexions elsewhere" evidence from St. Vincent to the Select Committee reports,

> and wished to leave the estate...I remember that one man told me that he had a wife at one place about five miles off and he wished to go and live with her, and cultivate a piece of land which he had; & others assigned similar reasons, that they had wives elsewhere; and those who came to me stated that they had wives and connexions on other estates.[44]

Family reunion was one overwhelming dynamic. Equally strong was the care of kin, particularly elderly kin, and the desire to make sure that children remained free and/or did not engage in field labour. In Barbados, as the Select Committee noted, parents removed their children from the estates and "carried them away and distributed them amongst friends and families."[45] Definition of family was inclusive and family members, or close friends, would be used to foster children, strengthening and widening kinship ties."There is a connexion of the negroes that is not generally known in this country [Trinidad]; that is, as godfathers and godmothers, which is as binding as the relation of the parents themselves."[46]

If families struggled to unite, they struggled also to lead independent lives. The primary concern of the planters was to maintain their labor force. Children, almost universally across the British West Indies, were withdrawn from field labor and in some cases, as in Barbados, from the estates altogether. More alarmingly for the planters, women, too, withdrew their labor, a particularly damaging action, from the planters' perspective, since women were the majority in the praedial workforce at the time of Emancipation. The view of the family order advocated by missionaries, abolitionists, and anti-slavery sympathisers was one that mirrored their own: discrete family units that displayed the appropriate gender decorum of the male breadwinner supporting a devoted, but dependent, wife and children.[47] Evidence from the Select Committee suggested that couples may have bought into this particular gender ideology, as men looked out for land "where they can go and live and allow their wives to sit down, as we call it, and take charge of the children,"[48] and women "who used to work, refuse to labour now on the plea of being married"[49] and, employed "in a domestic capacity providing comforts for their husbands, making their homes comfortable."[50]

However, given the low wages, particularly for field laborers, few men could have afforded to support their wives and children, and few women could have afforded to earn nothing. Women's withdrawal from field labor may have had an alternative motive. For the former slaves emancipation signified not only freedom from slavery, but freedom to assume control over the economic, social, and cultural conditions of their lives. As Woodville Marshall has argued, the former slaves had clear ideas of what freedom entailed: equality before the law, control over labor time, permanence of freedom, and freedom to practice religion. Implicit in this was a desire to reconstitute family life and to maintain control over how time and roles were allocated within. "Blacks" as Marshall indicates, "generally insisted that women and children should work a shorter week than the men."[51] A St. Vincentian planter calculated that "in all there was a loss of 579 days of field labor of males, and 1,255 of female.....I should think that a proportion of about two thirds of the women [have retired from field labour]." [52] The degree of labor withdrawal differed from island to island,[53] and according to the calculations of those providing evidence. Rather than this signalling the start of domestic dependence, however, Marshall suggests that

> [c]learly this was done mainly to maximise the family effort in the provision grounds and local market; the women, as hucksters, insisted on additional time to prepare for the market; and the children, when not at school, could increase the domestic labour supply.[54]

Moreover, market gardening and/or plantation piecework, as developed in some colonies, provided women with the ability to earn a living and the flexibility to care for children, particularly important for women household heads. The reconstitution of families in the period following emancipation challenged the European imposition of family models and, as Mimi Sheller has observed, manipulated European family ideology to the best advantage of their own families by, for instance, insisting on withdrawing their labor from the plantation on the grounds that they were wives and mothers.[55] The families that evolved may be seen as part of the popular resistance to the planters' hegemony over economic and political life, for they asserted an alternative or oppositional ideology that controlled the reproduction of the single commodity the planters needed most of all, and that they universally bemoaned was in short supply—the labor force.

***

While emancipation in 1834 may have sounded the death knell of slavery in the British colonies, it did not eradicate the anti-black sentiments that had accompanied it. The abolitionists, and the missionaries in the West Indies, may have lauded the "great experiment" that the ending of slavery promised, but their optimism proved short-lived. The supply of funds and resources to the colonies began to diminish, and within twenty years of emancipation, the former slaves began to lose the political patronage of their major supporter.[56] The planters, and their supporters, had never considered emancipation to be an appropriate move in any case. Their key concern was in maintaining a ready and steady supply of labor by the cheapest means possible. In their view, the former slaves were incapable of a work ethic and, therefore, responsible behavior in the labor market or, indeed, elsewhere. Without the imposed discipline of the slave regime, or self-imposed discipline of Christianity, the former slaves stood in danger of reverting to their former barbarous state. "There are no people there in the true sense of the word," argued J.A. Froude, "with a character and purpose of their own." [57] And, as an English visitor to Jamaica commented,

> The vices of slavery have not been removed by freedom, as they have received but little instruction. ...They are idle and wretched, and the rate of mortality is high amongst them. Marriage, as in the time of slavery, is but lightly regarded. ...If left for many years without European influence, they will, I fear, fall into as low a position as some of the worst tribes of Africa.[58]

As the nineteenth century progressed, poverty crippled the population and riots racked the region.[59] From 1843 (the first postemancipation census), colonial administrators were much exercised by the link between what they perceived as the sexual immorality of West Indians (as evidenced by the high rates of illegitimacy) and lack of citizenship (as evidenced by the social disturbances). And, for the first time, census data began to be sufficiently detailed to corroborate the profile. The 1871 census of Barbados, for instance, indicates that out of a total population of 162,042, only 13,372 men and 13,996 women were married. By far the majority of married couples were found in the older cohorts, not in the cohorts of sixteen to twenty years and twenty to thirty—the years of primary child bearing.[60]

For the colonial governments, citizenship and social stability were closely related to domestic stability. This theme was repeated by West Indian colonial governors and by the Registrar Generals of Barbados, of Jamaica, of Trinidad and of Tobago throughout the nineteenth and twentieth centuries. The 1891 West Indian census made woeful reading. The Registrar General of Jamaica, for instance, noted that "for the half year to 31st March 1890, the number of illegitimate births registered was...equal to an annual rate of 61.7 per 100 births and for the year ended 31st March 1891 the number was...60.7 per 100 births... " continuing that, as a result, "the foundational elements of good citizenship are thus lacking and the progress of the State is hindered."[61]

In a more optimistic vein, the Registrar General of Tobago, noting the decline in the rate of illegitimate births (from 57.80 percent of the estimate population in 1889 to 52.73 percent in 1891), commented that "[I]t is to be hoped that the increased marriage-rate now recorded may continue and increase until that dark stain of a former state of things be wiped out, and the home life of our people become what it should be, and must be, before any real moral or social progress can be made."[62] The optimism was echoed by the Registrar General of Barbados:

> In 1871-81 the number of married persons increased by 2,972 concurrently with an increase in the population of 9,818; and in 1881-1891 the population increased by 11,007 or 6.4% while the number of the married increased by 4,380 or 14.4 per cent. This is a highly satisfactory result, speaking well for the improvement that must have taken place in the moral tone of the people since 1861, and indicating, moreover, a decrease in the proportion of illegitimate births, which, from every point of view, is a subject for congratulation.[63]

Yet the 1921 census was recording illegitimacy rates of 59.2 percent for Trinidad (and 89.5 percent within its East Indian population, largely because neither Hindu nor Muslim marriages were legally recognized);[64] for Barbados, the same census recorded the illegitimacy rate as 67.66 percent,[65] although there had been a slight increase in the marriage rate between 1871 (when it stood at 16.9 percent of the population) and 1921 (when it stood at 21.6 percent of the population). Of these proportions, the ratio of married to single white people was approximately 1:2, for the black population 1:4, and for the mixed population 1:3.5. In 1946, the illegitimate birth rate for Barbados remained high, at 53.74 percent.[66]

By 1943, however, the Jamaican census had begun to refine its data and for the first time records not only rates of marriage, but also those living in common-law unions, a category adopted by the West Indian Census of 1946. From this, a more nuanced breakdown was possible into which the high rates of illegitimacy could be located, and from which a clearly defined pattern of union emerged, along broadly racial lines: for blacks and "coloreds," the rate of marriage was significantly lower than white, European or other racial and ethnic groups, while single status and common-law unions were significantly higher. "The marriage rate works out at 272 per thousand," commented Sir Frank Stockdale, the Comptroller of Welfare and Development, "a figure which compares very unfavourably with the rate of 645 for Great Britain obtained in the 1931 census."[67] When, however, this was broken down by age cohorts, it was found that as the groups increased in age so did the rate of marriage, with a corresponding decline in common-law unions and single status.

The census revealed, therefore, that the majority of Jamaicans—and the majority of Jamaicans were black and colored—displayed patterns of union formation that were sharply at variance with those of the white minority populations and the European pattern of union formation. At the same time, the census also revealed that although a significant proportion of mothers were married (92,029 out of a maternal population aged fifteen years and over of 258,842) most of these were over thirty. The majority of women producing children, however, were to be found among the fifteen to twenty-nine age group, the age cohort most characterized by single status (33,538) or common-law status (24,404). Only 16,092 of this age group were married. In percentage terms, 39.2 percent of single mothers, 17.5 percent of married mothers and 44.2 percent of common-law mothers were aged fifteen to twenty-nine.[68] The West Indian Census of 1946, which adopted the Jamaican classification, revealed a similar profile for Barbados in which

[t]he married population represents 39.92 per cent. of all males and 32.51 per cent. of all females aged fifteen years and over. Among males the proportion is only 8.40 per cent in the 20-24 age group, but thereafter rises rapidly. It reaches 67.68 per cent. in the 55-64 age group. Among females the married proportion at ages 20-24 was 19.27 per cent. and rose to 48.60 per cent in the age group 35-44. ...The married proportion among Whites was significantly higher at all ages and for both sexes than among the Black or Mixed groups.[69]

The Registrar General went on to observe that "the contraction in the proportion of common-law status in the higher age groups is an indication that common-law status is forsaken with advancing age."[70] The 1946 West Indian census also revealed a further discrepancy: that black and colored women tended to have children significantly younger than their white and European counterparts (between twenty and twenty-four white women had an average of 0.43 children, black women had an average of 1.13) and they also tended to have more children overall (by the ages forty to forty-four, white women had an average of 2.24 children, black women an average of 3.77.[71]

***

Between 1935 and 1938 major riots erupted in the British West Indies. A Royal Commission, under the chairmanship of Lord Moyne, was set up to investigate the causes of the disturbances. Lord Moyne's findings pointed to the poverty prevalent in the West Indies as direct cause of the riots, aggravated by what was perceived as the lack of a culture that could provide some form of social cohesion. Not only, in the view of the Commissioners, had West Indians lost all vestiges of cultural form for, as they put it (somewhat disingenuously, given the circumstances), "The Negroes...transfer to the West Indies...did not involve the transfer of any important traces of their traditions and customs, but rather their complete destruction. ...[A]nd no systematic attempt was made to substitute any others,"[72] but the bedrock of social organization, marriage, "was, for historical reasons, never the rule in the West Indies and the illegitimate birth rate was always high."[73] Explanation for this was found in overcrowded living conditions, poor education and "the absence of a strong opposing public opinion among a people whose immature minds too often are ruled by their adult bodies."[74] Although the publication of the Moyne Commission report was postponed until after the Second World War, interim measures for reform were put in place. Universal suffrage was recommended to be introduced, as was a notion of, and money for, development. £1 million per year for twenty years was provided to support the West Indian Welfare Fund to improve social welfare and stimulate development. Sir Frank Stockdale, agrarian adviser to the Colonial Office, was appointed the first Comptroller of Social Welfare and Development. For him, as for Lord Moyne,[75] "many if not most of the social problems of the West Indies centre round weaknesses in family organisation."[76] With weak families, social stability was unlikely to improve. "Village life in its social and even administrative aspects depends for its vitality on the strength of the family organization underlying it, and if the family is weak—as an institution—so is the village. ...The creation of a means of associating people together in some sort of common social bond is therefore the first task of social workers in the West Indies."[77]

In 1941 Sir Frank appointed as social welfare advisor Thomas Simey, the Charles Booth Professor of Social Science at the University of Liverpool, a key proponent of "modern sociology" and of the burgeoning field of social policy. Simey was invited to undertake a scientific analysis of the West Indies that could form the basis for formulating social policy and reforming the administrative framework. The result was published in 1946 as *Welfare and Planning in the West Indies*, and was the first (British) scholarly attempt to get to grips with the sociology of the region. Simey believed profoundly in the "applied science of social engineering"[78] and his starting point, shared with Sir Frank Stockdale, was the family. It was, he argued, "the outstandingly important social institution of the West Indies."[79]

By the time Thomas Simey came to investigate the West Indies, two new and influential explanations for African-Caribbean family "deviancy" were in the public arena. Both originated from America and from concern over the condition of African-American families that, like their African-Caribbean counterparts in the British West Indies, displayed high levels of illegitimacy, high rates of cohabitation, and low rates of marriage. Franklin Frazier, an American anthropologist, published in 1939 *The Negro Family in the United States*.[80] The character of contemporary African-American family structures, he argued, could be traced to slavery, which had stripped the African male of his culture and in so doing had distorted the institution of marriage and the sanctity of the family. Two years later, in 1941, another American scholar, Melville Herskovits, argued in his book *The Myth of the Negro Past* that although slavery had, clearly, disrupted family formation, the patterns of family life noted for African-Americans throughout the New World suggested that "slavery by no means completely suppressed rough approximations of certain forms of African family life."[81] Simey, in this debate, sided with Frazier. "The contemporary looseness of the family structure in the British West Indies" he wrote magisterially, "requires no further explanation than this."[82] And how was this contemporary looseness manifested? Borrowing from Lewis Davidson's typology of family based on his analysis of the 1943 Jamaican census, Simey observed four principal forms of West Indian family organization:

> a) *The Christian Family*, based on marriage and a patriarchal order approximating to that of Christian families in other parts of the world;
>
> b) *Faithful Concubinage*, again based on a patriarchal order, possessing no legal status but well established and enduring for at least three years;
>
> c) *The Companionate family*, in which the members live together for pleasure and convenience and for less than three years;
>
> d) *The Disintegrate family*, consisting of women and children only, in which men merely visit the women from time to time, no pattern of conduct being established.[83]

By far the majority of families, as revealed in the Jamaican census of 1943, were in the third and fourth category, of companionate and disintegrate families. "Such evidence as there is," he concluded, "goes to show that in the majority of cases the relationships between the sexes which lead to the procreation of children are temporary, and the institution of marriage is unstable. The family group is, indeed, one which is brought together in a very casual way and this obtains for the Christian as well as the Disintegrate family."[84]

Material and moral impoverishment of the family led to impoverishment of social life, and of the community as a whole. This, coupled (as both cause and effect) with the pernicious divisions of race and color that prohibited social and political mobility, amounted to a damning indictment of the contemporary West Indies, and an explanation of what Simey (in line with the contemporary fascination with social psychology, and borrowing from Dollard's influential study of the Deep South)[85] considered to be the "inferiority complex" of black West Indians.

Simey's concern with citizenship, poverty, and family form mirrored thinking in the metropolis. Like his influential contemporaries, William Beveridge and Richard Titmuss, Simey saw social policy as the way to remedy social ills. If the structures of social instability could be identified then a solution could be engineered. The legacy of slavery, particularly as it was reflected in family forms, and the constraints of poverty, as the prime causes of social instability and injustice, were capable of being restructured out of the social equation in much the same way as the inequalities of class, poverty, and poor health were being restructured out of the postwar British equation. Although Simey has been criticized for pathologizing the West Indian family,[86] he was one of the first scholars to attempt an explanation of what appeared to him as an intractable, alien, and unsatisfactory family form, in order to seek a solution to the overriding poverty of the West Indies and the ever-present threat of social unrest.

Like most scholars from his generation and background, he assumed that the European model of the nuclear family was the norm and the yardstick against which other family groupings should be measured. Family and households should, in this view, be coterminous. To his dismay, "not a single [household] consisted only of parents and their children."[87] Simey's endorsement of Frazier's explanatory thesis on what was seen as family breakdown led to a widespread acceptance of the view that slavery, by emasculating men, "led" as the Jamaican sociologist Orlando Patterson later argued, "to the breakdown of all forms of social sanctions relating to sexual behaviour, and with this, to the disintegration of the institution of marriage both in its African and European forms."[88] Women emerged as heads of families and households, a status confirmed during slavery by the laws of inheritance (a slave inherited its status from the mother) and endorsed post-Emancipation by male absence (often through migration) and the assumed marginal role men occupied within families.

This emphasis on women as sole household and family heads—so-called "maternal families" or "matrifocal families"—became the defining feature of subsequent studies of African-Caribbean kinship such as Fernando Henriques's *Family and Colour in Jamaica* (1953), R. T. Smith's *The Negro Family in British Guiana* (1956) and Edith Clarke's *My Mother Who Fathered Me* (1957). Henriques injected a correlation between class, color, and what he termed "maternal families." For the middle classes (predominantly, but not exclusively, "brown"), or those who aspired to them, "The fundamental unit of the middle class family is the paternalistic, monogamous, Christian family."[89] These families employed servants, and nannies, attended church, differentiated themselves from the lower classes in expectations for, and attitudes toward, their children and, above all, tended not to live in extended family groups. But the most important difference, Henriques argues, "between the family groupings of the lower and middle classes is the almost complete absence, except fortuitously, of the maternal family in the middle class."[90]

A comparable emphasis was placed by Edith Clarke. Clarke, who had been a doctoral student under Malinowski at the London School of Economics, was a civil servant, secretary to the Board of Supervision in Jamaica (which had responsibility for Poor Relief), and director of Jamaica Welfare Ltd., founded by Norman Manley (later to become Prime Minister), with whom she worked. Invited by the Colonial Social Science Research Council in Britain to conduct a study on Jamaican family life, the result was *My Mother Who Fathered Me* (1957)[91] Based on detailed data and anthropological fieldwork in three pseudonymous locations—Orange Town, Mocca, and Sugartown—which broadly correlated with class, family "deviancy" as identified by the maternal family (which she attributed to slavery and its aftermath) was identified, but located among the lower class—a feature of the residents of "Sugartown," the case study of the predominantly rural working class. Such families may consist of mother and children, but often included maternal grandmothers, with little or no paternal involvement. Evidence of female fertility in this community was almost a prerequisite to a relationship.[92] And, as with Henriques before her, and others after her, Clarke observed that there was a range of family forms functioning in the Caribbean, including households that contained several generations, but no nuclear family, who were linked not by conjugality but consanguinity. Household and nuclear family in the Caribbean were, therefore, not necessarily coterminous.

Clarke, Smith, and Henriques were working at a critical time in the history of the West Indies, as the region moved first to its experiment as a Federation of the West Indies (1958-1961), and then to Independence in the 1960s. The fledgling nations needed to know how life styles would contribute (or not) to the nation-building endeavor, and how these would impact on the structures of government and policy then being put in place. "So many of us at the centre," commented Sir Hugh Foot, the former Governor of Jamaica, in the 1957 Foreword to Clarke's book, "know so little about the lives and the homes and the families of the great bulk of the Jamaican population....We build a superstructure, without a real knowledge of the foundations."[93] This early work pointed to a strong correlation between family type, social class, and color a view endorsed by M.G. Smith's interpretation of Jamaica as a plural society, in which social sections lived parallel but essentially autonomous existences.[94]

The studies that followed in the 1970s, 1980s, and 1990s began to nuance the typologies of families and to explore the functions performed by flexible mating behavior in terms of family survival, seeing these as adaptations to the particular constraints imposed by, and solutions to, poverty in the region. At the same time, an understanding of gender pointed to the advantages secured by women for themselves and their families in mother-headed households, in the ways women could see childbearing and children as a way into accessing male income, and to question assumptions on male marginality in conjugal households.[95] Equally, the plural society became increasingly untenable as a range of scholars argued for a society linked by a common, creole culture, unique to the region, forged by its particular histories and cultural fusions and connected, paradoxically, through its divisions.[96] In this perspective, differences in creole family formations did not conform to class and color lines, but could be seen as part of a continuum that ran through the whole society. As R.T. Smith was to argue later, "the family structure of different classes, and racial groups can be understood as variations on a common structural theme."[97] Furthermore, increasing prosperity since Independence had not been accompanied by a change in kinship and family practices, as would be expected if family types were simply a reflection of class and income. On the contrary, as Douglass argued, "practices and patterns of kinship remain today much as they were just after emancipation over 150 years ago."[98]

***

As we have seen, these practices and patterns of kinship can be traced to slavery and were consolidated post-Emancipation. The networks they generated, and the values they endorsed, provided the structures necessary for sustenance, for migration, and ultimately for identity across generations and oceans. These family forms were consistently misunderstood and misrepresented by colonial and church authorities, and later by many of the early scholarly studies. The Caribbean represented from the beginning, and continues to represent to the present, a unique and extraordinary history, for which there was no precedent for understanding. Governors, commentators, and scholars filtered their view through white, European lenses and, convinced that there was no "native" culture or social organization among the slaves and their descendants, continued to be baffled by what they found, and to flounder for appropriate analytical tools.[99] As Sidney Mintz has argued: "It was not that their cultures were terribly familiar, so much as that they seemed so pathetically *hybrid*. No matter from what perspective one observed them, what they did, and what they were supposed to think, they and their lifeways seemed faded: a patchwork, tattered, makeshift, and, worst of all, *mongrel*. Anthropologists generally wanted to study (though again, none would have used the word) *pure* cultures" (original emphasis)[100] As a result, the cultural logic of the Caribbean and its families took a long time to be recognized.

Notes

1. JI 028/1/1/4/25. All such references relate to interview data (accession number, generation number, tape and page reference) from Living Arrangements, Family Structure and Social Change of Caribbeans in Britain (ESRC L315253009). Data deposited at Qualidata Archive, University of Essex.
2. Richard Sheridan, *Sugar and Slavery. An Economic History of the British West Indies, 1623-1775,* (Kingston: Canoe Press, 1994 [1974]).
3. Sidney Mintz, "The Caribbean as a Socio-Cultural Area" *Journal of World History,* 9, 4 (1966): 914-5.
4. See Peter Hulme, *Colonial Encounters. Europe and the Native Caribbean 1492-1797* (London: Routledge, 1986).
5. Raymond T. Smith, *Kinship and Class in the West Indies. A genealogical study of Jamaica and Guyana,* (Cambridge: Cambridge University Press, 1988),2.
6. Elsa Goveia, "The West Indian Slave Laws of the Eighteenth Century" in *Caribbean Slave Society and Economy,* eds. Hilary Beckles and Verene Shepherd (Kingston: Ian Randle Publishers, 1991), 350-351.
7. Edward Long, *The History of Jamaica,* Vol. II, (London, 1774), 353.
8. Ibid., 383.
9. Ibid., 410.
10. Elsa Goveia, *Slave Society in the British Leeward Islands at the End of the Eighteenth Century* (New Haven and London: Yale University Press, 1965).
11. Woodville K. Marshall, ed. *The Colthurst Journal* (New York: KTO Press, 1977), 135.
12. *A Jamaican Planter* (London:1815), 27-28.
13. Edward Bridges, *The Annals of Jamaica* Vol. II, (1827), 4.
14. Long, *History,* Vol. II, 265.
15. Ibid., 281.
16. Long, *History,* Vol. III, 328.
17. Douglas Hall ed., *In Miserable Slavery. Thomas Thistlewood in Jamaica, 1750-86* (London: Macmillan, 1989),37, 63.
18. Philip Wright ed., *Lady Nugent's Journal of Her Residence in Jamaica from 1801 to 1805* (Kingston: Institute of Jamaica, 1966), 29.

19. Roderick A. McDonald, ed., *Between Slavery and Freedom. Special Magistrate John Anderson's Journal of St. Vincent during the Apprenticeship* (Kingston: University of the West Indies Press, 2001), 168.
20. Barry Higman, *Slave Population and Economy in Jamaica 1807-1834,* (Cambridge: Cambridge University Press, 1976); Barry Higman, *Slave Populations of the British Caribbean 1807*-1834 (Kingston: The Press, University of the West Indies, 1995 [1984]). See also Michael Craton, "Changing Patterns of Slave Families in the British West Indies" in Beckles and Shepherd, *Caribbean Slave Society.*
21. William Dickson, (1815), 360.
22. Long, *History* Vol. II, 415-416.
23. William Sells, *Remarks on the Condition of the Slaves in the Island of Jamaica,* (London,1823), 31.
24. Sir Charles Brisbane, *A Communication from Sir Charles Brisbane, K.C.B., Governor of Saint Vincent, to the House of Assembly of that Colony,* (London,1823), 55.
25. Jean Besson, *Martha Brae's Two Histories: European Expansion and Caribbean Culture-Building in Jamaica* (Chapel Hill and London: University of North Carolina Press, 2002), 27. See also Higman, *Slave Populations.*
26. McDonald, *Between Slavery,* 160.
27. Sells, *Remarks,* 28. The slave trade was abolished in 1807.
28. Orlando Patterson, *The Sociology of Slavery* (London: MacGibbon and Kee, 1967),170. George Lamming 's novel, *In the Castle of My Skin* (1953), engages with this terminology in his depictions of "Ma" and "Pa," who represented the generic ancestors and elders of the village. See also the obituary of Ivy Jordan cited in the prologue.
29. Cited in Patterson, *Sociology,* 170.
30. Joseph Sturge and Thomas Harvey, *The West Indies in 1837* (London: Dawsons of Pall Mall, 1968 [1838]), 142.
31. Hilary Beckles, *Natural Rebels. A Social History of Enslaved Black Women in Barbados* (London: Zed Books Ltd., 1989), 120.
32. Long, *History,* Vol. II. See also Jerome Handler and F. Lange, *Plantation Slavery in Barbados: An Archaeological and Historical Investigation* (Cambridge: Cambridge University Press,1978).
33. Pedro Welch, "Forging a Barbadian Identity: Lessons from the 1816 'Bussa' Slave Rebellion" in *The Empowering Impulse. The Nationalist Tradition of Barbados* eds. Glenford Howe, and Don Marshall (Kingston: Canoe Press, 2001).
34. Marshall, *Colthurst,* 121.
35. Command Paper 479, Select Committee on West India Colonies 1842, para. 728.
36. The census, otherwise, is little more than a headcount with no information on marital status and, in the case of Barbados, no information on race and color.
37. Command Paper 426, Population of the British West India Islands and British Guiana according to the last census 1845.
38. Select Committee 1842, para.1757.
39. Select Committee 1842: para. 3149.
40. Marshall, *Colthurst,*79.
41. Sir Robert Schomburgk, *The History of Barbados* (London,1848), 89.
42. Schomburgk, *History,* 89.
43. Keithlyn B.Smith and Fernando C.Smith, *To Shoot Hard Labour. The Life and Times of Samuel Smith, an Antiguan workingman 1877-1982* (Scarborough, Ontario: Edan's Publishers, 1986), 29.
44. Select Committee 1842, paras. 485, 490.
45. Select Committee 1842, para. 1452.

46. Select Committee 1842, para. 1280.
47. Catherine Hall, "White Visions, Black Lives: the Free Villages of Jamaica" *History Workshop Journal* 36, Autumn, 100-132.
48. Select Committee 1842, para. 274.
49. Select Committee 1842, para. 334.
50. Select Committee 1842, para. 303.
51. Woodville K. Marshall, "'We be wise to many more tings': Blacks' Hopes and Expectations of Emancipation" in *Caribbean Freedom. Economy and Society from Emancipation to the Present* (Kingston: Ian Randle Publishers, 1993).
52. Select Committee 1842, para. 299.
53. Bridget Brereton, "Family Strategies, Gender and the Shift to Wage Labour in the British Caribbean" in *The Colonial Caribbean in Transition. Essays on Post-emancipation Social and Cultural History* (Kingston: The Press University of the West Indies, 1999). Select Committee 1842.
54. Marshall, "We Be Wise," 17.
55. Mimi Sheller, "Quasheba, Mother, Queen: Black Women's Public Leadership and Political Protest in Post-Emancipation Jamaica, 1834-1865" *Slavery and Abolition* 19,3, 1998, 90-117.
56. Hall, "White Visions."
57. J.A.Froude, *The English in the West Indies or the Bowl of Ulysses* (New York: Charles Scribner and Sons, 1888), 347.
58. cited Hall, "White Visions," 127.
59. Dominica 1844, British Guiana 1856, St. Vincent 1862, Jamaica 1865, Barbados 1876, Trinidad 1884.
60. CO 31/62, Barbados Census 1871, Appendix G.
61. CO 140/208 Appendix to papers of Legislative Council of Jamaica 1891.
62. CO 298/47 Deputy Registrar General's Report for Tobago for the year 1890. Papers presented to the Legislative Council of Trinidad, 1891.
63. CO 31/79. Registrar General's Report, presented to the meeting of the House of Assembly 17 November, 1891, Bridgetown, Barbados.
64. CO 298/122 Vital Statistics. (Report of Registrar General for Trinidad 1921.
65. CO 31/107. Documents laid at a Meeting of the House of Assembly, Bridgetown, Barbados 1921.
66. CO 31/137 West Indian Census 1946.
67. Sir Frank Stockdale, *Development and Welfare in the West Indies, 1943-44.* (London:HMSO,1945), 81.
68. Census of Jamaica 1943. Tables 38 and 39.
69. West Indian Census 1946. Part C, chapter 5:xxv.
70. Census 1946:xxvii.
71. Census 1946:xxix.
72. CO 967/118 The West India Royal Commission 1938-39, (1945), 29.
73. Royal Commission 1945, 422.
74. Royal Commission 1945, 221.
75. Lord Moyne had observed that "the argument that the man is head of the household and is responsible for the financial upkeep of the family has less force in the West Indies, where promiscuity and illegitimacy are so prevalent and the woman so often is the supporter of the home" (Royal Commission 1945:217-220).
76. Sir Frank Stockdale, *Development and Welfare in the West Indies 1940-1942* (London: HMSO 1943),52.
77. Sir Frank Stockdale, *Development and Welfare*, 1945, 82
78. Thomas Simey, *Welfare and Planning in the West Indies* (Oxford: Clarendon, 1946), 237.

79. Simey, *Welfare*, 79.
80. Franklin Frazier, *The Negro Family in the United States* (Chicago: University of Chicago Press, 1966 [1939]).
81. Melville Herskovits *The Myth of the Negro Past* (Boston: Beacon Press,1958 [1941]),139.
82. Simey, *Welfare*, 51.
83. Ibid., 83.
84. Ibid., 84.
85. John Dollard, *Caste and Class in a Southern Town* (New York: Doubleday Anchor Books 1957 [1937]).
86. See Christine Barrow, *Family in the Caribbean. Themes and Perspectives* (Kingston: Ian Randle Publishers, 1996).
87. Simey, *Welfare*, 84.
88. Patterson, *Sociology*, 159.
89. Fernando Henriques, *Family and Colour in Jamaica* (London: Eyre and Spottiswoode, 1953), 149.
90. Henriques, *Family and Colour*, 150.
91. Significantly, Clarke borrowed the title of her book from a phrase used by George Lamming in *In the Castle of My Skin*, one of the iconic books of the early Independence movements.
92. Edith Clarke, *My Mother who Fathered Me. A Study of the Families in Three Selected Communities of Jamaica* (Kingston: The Press University of the West Indies 1999 [1957]), 65. See also Peter Wilson, "Reputation and Respectability: A Suggestion for Caribbean Ethnology" *Man* 4, March (1969), 70-84, for how men exploited reputations of virility.
93. Sir Hugh Foot in Clarke, *My Mother*, viii.
94. "Differences in family types correspond with…differences in the kinship systems of the social sections." M. G. Smith, *The Plural Society in the British West Indies* (Kingston: Sangster's Book Store in Association with University of California Press, 1974 [1965]), 164; Henriques, *Family and Colour*.
95. George Roberts and Sonja Sinclair, *Women in Jamaica: Patterns of Reproduction and Family* (New York: KTO Press, 1978); Hyman Rodman, *Lower Class Families: The Culture of Poverty in Negro Trinidad* (London: Oxford University Press, 1971); Hymie Rubenstein, *Coping with Poverty: Adaptive Strategies in a Caribbean Village* (Boulder: Westview Press, 1987); Sally W. Gordan, "I go to 'Tanties': The Economic Significance of Child-Shifting in Antigua, West Indies," *Journal of Comparative Family Studies* 18, 3 (1987):427-443; Marietta Morrissey, *Slave Women in the New World: Gender Stratification in the Caribbean* (Kansas: University Press of Kansas,1989); Marietta Morrissey, "Explaining the Caribbean Family: Gender Ideologies and Gender Relations" in *Caribbean Portraits. Essays on Gender Ideologies and Identities,* ed. Christine Barrow (Kingston: Ian Randle Publishers, 1998); Christine Barrow "Caribbean Masculinity and Family: Revisiting 'Marginality' and 'Reputation'" in *Caribbean Portraits* (1998); Jean Besson "Changing Perceptions of Gender in the Caribbean Region: The Case of the Jamaican Peasantry" in *Caribbean Portraits* (1998); Mindie Lazarus-Black, "Why Women Take Men to Magistrate's Court: Caribbean Kinship Ideology" *Ethnography* 30, 2 (1991):119-133. For an overview see Christine Barrow, *Family in the Caribbean. Themes and Perspectives* (Kingston: Ian Randle Publishers, 1996); Godfrey St. Barnard, "Demographic characteristics of families and living arrangements in the Commonwealth Caribbean" in *Caribbean Families in Britain and the Transatlantic World,* eds. Harry Goulbourne and Mary Chamberlain (London: Macmillan, 2001). See also Rhodha Reddock, *Women and Family in the*

Caribbean: Historical and Contemporary Considerations: With Special Reference to Jamaica and Trinidad and Tobago (St. Augustine: Caricom Secretariat/Women and Development Studies Group/Center for Gender and Development Studies, University of the West Indies, 1994) for a summary of the impact of economic change and political perspectives on women and families.

96. See Edward Kamau Brathwaite, *The Development of Creole Society in Jamaica 1770-1820* (Oxford: Clarendon Press, 1971); Sidney Mintz and Richard Price, *An Anthropological Approach to the African-American Past, A Caribbean Perspective* (Philadelphia: Institute for the Study of Human Issues, 1976). Contemporaries of M. G. Smith at the University of the West Indies, Mona, such as R. T. Smith or Lloyd Braithwaite, criticized the "plural" thesis from the beginning.

97. Raymond T. Smith, *Kinship and Class in the West Indies*, 7; See also Jack Alexander, "The Role of the Male in the Middle Class Jamaican Family: A Comparative Perspective" *Journal of Comparative Family Studies,* 8, 3 (1977):369-389; Jack Alexander, "Love, Race, Slavery and Sexuality in Jamaican Images of the Family" in *Kinship Ideology and Practice in Latin America,* ed. Raymond T. Smith (Chapel Hill: University of North Carolina Press, 1984):147-180; Lisa Douglass, *The Power of Sentiment: Love, Hierarchy and the Jamaican Power Elite* (Boulder: Westview Press, 1992); Virginia Young, "Household Structure in a West Indian Society" *Social and Economic Studies* 39:3 (1990) 147-77.

98. Douglass, *The Power of Sentiment,* 15.

99. Michel-Rolfe Trouillot, "The Caribbean Region: An Open Frontier in Anthropological Theory" *Annual Review of Anthropology* 21 (1992):19-42.

100. Sidney Mintz, foreword, in Jean Besson, *Martha Brae's Two Histories: European Expansion and Caribbean Culture-Building in Jamaica* (Chapel Hill and London: University of North Carolina Press, 2002), xv.

Part 2

Narratives of the Family

3

"Praisesongs" of the Family

Let me start with two stories. Beryl was born in Jamaica in 1935:

> Most of all...the love...was a crucial part of my childhood and I think it made me into a whole person. That I remember, the community love. People just loved you. I mean, if you were naughty, down the road, and Aunt B., or Mrs S., saw you, she belted you. And she knew that you were Miss A.'s daughter and you were out of order. People who I pass and didn't say 'Good morning', they'd say 'Come back here, you. Did you see me?' 'Yes ma'am.' 'Why didn't you say "Good morning"?' 'I don't know, ma'am.' Wallop, wallop, wallop. 'Getting too big for your boots.' And so the community had a parenting responsibility.[1]

Avis was born in Barbados in 1940:

> [M]y Mum has always been a wonderful woman...I remember her as being very beautiful and with long hair...[and] my grandmother was very beautiful...[and] my great-grandmother...when [my grandmother] died I was ten...and people...say "Oh, she's going to come back and pull your leg" because she loved me so much and I remembered, when she died, they passed me over the coffin, underneath again, saying that that'll keep them away from you. ...It is said that when they love you they come back and take you. So they pass me over the coffin, and under. They lift me up, say "Where is Avis? Where is Avis? Avis, Avis, come here." Up over the coffin and under again.[2]

We read such passages as episodes or anecdotes from individual lives but in this chapter I want to think in more complex ways about the relation between individual memories and their cultural contexts. Memories share meanings and understandings, language and images, dreams and nightmares. Of these, perhaps language is the most central for, as Ernst Gellner argues,

> How many things would we do altogether, if the concepts of those things were not built into the language of our culture?...Words are a very great deal: the rules of their use is wound up with—though not in any simple or obvious way—the activities and institutions of the societies in which they are employed. They embody the norms - or, indeed, the multiplicity or rival and incompatible norms—of those societies.'[3]

The relationship between language and thought, language and experience and—necessarily—language and memory has long been recognized in philosophical and anthropological research. Metaphors, rhetoric, sayings that punctuate life-story narratives all signify values and priorities, ways of looking at the world and interpreting it for, as Edward Sapir observed, "we see and hear and otherwise experience very largely as we do because the language habits of our community predispose certain choices of interpretation."[4] The language of the Anglophone Caribbean is, however, laced with loan words reflecting its hybrid cultural history, and shaped by grammatical structures that indicate African as well as European origins. There is in Caribbean English usage what Kamau Brathwaite terms a "bi and inter-lingualism [which] is a feature of our culturation,"[5] reflecting parallel thoughts, classifications and interpretations between standard and Creole English. People may speak the same language, but the meanings and symbolic structures may not be the same.[6] The linguistic turns, the metaphors, the sayings of Creole English require interpretation, for the language and the thoughts are "collaborating," in Benjamin Lee Whorf's words, with cultural practices

> where the "fashions of speaking" are closely integrated with the whole general culture...and there are connections within this integration, between the kind of linguistic analyses employed and various behavioural reactions and also the shapes taken by various cultural developments.[7]

In the Caribbean, the link between language and concept has been complicated by the complexities of its language history and the processes of language acquisition, the retention of symbolic meanings and the corrosive and creative effects of translation. The work of Maureen Warner Lewis demonstrates that African language retentions were far higher than was hitherto thought to be the case,[8] which leads one to speculate that there were far greater levels of cultural retention conveyed through the medium of language than had perhaps been considered. Indeed, if Warner Lewis conjecture is correct, it was primarily in the areas of domestic and ritual activity that the widest vocabulary, syntax, and (one assumes) sayings were retained, the cultural meanings of which may not necessarily have become realigned as the words were translated into European languages. Thus it is

> not only that African culture overseas has been retained by way of ritual act and secular mores, but also that such customs had formal and systematized literary vehicles to sustain and articulate them.[9]

And as she also points out, the "target" language would more likely have been Creole than standard English or French, and as such a hybridized form incorporating conceptual, syntactical and lexical "Africanisms" (as well as "Europeanisms," and subsequently, "Indianisms"). This holds interesting implications for the conceptual framework of the West Indies, not least in terms of attitudes toward families, as we shall see.

***

Recent work not only reiterates the importance of the frameworks for recall, but highlights the importance of the cultural narrative, the ways in which a society (or a nation) tells the story of itself.[10] While the personal narrative may be seen as the property of the individual—intrinsic to, and defining of, the individual—the plot that it follows may reflect and conform to the cultural narratives to which any one individual is exposed at any one time. Similarly, people may relate their life stories (and the stories in their life) according to the repertoire of genre available to them. Storytelling—whether our own or that of another—is a universal and central characteristic of all human endeavor. All stories—from the personal anecdote to the scientific theory—follow conventions: of process and purpose, presentation and style, place and performance. Broadly speaking, these conventions alert us to the type or genre of story we are hearing, reading, or seeing. We distinguish a scientific text from a history, a theological treatise from a fairy story, a novel from literary criticism, a joke from an eulogy. At the same time, when we tell a story, we choose the genre appropriate to the occasion,[11] we abide by (what Elizabeth Tonkin calls) "the conventions of discourse.[12] It is this choice that provides both meaning and understanding.

While we are familiar with genre in written and oral tradition, the notion of oral histories and life stories being subject to comparable typologies is less obvious. It appears to run counter to common sense. The life story is, after all, a particular construction in itself. At its most basic, a life story is the result of the interaction between the interviewer and the interviewee. It is determined by the culture of the interview, the nature and form of the questions asked, the skill of the interviewer, the relationship between interviewer and interviewee, and the place where the interview occurs. In this sense, a life story interview is essentially dialogic. It also constitutes, as Portelli[13] (1998) and Chanfrault-Duchet argue, a genre of its own.

> Thus life story is the product of a ritualised speech act, which results from the conjunction, in the 1970s, of a genre, autobiography, with a new medium, the tape recorder, within the institutional framework of social science. Life-story is thus at first a methodological tool used to collect information from social categories (among them women) which, although social actors, do not have access to the public stage. But considered as a genre, it can be viewed as an object created by the form and the contents, which produces meaning, just like a literary form.[14]

When the oral historian or the sociologist collects life stories, they collect a particular story, at a particular time, and in a particular location. What the historian may hear may never have been told, in that form, in that sequence, in that time frame, before. For the most part—even within the interview—people remember their lives in fragments, in Walter Benjamin's words, "moments and discontinuities."[15] To suggest that oral histories contain genres hints that our informant is engaged in a performance that somehow detracts from the authenticity of the memories recounted.

Yet, when collecting life stories, one is struck by the similarities between them, and by recurring themes of content or intent. It is not just, or always, the experience that is shared and that explains such similarity. It is also the understanding and interpretation that is shared which gives that kind of story, at that time, a priority and value, a moral and an emphasis, which explains or exonerates behavior, which reinforces a particular cultural or social code. It is these that constitute genres, and that determine the form and the content of the account.[16] How people present themselves—and that includes the silences as well as the articulations—may reveal as much about their values as their experiences and as much again about cultural practices. What is remembered, when, and why is molded by the culture in which they live, the language at their disposal, and the conventions and the genre appropriate to the occasion. In turn, cultural practices become manifest in the content, intent, and form of stories, emerging out of the traditions and genres of storytelling. Memories refer to, and reflect, the deep imaginative structures of the social mind. These are our cultural templates. It is through genre that particular kinds of comments may be made and understood. But, as Elizabeth Tonkin has pointed out, in order to understand the content and import of what is being said, it is essential to understand the genre through which the words are spoken.

***

If we heard Beryl's description of a Caribbean neighborhood once, we heard it repeated over:

> You have to be respectful of everybody. If you meet me in the road doing something, you could (chastise) me and send me home. ...And anything we give. When they bake, long time...they're making sure that they bake and they put aside that...this part for Mr. Joe, this is for this body, this is for that body. There's so much in this giving that even you have, and they have something, they will still send you something, to give, you know...people used to live nice a long time...they were a happy time...that was the way people was, long time.[17]

And over,

> If I did something wrong...I would have been told off, you know? Yes, there was this freedom...if you see a child doing something wrong, you will correct it, black, yellow, brown or white. I mean, you didn't have to wait, you know. ...We were free. We were people. ...If I'm there and it's a mealtime, you would get a meal. If they're here and it's mealtime, they get. ...You see what I'm getting at?[18]

And over,

> In those days...you have to respect your elders. If you see somebody coming...who is older than you, you had to show respect...otherwise they might give you a smack, or they might go and tell your parents, then you get another one on top of it! Take, for instance, you see somebody, an adult person...and you don't say "Good morning" or "Good afternoon"... they'll call you "Don't you see me?" "Don't you have any manners?" [19]

Again,

> All the neighbours we used to call Uncle and Aunt...all the adults, when you were growing up...we had uncles and aunts all over the place...[I played with] the kids in the area...everybody was in the street, playing, yes...[But] if you did anything wrong, your mother would soon know. Somebody would tell her. She would soon know, don't worry![20]

Despite the differences in these accounts, the repetitions are frequent and striking. What are we to make of this? The most obvious interpretation looks to the peculiarities of memory itself. There may well be a point of comparison between the golden then and the gilded now. It is not only in the Caribbean, of course, that the elderly look back on childhood through rose-tinted spectacles. Such points of comparison are part of the stock in trade of the fifty somethings everywhere. They are part and parcel of the repertoire—some might say clichés—of popular memory. Questions can often reveal examples of dissent in this world of unity, but the first order memory (if we can call it that) is one of harmony. These descriptions may be less a statement of how things actually were but of what they should have been, a form of what Alessandro Portelli[21] would call "uchronic" memory, an explanation of a change over which they were powerless. Alternatively, what we hear is how people conceive of experience and change. The past may well have been a more pleasant place, and we hear the loss of belonging, the loss of innocence, of a past in the process of becoming mythologized, a present in the process of being demonized, and a future absolved of responsibility.

But while the sentiments may be universal, the language and the metaphors are not. The description is couched, more often than not, in the language of the family, the relationships described in terms of the metaphors of family. Sometimes family and neighborhood were literally synonymous, but not always. Moreover, in these cases, the ages of the informants range from forty to eighty. Is this a literal description of a common and shared experience? Or a prescription of an ideal order? One interpretation could be that the family is used as both a metaphor and a blueprint for social organization. The gridlines of vertical and horizontal relationships within families and neighborhoods are characterized (at least in the Caribbean) by notions of responsibility and obligation, respect and authority, while the use of terms such as father, uncle, brother, mother, aunt, sister not only clarify status and respect, but also actual and anticipated behavior (see chapter two). Once outside the Caribbean, they became the blueprint for the networks of migration itself, and extended into the patterns of the settlement process and the formation of migrant organizations. They may have been, in Raphael Samuel's telling phrase "perceptions of the past which find expression in the discrimination of everyday life."[22]

There is perhaps another, related, reading. What we hear is a description of an idyllic—perhaps ideal—state of nature, a kind of Rousseau-esque vision, *une vie commune* where "all the individual consciences [were] in unison and combination."[23] In this idyll, the spats and squabbles which make up daily life for the rest of us seem never to have occurred or, at least, were never (or almost never) sung about, at least in the performances recorded. I use the term "sung" and "performance" here deliberately.

***

In Barbados, there was a genre of song called "banter," which survived well into the second half of the twentieth century. These were songs rooted in and inspired by village life. They were songs—a kind of melodious banter—primarily composed and sung by women. Far from celebrating the harmony of village life and the metaphoric security of the extended family, they recounted its crimes and quarrels, signalling the start of a squabble, detailing an actual one, or naming (by renaming) and (thereby) shaming a miscreant:

> ...Ratty girl if I did you,
> Uh would hide muhself beneath a shoe
> Fuh de tiefin'deed dat yuh serve Leslie,
> Yuh name shall be written in history.[24]

In the Caribbean we find reworkings of a variety of cultural forms, practices and artefacts, from Anansi stories to belief systems, to musical rhythms and dance forms, to cuisine and the decorative arts, whose origins can be traced, via slavery and subsequent importations, to Africa. Over time such cultural imports—and bear in mind that we are not talking one African culture here, but many, not one time frame, but several—have become both syncretized and creolized. They have responded, in the dynamic way of all cultures, by adapting and absorbing the waves of world influences on the Caribbean, creating something new, unique, and equally dynamic in the process.[25] There is nothing in the Caribbean that we can say is "purely" African (any more than it is "purely" European, or Indian). Any clues we may find in the contemporary Caribbean will be light years and cultural worlds apart from its original or contemporary equivalent. Nevertheless, we can still pick up and explore the traces. The anthropologist Sidney Mintz made an important point (he made many) when he argued that

> The glory of Afro-Americana inheres in the durable fibre of humanity, in the face of what surely must have been the most repressive epoch in modern world history. It depended—had to depend—on creativity and innovation far more than on the indelibility of particular cultural contents...we need to discover what actually happens when such new forms—be they musical, linguistic, political or whatever—take shape. In the case of music, the clues are especially plentiful.[26]

Let us take music and other aesthetic forms that conform to principles of composition. In Africa, the praise poem or praisesong is a particular aesthetic device that appears to be common throughout the continent south of the Sahara. Leroy Vail and Landeg White[27] have explored its use in Southern Africa; it has been noted by Elizabeth Tonkin[28] in her work on the Jlia of Liberia, researched in depth by Karin Barber[29] in her work on the Yoruba. The style and purpose of the praise poem reflects regional and cultural differences. Some trace the lineage of an individual, others that of a community, offering praise, or confirming authority. Some trace the history of a group, others its mythologies. They may be used to provide a safe stylistic house for social commentary and criticism, or to extol the virtues and achievements of a local hero or "Big Man." Most are told or sung by men but some—such as the Oriki among the Yoruba—are sung by women. Some are straightforward, some elliptical. Some are formal in content and construction, some value improvization of theme and style. They may offer a history and a judgment, an interpretation and a prescription. They may be used to entertain or to teach. They cover a variety of themes and are presented in a variety of formats, sung or spoken, poem or prose. They are one in a range of cultural devices or performances through which the past is made to live in the present, regardless of whether the theme of the song is contemporary or historical. The link with the past is as much through the performance, style, and intent as through the content. Moreover, particular kinds of criticism may be legitimately voiced only through this aesthetic. Leroy Vail and Landeg White in their work on Southern Africa cite, for instance, two singers from Mozambique who could justify their song, which indicted a harsh colonial official, on the grounds that

> It was "all right" the men said because the complaint was expressed in song. To say such things outside the song "would be just insulting him…just provoking him" but so long as it was done through singing "there will be no dispute."[30]

They could say in song what they could not say in speech. Throughout the West Indies there is a tradition which uses the aesthetic of song to voice commentary, criticism, or complaint. This particular use of song was first identified during slavery[31] and it is not unreasonable to assume that its use then may be traced to African societies where song was, and is, put to comparable use. The use of song as social commentary, and criticism, continues to the present in the Caribbean. Calypso is perhaps the most well-known contemporary example, or manifestation, of this although even the more recent musical innovations of reggae and ragga, rap and dub can be seen to fall within this tradition.[32] Gordon Rohlehr,[33] in his work on the history of calypso, suggests a link between contemporary calypso and the praisesong of Africa, particularly in the roots of political calypso. While calypso developed along a particular trajectory evolving a particular narrative and compositional form, there were other traditional songs in Jamaica or Barbados, for instance, identifiable until well into the twentieth century, which performed a comparable function. For example,

> Oh, poor Millie!
> Millie gone to Brazil
> She ent tell nobody
> Wire up round she waist
> And the razor cut up she face.
> I went to the walk
> And the sister say Lord!
> And Millie gone to be wed.

In style, it is elliptical, relying on local knowledge for its meaning. My informant felt compelled to explain it to me. It is, in fact, a satirical rendition of the cynical excuse offered to the police by a man accounting for the disappearance of his lover. In fact, far from Millie eloping to Brazil (at the time, the 1920s, a familiar, though distant, migrant destination), she had been brutally murdered by him.

The Caribbean sociologist Rex Nettleford[34] argues that many elements of contemporary Caribbean carnivals—from the grand spectaculars of Trinidad, to Jon Konnu in Jamaica, or Belize or the Bahamas, or the Tuk band in Barbados—can be traced to their African origins, not only in the visual traditions and impacts of the mask but in the historical license they provided to invert the social order and to invite and legitimate, through song and dance, commentary and criticism. Even more directly, Lorna McDaniel's work on the *Big Drum Ritual of Carriacou*[35]—subtitled *Praisesongs in Rememory of Flight*—chronicles and codifies the extant musical and poetic texts of Carriacou. Not only does she display their African genesis, she uses them to explore the history and social politics of pre- and post-Emancipation Carriacou and Grenada. Similarly, Maureen Warner Lewis's[36] work on the Yoruba imprints in Trinidad, and among the Maroon communities of Jamaica and Suriname,[37] suggests that vibrant vestiges of African song culture and storytelling modes remain.

Song and poetry is one cultural form. Prose is another. While the notations may be different from music, the stylistic devices that conduct the rhythms of prose hint at more formal cultural practices. Visitors to and commentators on the West Indies noted the love of what they saw as the grandiloquence of the slaves. The Jamaican Edward Long, in his *History of Jamaica*, recorded how the slaves

[g]ive their dogs as many names as a German prince; or more frequently call them by a whole sentence, as, *Run-brisk-you-catch-'um-good*, etc. ...The better sort are very fond of improving their language, by catching at any hard word that the Whites happen to let fall in their hearing; and they alter and misapply it in a strange manner; but a tolerable collection of them gives an air of knowledge and importance in the eyes of their brethren, which tickles their vanity, and makes them more assiduous in stocking themselves with this unintelligible jargon.[38]

"A negro wd. Make a capital *special* pleader," commented John Anderson, echoing Joseph Sturge and Thomas Harvey's observations on the oratorical skills of the apprentices, developed in bondage, which, as McDonald argues, could be used to "manipulate a system where the formal relations of power and control were so disadvantageous to them."[39] Bryan Edwards, the eighteenth-century Jamaican slave owner similarly observed, in 1793,

Among other propensities and qualities of the Negroes must not be omitted their loquaciousness. They are as fond of exhibiting set speeches as orators by profession; but it requires a considerable share of patience to hear them throughout; for they commonly make a long preface before they come to the point, beginning with a tedious enumeration of the past services and hardships.[40]

Edwards commented later, "Yet I have sometimes heard them convey strong meaning in a narrow compass."[41] suggesting that there were levels of linguistic codes that varied according to the context and function of the narrative. They could be a pithy proverb (of which many examples remain in the contemporary Caribbean) or language used as ornamentation, mask, and subversion. What Edwards, perhaps unwittingly, observed was both the performance, albeit in Creole English, of an older African oral tradition that prized prose renditions, displays of linguistic pride and skill that elevated the storyteller and, by extension, the story told. They were also a display of the slave's command over, and innovatory skills in, the language of the "massah." As such, they were a display of political resistance which almost certainly went over the head of the master. Gordon Rohlehr suggests that, in the case of Trinidad, the linguistic virtuosity displayed in the calypso of the late nineteenth and early twentieth centuries symbolized and marked a mastery over English, at a time when the struggle between French Creole and English was at its most pronounced.[42] In Barbados, the custom of "speechifying," practiced until late into this century, was another form of display of linguistic virtuosity, often performed by a moonlighting school master who would incorporate Latin into his repertoire. Particular versions of prose, therefore, may also be seen as part of the cultural performances of the Caribbean, part of the genres available through which a particular kind of comment may be made, and more particularly, recognized for what it is.

***

At certain points in the interviews, the narratives sprang to life as if there were a shift of register. It happened when certain themes were introduced. Not all the time, not every time, but with sufficient regularity to suggest a pattern. Thus these stories—highlighted here—of community life, these idyllic, ideal worlds, denoted such a shift. What may be identified is a formulaic genre in many of the narratives, distinguished by their common theme, purpose, and style, by content, intent, and device. As such, we need to understand the genre in order to understand their import. The genre, I would suggest, is part of a cultural template which in this case functions didactically and critically, as a powerful reminder of, and lesson for, a particular set of communitarian values. These are less a description of the past, but more a prescription, a manifesto, of how life should or ought to be, conveying social principles and a social world characterized by order and respect, singing the praises of ideal types. It is emblematic, symbolic short-hand for a particular [cultural] worldview. In this, the formulaic, almost ritualistic, descriptions become mnemonics in which prescriptions are both encoded and remembered. In the cases of the Yoruba in Trinidad, for instance, the remnants of song and poems suggested

> not only that African culture overseas has been retained by way of ritual act and secular mores, but also that such customs had formal and systematized literary vehicles to sustain and articulate them.[43]

While the case of the Yoruba is quite specific (since for the most part their arrival in the West Indies is relatively recent), the use of such forms to transmit values may well predate the Yoruba and some may even be interpreted as vestiges of African praisesong, in function if not always in form.[44] Many reveal the values and philosophies that underpinned social organization, inform cultural representation, and provide an idiom through which African-Caribbean peoples converse, and survive, in the Caribbean and beyond. Conveying meaning through metaphor is not only a practice with a long African pedigree; it was also (arguably) a way of hoodwinking the plantation and colonial world.[45] Brathwaite's inter-linguality had a political as well as an aesthetic purpose.

From this perspective, while the praisesongs of lineage, of history, had no resonance in slavery—and thus no relevance for survival (although Lorna McDaniel argues a strong case for adaptation)—what we may have are vestiges of their prescriptive purpose, and a praise, a thanksgiving, a prayer to the past and its people that made them, like Beryl, "a whole person." Perhaps what we have is an echo, a praisesong stripped of its particularities and presenting itself in the bare bones of principle. In this template, there is no room for disharmonious behavior. Another (calypso, banter) exists for the purpose. These are, perhaps, no more than fragments of a more coherent order where, as the African-American scholar Henry Louis Gates commented,

> To reassemble fragments, of course, is to engage in an act of speculation, to attempt to weave a fiction of origins and subgeneration. It is to render the implicit as explicit, and at times to imagine the whole from the past.[46]

These are "first order" memories, or accounts. It would be a mistake to view them as a simple first pressing. They are more of a distillation, or compression, of a cultural practice. Seen this way, its aesthetic is of equal value to its content, conveying a comparable authenticity.

Let me turn now to the second story. Again, if we heard this once we heard it over and over. References to spirits, and spiritual metaphors are a recurring theme in many West Indian narratives. Both old and young talk of themselves as "spiritual" people. Family members are often described in religious terms, mothers and grandmothers, are "saints," they are "angels," they are "blessed." (See chapter six for further discussion on the language and role of grandparents.) Saints and angels, the metaphors of Christianity, run in parallel with other metaphors, of duppies (ghosts) and the spirit of the dead, an interest in lineage, a reverence for the "old ancestant," an abiding trust in kinship, and a powerful sense of lineage. "When you are looking at me," Beryl remarked, "you're looking at my mother. I am the image of my mother." "I was never lonely," another informant remarked (about her migration to England), "I carried my family within me." "I was a grandmother child," Beulah, a Barbadian woman born in 1950, told me, "My great-grandmother was everything to me. I can feel her presence even now."

In these interviews, the women knit into their narratives of self powerful identifications with family and in particular with mothers and grandmothers. "We were all full of my grandmother," the Trinidadian Dionne Brand wrote in her short story "Photograph."[47] "[S]he had left us full and empty of her." Images of mothers and grandmothers provide intimacy (Beryl, for instance, playing with her mother's long hair). They even elide (Anne-Marie was born in London in 1972 and referred to her grandmother as "Mother" because "everyone does. Her children do, her grandchildren do, her great-grandchildren do. Everyone does").[48] These descriptions suggest lineage and tradition, explanation and validation. The "grandmother child," the lady in whom you see her mother, or who never felt lonely because of the family within her. These were all migrant women who left behind, were absent from, family and kin in the West Indies. This sense of the spirit of kin and particularly ancestral kin, is a strong element in West Indian culture and acts as a powerful binding force and dynamic in families, echoed often—perhaps shaped by—the ritual language used to describe it. Such metaphors reveal a more profound sense both of self, of women, of the vitality of lineage, kinship and family in the construction of subjectivity, and offer us considerable insight into the values, forms and power relations of African-Caribbean families.

In this, women's roles as kin and mothers are shaped by a specific "cosmology" that may place them at the center of an exchange of lineage, as Virginia Kerns so perceptively observed in 1984 in her work on the Garifuna of Belize.[49] This feature, as Constance Sutton noted, has remarkable parallels among the Yoruba.[50] As such, this may help reinterpret the much-vaunted "matrifocality" of West Indian family life, and deflect attention away from what she describes as the "power by default" theses which centers African-Caribbean women as powerful only because their men are absent through migration or poverty.[51] It makes sense of, and provides cultural meaning to, a range of identifiable social characteristics such as the importance of consanguineous (as opposed to conjugal) links, of family reunions and rituals (notably funerals), of child fostering, and so forth, all of which have been regarded in the literature as part of the default syndrome which (analytically, at least) renders women's roles as secondary and derivative. In this reading, therefore, women are placed at center stage, as the life bearers, the carriers of lineage, and the ones primarily responsible for cultural and familial continuity. Mothers are angels and saints not (just) because they display abundant goodness or patience, but precisely because they represent a living link with the dead, and are the guardians of the future. They are powerful beings in societies that remain officially patrilineal and patriarchal. Indeed, it is mothers who, through their children, link the fathers and their families.

Caribbean women (and men) may have a different sense of self from that which we, as Europeans, may understand with our emphasis on individuality and autonomy. It conforms to an alternative narrative of self, which enfolds within it an acknowledgement of lineage, and their place within it. This place necessarily shifts along with the course in the life cycle. In this sense, it is much to do with origins as continuity,[52] an awareness of the roles women play in their own life cycle and that of their families. Women, in other words, may have a plural sense of self, fashioned by the roles they perform, and their positioning as intermediaries in their lineage. Indeed, a sense of self emerges precisely out of the cooperation that is integrally involved (with younger and older family members) in the act of positioning, the tensions and ambiguities of adjusting the individual within the social. They may even invoke a variety of terms to talk about the self, as Gloria Wekker[53] notes in relation to Afro-Surinamese women, calling in the ancestors and spirits, and using their voices to mask both criticism and affirmation.

While I talk of a plural sense of self, the term polyvocality may be more appropriate. The historian, sociologist and novelist Erna Brodber wrote of one of her characters that "The voice belongs to the family group dead and alive. We walk by their leave, for planted in the soil, we must walk over them to get where we are going."[54] "This account of my life," Jamaica Kincaid wrote in her novel *The Autobiography of My Mother,* "has been an account of my mother's life as much as it has been an account of mine, and even so, again it is an account of the life of the children I did not have, as it is their account of me."[55] In our "noisy" narratives (to use Kristeva's term) individuals spill into families—siblings, who often do not share paternity, nevertheless grow up together "as part of the family...because that is the order of the day."[56] "[I]n my mum's family, to be quite honest, I just lumped everybody together, if she's my auntie, she's my auntie"[57]—and families spill into the community.

> My mother was plump, georgeous. She was everybody's mum...everyone would be crying out as they're passing "Hallo grandmother"...or "Hallo, mother."[58]

And generations, as we have seen, elide into each other, speak to each other, live through each other, and hold the potential to enter each other. There is a polyvocality and a fluidity. What seems to link the oral narratives (and much of the literature) is the lack of boundaries, whether genealogical, political,[59] or cultural. The Martiniquian novelist Chamoiseau talks in his novel *Texaco*[60] of the "boundless" city. What links the experience of West Indians—of migration, the migrant, and those left behind—is this sense of boundlessness, of an ever permeable membrane through which emotions, subjectivities, identities flow, the generations and the genders become repositioned, boundless, as grandmothers are reborn as mothers, mothers emerge as breadwinners, siblings are cojoined through their mother, and lineage, the "old ancestant" unifies.

I think we can push this further. Karin Barber's work on the Oriki —a very particular form of song composed and performed by Yoruba women—commented that while the women may compose songs for the men, specific songs for individual women are rare. Far more common are songs that salute mothers, or motherhood, in general. At the same time, part of the performers' art is to give voice to a range of generations through eliding the genealogical boundaries. There is always an indeterminacy, and a confluence of identities. But I do wonder whether what we have here is not evidence also of another cultural template, another vestige of a praisesong, a celebration of—and a prescription for—all mothers.

The Big Drum Ritual of Carriacou venerates ancestral heroes such as Cromanti or Cudjo and, as Lorna McDaniel argues, in much the same way:

> [T]he calypso, parang, myth, Nancy stories and the political slogan become compositional scores, praisesongs of cultural knowledge that enliven the ancestors and the disremembered.[61]

***

I have pointed here to two possible "compositional scores"—the community as family, the mother as the source of lineage, but there may be others. Elsewhere, for instance,[62] I have looked at the stories men told of migration, in which their curiosity leads them into scrapes, but whose ingenuity enabled them to escape and emerge as triumphant and autonomous heroes. In many ways the scores of their stories resemble those of Anansi, the eponymous hero of Caribbean (and West African) folklore. I suspect there are more, stories of "fathers,"[63] for instance, or stories that are gender specific. What McDaniel calls compositional score I would term a cultural template. These templates are multilayered and polyvocal. They recall a textured memory of the past as a prescription for the present, praisesongs, indeed, of cultural knowledge.

What are we to make of these fragments? Without wishing to devalue the informational content of oral sources, we must, nevertheless, be aware of the importance of the aesthetic as an additional source of meaning, and the vitality of aesthetic as a mnemonic, through which values are learned and conveyed. Perhaps we can use it to rethink the role and position of kinship and lineage in African-Caribbean families and the ways in which those prescriptions continue to be conveyed throughout the Caribbean and its Diaspora. It has been argued that West Indians abroad develop a heightened awareness of political and cultural identity, based, as R.T. Smith suggested, on "a created, valued way of life that is creole."[64] Perhaps at the heart of that "creolity" is the family, and at the heart of the family are the praisesongs in which its values and prescriptions are encoded and transmitted.

Notes

1. JA 028/2/1/1/9.
2. BF 069/2/1/2/15.
3. Ernst Gellner, *Thought and Change* (London: Weidenfeld and Nicolson 1964),195.
4. Edward Sapir, quoted in Benjamin Lee Whorf, *Language, Thought and Reality* (Cambridge, Mass: The M.I.T.Press, 1956), 134.
5. See introduction by Edward Brathwaite to Roger Mais, *Brother Man* (London: Heinemann, 1974).
6. See also Carolyn Cooper, *Noises in the Blood* (London: Macmillan, 1993) for a fuller discussion of the levels of African narrative retentions and conventions in Caribbean orality and poetry.
7. Benjamin Lee Whorf, *Language, Thought and Reality,* 159.
8. Maureen Warner Lewis, *Trinidad Yoruba. From Mother Tongue to Memory* (Kingston:The Press, University of the West Indies, 1997).
9. Maureen Warner-Lewis, *Guinea's Other Sons. The African Dynamic in Trinidad Culture* (Dover, Mass: The Majority Press, 1991), 113.
10. Kate Hodgkin and Susannah Radstone, *Contested Pasts. The Politics of Memory* (London: Routledge, 2003).
11. For a more detailed discussion see Mary Chamberlain and Paul Thompson, introduction to *Narrative and Genre,* Routledge Studies in Memory and Narrative (London: Routledge, 1998), 1-22.
12. Elizabeth Tonkin, *Narrating Our Past. The Social Construction of Oral History* (Cambridge: Cambridge University Press, 1992).
13. Alessandro Portelli, "Oral History as Genre" in Mary Chamberlain and Paul Thompson, *Narrative and Genre.*

14. Marie-Francoise Chanfrault-Duchet, "Textualisation of the Self and Gender Identity in the Life Story" in *Feminism and Autobiography. Texts, Theories, Methods*, eds. Tess Cosslett, Celia Lury, and Penny Summerfield (London/New York: Routledge, 2000), 62.
15. Walter Benjamin, "A Berlin Chronicle" in idem., *One Way Street* (London: Verso, 1997), 316.
16. For a fuller discussion of this see Chamberlain and Thompson, 1998.
17. TM 098/1/1/1/2-6.
18. TP 108/2/1/1/1/8.
19. JG025/2/1/1/16.
20. TC 029/2/1/1/9-10.
21. Alessandro Portelli, "Uchronic Dreams" in Raphael Samuel and Paul Thompson, *The Myths We Live By* (London: Routledge, 1990).
22. Raphael Samuel, *Theatres of Memory* (London: Verso, 1995), 17.
23. Jean-Jacques Rousseau, *La Nouvelle Héloise* (Oxford: Woodstock Books, 1989).
24. Trevor Marshall, Peggy McGeary, and Grace Thompson, *Folksongs of Barbados* (Bridgetown, n.p., n.d). The classification of "banter" songs is attributed to Marshall et al.
25. For a discussion on the processes of cultural formations and transformations in the Caribbean, see Edward Kamau Brathwaite, *The Development of Creole Society in Jamaica 1770-1820* (Oxford: Clarendon Press, 1971) and Fernando Ortiz, *Cuban Counterpoint: Tobacco and Sugar* (Durham and London: Duke University Press, 1995). Ortiz developed the notion of "transculturation," the process by which cultures were uprooted from one context, and created anew in another through the mixing and blending of peoples and circumstances encountered there.
26. Sidney Mintz, *Caribbean Transformations* (New York: Columbia University Press, 1989 [1974]), 14.
27. Leroy Vail and Landeg White, *Power and the Praise Poem: Southern African Voices in History* (Charlottesville: University Press of Virginia; London: James Currey, 1991).
28. Elizabeth Tonkin, *Narrating Our Past*.
29. Karin Barber *I Could Speak Until Tomorrow: Oriki, Women and the Past in a Yoruba Town* (Washington, D.C.: Smithsonian Institution Press, 1991).
30. Vail and White, *Power and the Praise Poem*, 41.
31. Orlando Patterson *The Sociology of Slavery*.
32. Louis Regis, *The Political Calypso. True Opposition in Trinidad and Tobago 1962-1987* (Kingston: The Press The University of the West Indies, 1999).
33. Gordon Rohlehr, *Calypso and Society in Pre-Independence Trinidad* (Port-of-Spain, Gordon Rohlehr, 1990).
34. Rex Nettleford "Implications for Caribbean Development" in John W. Nunley and Judith Bettelheim ed. *Caribbean Festival Arts* (Seattle and London: St. Louis Art Museum in association with University of Washington Press, 1998).
35. Lorna McDaniel, *The Big Drum Ritual of Carriacou: Praisesongs in Rememory of Flight* (Gainesville: University Press of Florida, 1998).
36. Maureen Warner Lewis *Guinea's Other Sons: The African Dynamic in Trinidad Culture* (Dover, Mass.: Majority Press, 1991).
37. Marjorie Whylie and Maureen Warner-Lewis, "Characteristics of Maroon Music from Jamaica and Suriname" in E. Kofi Agorsah, *Maroon Heritage. Archaeological, Ethnographic and Historical Perspectives*, ed. E. Kofi Agorsah (Kingston: University of the West Indies, Canoe Press, 1994).

38. Long, *History,* vol. II, 427. For an excellent discussion on contemporary naming practices see Richard D. E. Burton, "Names and Naming in Afro-Caribbean Culture" *New West Indian Guide* 73,1 and 2 (1999), 35-58.
39. McDonald, *Between Slavery,* 150n.
40. Bryan Edwards, quoted in Rohlehr, *Calypso and Society,* 57
41. Ibid.
42. Ibid.
43. Maureen Warner-Lewis, *Guinea's Other Sons*, 113.
44. See Lorna McDaniel, *The Big Drum Ritual of Carriacou* and Maureen Warner-Lewis, *Guinea's Other Sons;* Maureen Warner-Lewis, *Trinidad Yoruba*.
45. See also Diane Austin-Broos, "Women and Jamaican Pentecostalism" in *Caribbean Portraits;* Raymond T. Smith, *Jamaica Genesis* (Chicago: University of Chicago Press, 1997).
46. Henry Louis Gates, *The Signifying Monkey: A Theory of African American Literary Criticism* (New York: Oxford University Press, 1988), xxiv.
47. Dionne Brand, "Photograph" in *Sans Souci and Other Stories* (Toronto: Women's Press, 1989), 75.
48. TC 058/2/1/1/5
49. Virginia Kerns *Women and the Ancestors. Black Carib Kinship and Ritual*, (Urbana and Chicago: University of Illinois Press 1997 [1983])
50. Constance Sutton. "Introduction" to Kerns,*Women and the Ancestors.*
51. Ibid.
52. Ibid.
53. Gloria Wekker, "One Finger Does Not Drink Okra Soup. African-Surinamese Women and Critical Agency" in *Feminist Genealogies, Colonial Legacies, Democratic Futures,* ed. M. Jacqui Alexander and Chandra Talpede Mohanty (London: Routledge, 1997).
54. Erna Brodber, *Jane and Louisa Will Soon Come Home* (London: New Beacon, 1980), 12.
55. Jamaica Kincaid, *The Autobiography of my Mother* (London: Vintage, 1996), 227.
56. JI 028.
57. JB 008.
58. JI 028.
59. See, for instance, Linda Basch, Nina Glick-Schiller, and Cristina Szanton Blanc, *Nations Unbound: Transnational Projects, Post-Colonial Predicaments and Deterritorialized Nation States* (Langhorne, P.A.: Gordon and Breach, 1994).
60. Pierre Chamoiseau, *Texaco* (London: Granta 1997).
61. McDaniel, *Big Drum,* 166.
62. Mary Chamberlain, *Narratives of Exile and Return* (London: Macmillan, 1997).
63. Lord Melody's calypso in the early 1950s "Mama Look A Boo-boo" may well have been saying in song ("Daddy, why you ugly so?") what could not be said in speech.
64. R.T.Smith, *Kinship and Class.*

4

Continuities and Change

"The Caribbean islands early became settings in which peoples of very different pasts but fairly similar presents jostled together in new social settings. The cultural accompaniments have been heterogeneity and diversity, as well as a remarkable amount of innovation in style."[1]

The legacy of historical and cultural heterogeneity[2] in the Caribbean has resulted in a variety of family forms, not only between and within social groups, but also between and within families. Each family is a refraction of a highly complex grid of social and cultural influences where at any one time one form may take precedence over another, and where apparently competing or contradictory ideologies and practices can cohabit more or less compatibly. Families are micro-societies of their own, with their own histories and cultures, creating their own dynamics and ethos, continuities and ruptures, constantly evolving to accommodate growth and change—of individual family members and of the family as a unit. Family lives are complex, involving sets of evolving relationships and roles, which change over the life course of both the individual and the family, involving responses to space and circumstance, and adjustments to the configuration and reconfigurations of family membership and jurisdiction. Issues of choice, reason, and behavior in families are as much a function of consciousness and rationality as of emotions and inequalities.

In understanding families—any family—it seems more fruitful to focus not on one time frame or one set of relationships, such as the conjugal relationship or the mother/child relationship, but on multiple destinations. Any one individual will relate to family members through a fluid set of relationships. In the life of the family, different relationships become dominant or subordinate at any time while the roles any one individual will perform in a family are multifarious and multifaceted.

This chapter introduces three case studies of African-Caribbean families, to illustrate the variety of types possible within one family and the fluidity of roles and relationships within the family. It attempts to explore some of the constituent elements in family formation, to describe the everyday, interior experience and affective world of the family. The families have shaped, and been shaped by, migration and, in common with most of the families in our study, described themselves as "close," even though family members are geographically and genealogically dispersed.

Merle's Family

This first family illustrates the complexity of families, the importance of looking at the family in a wide and long-term context, and the tension (and its accommodation) between two sets of family ideologies and one set of family values. The family values were quite clear. Whatever disagreements or skirmishes may take place between family members, family loyalty and unity must remain paramount. This loyalty extends vertically and diagonally across the generations and horizontally between them, and exists independent of time and space. As one family member described it,

> we've always been a family that keep in touch with our families all over Jamaica...it is really important to us ...we always have family gatherings, just sit around and chat. Or if anything is happening in the family, a christening, a drink up, everybody get on the phone...it just keeps things alive...and you get to know your family that way...it is very, very important for people to just socialise with each other, really, especially the family.[3]

The oldest family member, Merle, was born in Jamaica in 1925. She was her mother's first-born child, although she had a brother on her father's side. Her parents never married and her father died when she was three. After his death, Merle went to live with her maternal grandmother, surrounded by kin on a complicated pattern of family land.[4] When she was nine, Merle returned to live with her mother and an aunt. Her mother by then had another child whose father she recalls as "kind and good" but whom she "didn't relish."[5] Her memories of her mother are ambivalent (Merle's daughter, Alana, refers to early maternal neglect), and "the most one that shows me love was my aunt."[6]

At fourteen Merle left school. She lived with this aunt, and with the exception of a short period as a domestic when she was sixteen, she did not work. Her then boyfriend helped support her until he suspected her of infidelity. He himself was married. The relationship turned violent, and Merle ended it, dismissing his attempts to woo her back, "You cannot love me..." she told her boyfriend "You have your woman inside. I am outside. So just leave me alone. But he wants to have her *and* have me." [7]

Shortly after, she met another man by whom she had two children, and whom she subsequently married when she was twenty-seven and her eldest child, Alana, was six. He was an agricultural manager. Although Merle did not work at any formal occupation she nevertheless supplemented the family income with rearing fowl and stock. In doing so, she was (like many women) participating in the informal economy. For many women in the Caribbean income-generating activity was confined to the informal economy, which satisfied the material needs of family support, paid lip service to the rhetoric of a "modern" division of labor, and rendered their contribution invisible to the state (and arguably emerged as a form of resistance to the regime and expectations of plantation labor, see chapter two). Its invisibility was not confined to the state. Another informant, Beryl, for instance, recalled,

> Mother did not work, no. No. She would be at home. Women hardly went out to work in those days, it simply wasn't done. They would take in washing for the local English-owned hotels, and she'd do washing, and the washing would be delivered, say, collected, and then delivered, say, perhaps a few days later. Yes. And Mother was what was called a "higgler"...My mother bought and sold things, so when my father cultivated all the stuff, and got it home after it had been harvested, my mother would go to...Kingston, and sell. And my mother would sell wholesale. She would be selling to hotels and all the people who owned shops in Kingston. She was back from market very quickly, perhaps one night away. And sometimes, she would sell in the local market, things like eggs and vegetables and fruits, and whatever was seasonal. And that's how, that's how we lived, and that's how most of the people lived.[8]

Many women were (and still are) able to exchange this informal activity for more formal labor participation when and if the circumstance could arise. In Barbados, for instance, data from the 1990 census revealed that 77.9 percent of women in the twenty to thirty-nine age group were employed—the group at the height of their reproductive years—while 47.8 percent of the forty to fifty-nine age group were employed.[9]

In 1962, Merle made the decision to come to England "for five years." She "partnered" the fare,[10] and joined a friend, and her cousin who had "come down" some years earlier, leaving her children with their father in Jamaica. It was an agonizing period. "I used to be so sad," Merle recalled "on the street, seeing people with their children, my heart aches, you know. I wanted to go back and get them here."[11] As a result, after three years, she sent for them to join her. "and when I get them here, it was the best thing in life."[12] Her husband, however, refused to join her. He claimed not to like the cold, but Merle "hear he have another woman living in the house."[13] Merle eventually divorced him in 1978.

There is no conflict between leaving children in the care of others (sometimes for extended periods) and securing work, nor is it, or was it considered (not least when Merle was young) a threat to the status and function of a husband if the wife provided or supplemented the family income. Throughout this study we hear similar stories of children left, for long or short periods, in the care of others while either one or both of their parents went to work. In this, African-Caribbean practice was in direct contrast to what was, until recently, considered (in a British and European context) responsible motherhood, where women were expected to remain at home to bring up children and pose no threat to the status of the husband by competing in the employment market. The high incidence of female employment in the Caribbean may be interpreted as a response to poverty, and/or as a response to particular employment opportunities (for instance, where male out-migration has been consistently high, as it was in Barbados during the first two decades of the twentieth century, providing full employment opportunities for women). It may also be seen as a cultural response, an assumption that women have equal if not primary responsibility for the material welfare of their children, or that women are expected to be economically autonomous, if not self-sufficient. As another informant put it,

> when it come to a home with children it means the mother had to, she had to bear the Atlas, she had to be the Atlas. So it goes on then…I… couldn't stand it because I like to know that my children wake up this morning and [I] … know where to get something to give them to eat. I don't mind myself but I hate to think that children are hungry.[14]

How else can we interpret Merle's decision to migrate? Her husband was a skilled worker (and employed). Although his skills would not have been transferable in Britain, given the contemporary wage differentials, he would have earned more than Merle. It was, however, Merle who took the initiative in migrating. Merle's decision to migrate was based on the calculation that in five years she could return to Jamaica with a capital sum to help the family and in the meantime send remittances to help support the children. Her income enabled the children to be educated privately; after they joined her in England, Merle continued to support them, working in a factory in North London. In the interviews, women as well as men took this initiative and even those women who migrated to join husbands or boyfriends fully expected to work on arrival, leaving any children in the care of kin. Providing or securing financial support for the children may be seen, therefore, as an expression of maternal love as well as a response to particular circumstances. As such, it may be interpreted as a value whose origins may be traced to Africa,[15] but which has now become embedded in contemporary African-Caribbean practices, as Mintz and Price suggest,

> The generation of separate and independent economic risk structures within a single family may be considered characteristically West African and African-Caribbean, as opposed to European or North American.[16]

This continues as a feature of some contemporary African societies. For instance, the pattern of maternal support and the values attached resembles contemporary urban Ghana where, as Gracia Clark observed, "biological motherhood remains a key responsibility, but one that logically or naturally mandates income-generating work rather than personal responsibility for childcare."[17]

In England, Merle lived with her cousin and shared the childcare with her. The arrangement worked well until her cousin decided to emigrate to Canada. She sold the house, with Merle and the children as sitting tenants, but the next owner made life unbearable. Unaware of her rights as a tenant, she left and rented other accommodation for herself and the children, and continued to work to support them.

Her daughter, Alana, was born in Jamaica in 1952. She was ten years old when her mother left for Britain, and although she thinks the "world" of both her parents, she has a particular affection for her father "such lovely memories." He was, for instance, immensely knowledgeable about horticulture, and passed on much of this knowledge and love of plants to her

> I keep bringing it up to my kids...showing them things that he's done...I remember him peeling two ripe bananas...and [he] said to me "That's the male one, and that's the female banana" and ...even now I tell the kids I work with, and many people when they're eating a banana..... "Do you know which banana you're eating?" And the way he described it...I'm just amazed.'[18]

Her father had been orphaned as a young child. She cherished the guidance he gave her, made all the more remarkable since, as a child, he had no one "behind him, to guide him, really...but, you know, I think by seeing things, he thought he'd try and do the best for us, really."[19]

By contrast, her mother she describes as a "very strong lady. Very strong. I think this is where I got it from"[20] Her mother's childhood she recounted as punctuated with moves between relatives "just from pillar to post really...as a youngster,"[21] as a result of the neglect of her mother. Yet this mother—Alana's grandmother—in old age doted on her granddaughter:

> I always looked forward to...Granny coming down to see us, you know, and bringing us little goodies....She even wanted to adopt me, really, and my dad...wouldn't have anything like that...she wanted to actually take me because...in West Indian families...they do sometimes...she used to spoil me rotten really. And, grown up now, I suppose I look at it in a way, yes, she was glad that I'm her grand-daughter, but because she didn't really give my mum the love she should have given her. I think she was just pouring it out on me, more than anything else.[22]

While Alana's relationship with her grandmother was good, that with her mother (like her own mother before her) was more ambivalent. Her mother's migration, for instance, forced a separation first from her mother (we "lost that mother and daughter relationship"),[23] then between her parents, and finally from her father: "he should have followed...I think that's a great pity in West Indian family, really. Well, that's the worst thing...when you have to travel...where by travelling...the relationship break up between the mother and the father. And this is what happened."[24] Reunion with her mother in England neither compensated for the loss of her father, nor for the time lost with her mother "we never did make up for lost time."[25] The day after she and her brother arrived, they began school and her mother returned to work. The experience was daunting, and she found an English school frightening.

> You're frightened to open your mouth because...you're going to speak different to them...and bearing in mind what you were taught when you're in the West Indies, that white people...are superior, you know, and certain things you can say, certain things you can't say...you just feel as if you're in prison, really...because you didn't want to do anything that was wrong, so you just—even if you wanted to ask the teacher a question, you didn't. You didn't do it. You just kept quiet And you just went through all the lessons not really understanding what you're doing although, basically, when I was in the West Indies, I was always a bright kid...but you still didn't want to open your mouth, just in case they're going to laugh at you and whatever.[26]

The experience of school was compounded by cramped and unsatisfactory living arrangements with her mother's cousin, "To me," Alana said, "it felt like...when you're in the West Indies and you see servants, you know? Like we were the servants, that sort of way, and you had rich relatives, that sort of thing, That was how it felt, living there."[27] And, like her mother, it was to her aunt (her father's sister) that Alana turned to in her teenage years "because I couldn't get on with my mum, I would run to her. She was my mum, you know? Any joy I'm sharing...she knows more about me than my mum knows...my aunt," she says "was like a rock, really." She was "very, very, very, very, very important."[28]

Alana, however, became pregnant when she was sixteen. According to Alana, Merle "hit the roof"[29] at the news. Merle herself concedes that she was "mad" and also, "sad"[30] by her daughter's pregnancy. The regularity with which unmarried daughters recall their mother's reactions to their first pregnancy indicate the shaming rituals that Edith Clarke[31] identified, where the daughter may even be temporarily exiled from the home before the mother forgives and embraces the grandchild. Jean Besson argues that these rituals are "rituals of reversal" where, far from suggesting loss of respectability, they indicate female reputation and "contribute significantly to a woman's status, symbolize her womanhood and, potentially, represent the beginning and continuance of the landholding family line."[32]

Merle recognized that "she [Alana] need her mother, so I got to stand by her. And I look after the child."[33] Although she could not afford to give up her job to take responsibility full time for her grandson, her help and support nevertheless enabled her daughter to cope and to return, in time, to her studies. Given the high incidence of lone parents and female-headed households in the African-Caribbean community in Britain and the Caribbean,[34] given also that Merle herself had had two children prior to marriage, and that neither her own mother nor her grandmother were married, why, therefore, the anger? Anger as ritual may provide one explanation, but there were also two practical reasons. First, Merle was "heartbroken" because Alana was due to sit her CSE (Certificate of Secondary Education).[35] The pregnancy, therefore, disrupted her education. For Merle (and for most West Indian parents) education was considered vitally important[36] and Merle had migrated (among other reasons) to improve the educational opportunities for her children. Second, she would have preferred for Alana to have been married. Merle herself had, indeed, married (albeit some years after the birth of her children). Although she and her husband lived apart for sixteen years, Merle only reluctantly agreed to divorce him in 1978, accusing him of little respect for their "marriage vow."[37] Her son who has two children has now married the children's mother, and "they does remain one family. For myself, it make me feel good. Although he have them out of wedlock, you see, but I don't put him down for that."[38]

And yet, Merle would not allow Alana to marry the father of her child. She felt that he was a bully and "I wouldn't put up with that."[39] Alana now has four children, all sons, by different fathers, with whom she has neither married nor cohabited. Merle appears reconciled to her daughter's life style, and even jokes. "I tell her off, but she only does produce all boys!"[40] Merle's judgment now is that Alana "is a determined girl and when she says no, she says no...she don't really have any luck with these men. And she should leave them well alone."[41] Indeed, leaving men well alone is now Merle's own position. She cohabited once, for a while, since her divorce but now "I never really want to have that problem, to bother with men. Go, go out, working, come back, cooking and all that."[42]

There appears to be little consistency in Merle's position. Marriage is both a desirable and, once secured, sacred state, conferring status on the parties involved and their children. It is an institution Merle values and endorses. Yet Merle herself cohabited before and after her marriage, had two children prior to her marriage, and did not force Alana into marriage, despite the pregnancy. Neither Merle's parents nor grandparents were married. Marriage, then, is separated from sexual morality, and reproduction and is neither necessary nor sufficient for the establishment of either a family or household. Indeed, she appears to hold in tandem two very different interpretations of the purpose and status of marriage, suggesting that marriage is still regarded as a symbol of status and fertility rather than a prerequisite to children.

The diversity of family life is most clearly brought out by the diversity within families and the contradictions or inconsistencies within them. In Merle's case (and others like her) there appears no apparent contradiction between holding two incompatible viewpoints —or what Giddens may describe as systems of 'mutual knowledge'— together within one frame of reference and practice. Although Giddens's notion of structuration relates more to the interdependence of production and reproduction in custom and practice, rather than the processes of (multi-) cultural change, his emphasis on the role of the past in the present, his insistence on the awareness, rationality and actions of social agents, and his recognition of the interplay between dominant and sub-cultures, may nevertheless open up insights into how two systems of "mutual knowledge" may operate simultaneously. In this view,

> ...the forms of social theory which have made little or no conceptual space for agents' understanding of themselves, and of their social contexts, have tended greatly to exaggerate the impact of dominant symbol systems or ideologies upon those in subordinate classes.[43]

Gidden's insight in many ways reworks W. E. DuBois's concept of "double consciousness."

> It is a peculiar sensation, this double consciousness, this sense of always looking at one's self through the eyes of others, of measuring one's soul by the tape of a world that looks on in amused contempt and pity. One ever feels his twoness, - an American, a Negro; two souls, two thoughts, two unreconciled strivings; two warring ideals in one dark body, whose dogged strength alone keeps it from being torn asunder.[44]

Here, as DuBois suggests, it is possible to internalize and balance two opposing ideologies and cultural practices, and at the same time to code-switch between them.[45]

In the case of the Caribbean, the influences on social and cultural practice are both plural, and contaminated (by history and change). At the same time, there have been historic tensions between who, at any one point, could lay claim to being the dominant culture—the numerically small elite, who controlled the formal frameworks of the society, or the excluded majority who filled the spaces ignored by them? Either way, part of the process of social and cultural accommodation has been the overlaying of spiritual, social and cultural imports so that vestiges of African, Asian or European influence (both dominant and sub-cultural) may overlay or be overlaid by each other, a process remarked upon by Melville Herskovits,

> To term an old deity by a new name is but one manifestation of a device which, *in the field of social organisation, has made for disregard of European sanctions underlying family structure while accepting European terminology relating to the family*...This principle of disregard for outer form while retaining inner values, characteristic of Africans everywhere, is thus revealed as the most important single factor making for an understanding of the acculturative situation (emphasis added).[46]

It is noted, in a linguistic context, by Warner Lewis (see chapter 3). If the process of what Herskovits calls acculturation permits one rationale to be superimposed on another practice, and if, as Giddens suggests, it is possible for two (or more) structures of mutual knowledge to inhabit the same space, then seeming irregularities or inconsistencies in social practices and their supporting values may seem less puzzling. The plurality of cultural influences in the Caribbean, the regimes under which acculturation and accommodation occurred and recurred, the indications of cultural discrepancies and ambiguities, suggest that a likely explanation may be found in identifying what may be parallel systems of "mutual knowledge" as they weave in and out of each other.

Again and again in the narratives informants insist that they are a "close" family, and that membership of that family is inclusive and extensive. The values of the family continue to be passed down, regardless. "We make sure" as Alana says "that...everyone knows everyone else, regardless of how you've moved on in your life."[47] And of her own children, Alana has observed, that although

> ...they're not for the same dad, but you'd never know it...because I bring the four of them up myself, and they just...gel together, you know, you would never know that they're different dads, because they're so close, you know, as a family.[48]

Both mother and daughter insist that the family is both close and important. Alana's brother is "the sort of person...we are that close that he thinks my kids, I mean, they're grown up now, they should be turning up on his doorstep 'hello uncle.'"[49] Aunts, uncles, and cousins in England, Jamaica, and Canada are in regular contact. Alana talks regularly with her father, and visits Jamaica every other year. The fathers of her children similarly play a part in their upbringing, and contribute (and extend) the family network. Her eldest son's father, for instance, "even yesterday, his dad came up to look for us, and he brought his other two daughters, and his two niece....So, my oldest son is Mickey. Any kids that his dad has got, you know, he knows all of them."[50]

Given the value of inclusive kin and the importance of family *qua* family, marriage unites two families and extends the family network for both direct descendants and for the children of either party prior to their union. Marriage is not just the union of two individuals, but of two lineages and, given the size and complexity of African-Caribbean families, two large and often global networks. The importance placed on marriage is as much to do, therefore, with its sanctioning of reproductive rights (or rites), as its acknowledgment of the union of two families, their networks, and by extension familial rights and responsibilities. Marriage is, for the most part, a formal procedure that requires the full knowledge and cooperation of both families. Occurring often late in the life of a couple, and after the birth of children, it becomes as much a celebration as a sanctioning of lineages.

What we may be seeing here is one institution with a dual meaning. First, the Christian meaning of marriage, a sacrament to sanctify the union of a couple and to bless their subsequent offspring, an institution which in its modern secular interpretation prescribes and sanctions a monogamous union, legitimizes the children, and is primarily exclusive in its application. Second, an alternative meaning that formalizes the union of two family groupings, is essentially inclusive in its application, and not time/conjugally dependent.

Seen from this perspective, the opprobrium attached to a young woman who bears her first child "out of wedlock" may have little to do with the moral outrage of sex before marriage and the social scandal of illegitimacy (except for some committed Christians) and more, perhaps, to do with producing children (and therefore precipitating the union of families) without the appropriate prior negotiations, knowledge and co-operation of family members. Another informant explained how, when courting, you may tell your parents, "and then they'd suck the air, they might think about it and... and they maybe checking out who, who they think is,"[51] Another informant, who fathered a child when he was sixteen, described the family reaction thus:

> The mother [of the pregnant girl] then brought her home to my [family], typical West Indian families, you know, "Your son got my daughter pregnant"...and my mother saying "Well, is it true?...If it is true, we'll look after the child"...And the aunt that was there...you know, the typical thing of, "Oh, the child is the spitting image of"... you know, of us, and together they used to look after the child.[52]

Pregnancy short-circuited both the negotiations, and the step into adulthood.

Alana's subsequent pregnancies attracted no opprobrium from her mother. Like her mother, Alana has worked continuously to provide financial support for her children. Like her mother, she decided not to cohabit, even though the father of her last child would prefer her to but,

> I haven't got the time to be just totally there for him. I've got other kids and...they're important to me as well, and I'm different directions you know, helping that son or doing this, or looking after my grand-daughter and...that sort of thing...and I find I couldn't be without that, you know?[53]

Despite an absence of marital bonds, despite a variety of household types, despite multiple membership of nuclear families, the family describes itself as "very close" and as "rooted" together, closeness and roots that embrace not only Alana's immediate family of both origin and creation, but also a wider circle of kin incorporated into the family through her own children and their fathers, and through her siblings and their children.

Dawn's Family

Many of the themes identified in the first family find echoes in the second family. Dawn was born in 1963 in Jamaica, migrating as a child to Britain with her mother and siblings to join her father who had settled in Birmingham. Dawn is a university graduate. She works full time, though she lists as her current occupations "a) part-time lecturer, b) a co-ordinator for supplementary school. And c) I work part-time at British Gas and d) I'm also a housewife and a mother." [54] As Tariq Modood et al. suggested, young African-Caribbean origin women in Britain have greater success in education and employment than their male counterparts (a finding that has echoes in the Caribbean.)[55]

Dawn is unmarried and has two children by different fathers, neither of whom make financial or other contributions to their children's welfare. She, her children and her boyfriend (whom she plans to marry, who is not the father of either of her children) live together in her parents' house. Given the equation between education, class and family type, her status as a salaried professional woman should suggest a pattern of domesticity and life style that conforms to a European model of family life. It is relevant to look therefore at the life choices made possible, and more particularly, at the cultural and family directives that helped shaped them.

Dawn is close to her family, a concept embracing grandparents and parents, siblings and cousins, uncles, aunts, and close family friends. Dawn's parents are active Christians and had married before giving birth to their children. Her father's parents had similarly been married (her paternal grandfather was a pastor) and had successfully raised twenty-four children, including one born "outside." Her mother's parents, by contrast, had not been married. Her maternal grandmother had four children, two by her grandfather, who also had a number of other children by different women, "...still blood related...so in my Mum's family, to be quite honest, I just lumped everybody together, if she's my auntie, she's my auntie....I can't really say who belongs to who."[56]

Despite the diversity of family form, both Dawn's parents, Elsie and Frank, in their recollections of their respective families of origin, stress comparable values. The legality of the parental relationship was of little importance compared to the quality of that relationship within the broader context of kinship. Elsie lived with her mother and her aunts "like one family."[57] Both stressed the closeness of the relationship with the wider family—"we're all a big circle together, big family, happy family, together."[58] The model of the wider family, and clear parental instructions "to grow up loving and nice and gentle to each other,"[59] ensured an environment of obligation, responsibility and family support. Both Frank and Elsie characterized their neighborhood in Jamaica as one of mutual support. "The district was like one big family."[60] The support expected, and provided, by the network of kin, affines and neighbors enabled Frank to leave Elsie and their first two children while he went to work first in America and then in England.

While support is one powerful family dynamic, there is also a powerful counter narrative. Frank returned from America, and migrated to Britain in 1952. Elsie commuted for several years between Jamaica and Britain (during which time Dawn was conceived) before she and the children eventually joined him, to discover that in the intervening years Frank had become involved in another relationship. Elsie left him taking the children with her. The balance in the family shifted dramatically and the narrative assumed a fresh and heroic dimension. Elsie returned to her original trade as a dressmaker, which enabled her to work from home, and (like Merle) to support her children.

> The business took off in a good way. And with that we knew that Mum couldn't do any housework, no cooking, no cleaning, no nothing, she just...didn't do none of that, she just sewed all the time. And we kids...we managed the house.. so that she could just sew.[61]

Indeed, Elsie was so successful that in time she refurnished the house, learned to drive, bought a car, and was buying a house with the help of her eldest son. At this point, when Dawn was thirteen, their father returned. To the children's dismay, their mother took him back. "Mum was saying to us that that she was going to find it in her heart to forgive him and hope that we would do the same too, and give him another chance."[62] Before her father's return, Dawn was close to her mother. After his return, we started to go our own ways, and each of us in our different way gave her a different kind of trouble...we wouldn't have dreamed of doing it before, but it was like rebellion. But never against Mum, because we understood.[63]

Dawn became pregnant when she was seventeen. She did not love the child's father. Shortly after, she and her son left home to cohabit with another man whom she later married and divorced. She has now met, and intends to marry, her current boyfriend. In between, however, she returned to her studies, and took a university degree.

One reading of Dawn's behavior is a simple teenage rebellion. The "simple" is, however, misleading. That her rebellion assumed the form of motherhood is both psychologically and culturally meaningful. This family placed a high premium on marriage—Elsie and Frank are active Christians. For them, marriage was a lifelong commitment. Throughout the separation from Frank, the question of divorce was never raised. Fidelity, loyalty, and forgiveness were values that Elsie cherished, along with an abiding commitment to her children. Merle, too, was reluctant to divorce her husband. They also placed a premium on marriage as the necessary precondition for having children, a condition that Dawn flaunted alongside cohabitation and divorce (from the father of her second child). But Elsie and Frank were not the only role models. Remember that her maternal grandmother had borne—and supported—all of her children outside of marriage, and although Elsie was "disappointed" by Dawn's behavior, she stood by her.

Dawn herself considers her role model to be her mother: "I think I just do [model myself on her]. I think I just do it without...I think most of it is subconsciously."[64] Elsie, like her mother before her, demonstrated both heroism and stoicism in her commitment to her children and their joint struggle for survival and success in Britain. What emerges in Dawn's narrative is a comparable story of heroism. Despite the demands of motherhood, the complications of her relationships with men, and the need to work to support her children, Dawn completed her university degree and has proved as successful as her siblings, who all went on to higher education or became trained professionals. As Elsie said "people say to me, 'It's because you're motherly,' and I'm proud of that."[65] And implied in this is perhaps a notion that "motherly" is as much concerned with material provision as emotional support, a principle well acknowledged by this family as much as by Merle and her daughter, Alana.

Annie's Family

A further variation is provided by the third family. Carmen was born in Britain in 1978, the only child of Annie, a Barbadian, and her Jamaican husband, Len. Annie and Len were married in 1974. Both came from practicing Christian families in their respective islands and believed in the importance of marriage as the context for bearing and rearing children. Annie's father, Theophilus (known as 'T') was (and still is) a lay preacher for one of the Pentecostal churches in Barbados and his presence (and most of his values) have dominated the life choices of his children and grandchildren.

T's father died before he "could creep," [66] He and his brother were brought up by his mother, a domestic servant, whose outspokenness won her few friends and cost her many jobs. "She wasn't" as T put it,

> euphemistic in her dealings. It is 'Yes', it is 'No'. So some people loved her for that, some people didn't. So it meant she's here today, next year she's there, and it goes like that.[67]

When T was thirteen, his mother lost her sight in an accident and he and his brother had to start work to support themselves and their mother. T became a tailor, and an auxiliary postman, converting when he was twenty "to the Lord." Although his mother was a religious woman and insisted that her sons attend church regularly "going to church isn't salvation...but when you are converted it is your giving over to God."[68] In 1944, when he was twenty-eight, T became a pastor and "after I gave my heart and life to the Lord, that came first."[69]

Although T's parents had not been married, his own religious beliefs precluded any premarital relationship. Indeed, one of the precipitating factors in his conversion was, as he described it, " ...feeling man and so, then the shame covered me."[70] In 1943, when he was twenty seven, he became "wifish"[71] and married. His bride was sixteen-years-old. According to their daughter Annie, the marriage was "arranged" after her mother's father had died. Her maternal great grandmother, although Christian, had originated in India and the family

> had the same principles of arranged marriages....Mother explained to us...that because her only brother was at sea when her father died, and she being the youngest, and being a girl, the Elders of the Church, and the Elder in the district where they were living, held a meeting and decided it would be best to have her married off...and she was married off at the age of 16 to my father who was 27 at the time.[72]

After marriage, T and his wife "didn't hesitate. Children came. And I mean, they just came, parcel and a penny."[73] In all, they had sixteen children of whom eleven survived. Annie was the second oldest.

Unlike the other two families, T was a constant presence throughout her and her siblings' childhood, ruling the family with strict, and often peremptory, discipline. "Dad," as she says,

> has always been, and I think always will be, a strict disciplinarian. Very, very, very devout Christian. You can't persuade him at all. We loved him, but we feared him…we have had the strap quite a lot, sometimes unfairly and unjustly. But what could you do? He never allowed you to explain yourself…if he wants to ask questions, it's after the punishment has been administered. So that's why you feared him….[But] I think it's because he was very fearful for us. I mean, he was proud of…us.[74]

As a result, the children tended to 'cling' to their mother who, Annie speculated, may have found the relationship with her husband overbearing,

> He sort of ruled…so my mother could not make decisions about certain things, you know, she always had to consult him. I probably think, as she matured and got older, she found herself very restrict[ed]….I think although she loved us, and loved my father, I think she felt that she was dealt a raw deal then, when she was mature, to the stage of "Now, well, look, here am I, married, and someone dictating and I can't make the decisions." You know, everything had to be vetoed by my father…. She couldn't just sit and say "Well, look, I'm off to town." It had to be something discussed, and he'd say "Alright, then, you go to town on such and such a day"….I think, deep down, you know, she felt that she shouldn't have been in that situation. And she would comment, many a time, and say how she always wanted to be a nurse, which I'm sure those were regrets, not so much because of my father, but what the family did.[75]

Nevertheless, despite these speculations and the many instances of what was considered unfair punishment and excessive discipline, they grew up "close" and, as a family, sharing every activity. The family was musical, for instance. Annie, along with her siblings, was taught the piano and the family would often enjoy musical evenings and events. The children would often accompany their father to revivalist meetings. Meal times were always a family activity, preceded by a sung Grace—a practice that Annie has continued with her own family (although "I mean, we don't *sing!*"[76]) Above all, as Annie recalled, their father "was very protective as well, for us as his children, and the wife…when it comes to the family, he's like a lion."[77] As a result, unlike many other families, there was very limited input from other relatives, including grandmothers. "My father," as Annie recalled, "was the type of person, he felt that his family was his responsibility, and he made the decisions and everything."[78] Her father did not allow family sentiment to stand in the way of principles, and on occasion had major disagreements, resulting in lengthy periods of estrangement, with his uncles and cousins (over family land) and even his mother, after she refused to obey his order not to help a man of whom he disapproved. His mother, however, held her ground and replied that "'you can't tell me that I am your mother. You won't be guiding me, I am to guide you'….And I tell her, 'Decide between the two of us.'"[79] T then moved out of his mother's home and it was only a subsequent illness that reunited them.

With his own children, however, he never failed to demonstrate trust and confidence. Annie was the first of his children to go abroad, and she went with his blessing to train as a nurse. Her departure was not without pain.

> The first shot I got, of grief, is the garments that she left in the wardrobe. You know, there was no use taking them to England, so they were left in the wardrobe. And a day everybody was out, and only us was home, and for some reasons, I had to go in the wardrobe and when I go in and open up, and saw these clothes, I tell you, it took only God to keep me alive. I then missed her. And believe you me, I wept like a child…that's my first grief of her going.[80]

Equally, he never failed to offer guidance and advice. When Annie was thinking of marrying an Asian, he counselled against it on religious grounds. She obeyed him and "that made me to love her for the more, you see."[81] At the same time, Annie—and from time to time her other siblings—entrusted their children to the care of her father and mother. Annie's daughter, Carmen, spent regular periods of her childhood with her grandfather in Barbados. "You can see the confidence, you see. And that tells you that your children…agree[s] with what training I have given…to trust your child with grand-parents…that unity, that fellowship, you know, it was rich."[82] Indeed, T continues to command obedience. Even now, when Annie goes home, she

> has to respect certain disciplines. I still couldn't have fellows…calling me up…he was right there by the phone… and my husband allow me to go anywhere on my own. And he would say "All right, he's not here"…and you know, if he was around, I would go and dress differently. I mean, I'm my own woman at the moment, so I am wearing trousers.[83]

And Carmen, when she visits, can make him smile but,

> …if there's anything he doesn't approve of…he'll show it, basically. And even now, even though I'm …17 now…and I wear shorts or whatever, he doesn't approve at all! He disapproves seriously! But he can only say, you know, 'Are you going to wear that

today?' And I say "Well, yeh, Grandad, it's hot!" I try not to be rude back, But I try to show that, okay, times is changing, you can't wear skirts down to your ankles, or whatever.[84]

Although T's narrative was one of unquestioned obedience from —and pride in—his children, and of a harmonious sequence in his relationships with them, for Annie as for her other siblings there were several points where this harmony was fractured. Far from migrating to Britain with his blessing, her decision to go was not taken "very kindly."[85] Indeed, she and her sister had to conspire to leave, a decision implicitly condoned by their mother. "I saw this as an escape route" Annie recalled,

> to try and be my own person and to see what material I'm made of, whether or not, you know, I still have to wait on my father's decision. I felt if I didn't do that, as my mum always said to me, "if you never leave home, you'll never marry" because no way would anyone ever, ever come…if you notice, the two of us who are away are married, and the two who are there…aren't.[86]

Far from accepting her father's advice on marriage, the decision was taken from her when her fiancé had to enter into an arranged marriage in his native India. When she subsequently did marry, her father's benign recollection "I have never even met the man, but if you says. It was quite acceptable"[87] disguises a very different circumstance where

> my mother came to the wedding. My father was not very happy from the word go. I mean, it was not so much the person I'm marrying …but parents think 'Right. I've educated you, you've done well, you can do better.' And I think, because I said he was working for London Transport, he was driving automobiles and so on, my father went berserk! He said 'Look, you can write to me and say this is nonsense, this is all done with, then we can talk. But' he said 'if you are insisting that you are going to marry this person' he said 'we're not talking.' So, he was very, very annoyed….[But] little by little, my father, I think mainly after Carmen arrived on the scene, he then really came around to accepting.[88]

Although Annie's Jamaican husband is very different from her father (as their daughter, Carmen, recalls, her father is not religious, rarely attends church, and had two children prior to marrying Annie), and despite points of open resistance to her father, Annie has continued many of his principles in her own family.

> I felt it was important that I really had the values of what I had to put up with, and also that I would bring her up that way, that she wouldn't be too dependent on me, but have great respect still for me. And that she will value, you know, the finer things of life, and especially behavior wise and suchlike.'[89]

Carmen was, therefore, brought up as a practicing Christian, for as she put it, "it's embodied in the whole family. It's hard not to be religious."[90] She has visited Barbados on a regular basis, often for extended periods, and has grown up close to her cousins and family in Barbados, as well as those family members present in England. Compared with her mother's childhood, Carmen's has been less strict. She is on good terms with both her parents, is succeeding well at school, hopes to go to University, to live eventually in Barbados and, like her parents, marry and have a family. She concedes that this is the ideal, but not the only, circumstance in which to bring up children. As for Annie, she would condemn her daughter's behavior if a child were born outside marriage, but would nevertheless continue to help and support her for "if I were to say 'Oh, you and the baby go' I don't think it would be fair."[91]

While in many ways this family contains elements common to our first two families—an insistence on closeness, on the importance of religion, and of marriage—there are striking differences. The role of the father, for instance, was very different in this family. T dominated his family, controlling his wife and children, and attempting to control his mother. He was prepared to estrange himself from other family members (including, for a time, his mother and daughter) rather than seek a compromise. For him, religion came before family, and his strict interpretation of the Bible led him to insist that he hold unchallenged authority within the family. He would not counter "outside" relationships either before or after marriage. Above all, it was the discipline for which he was remembered, recalling Edith Clarke's observations of fathers, that

> where the mother was indulgent, hasty in her angers but quick to be kind again, the father was remembered for his strictness. As an Orange Grove farmer said, "You could not fool with your father."[92]

Yet Annie's father was not unique in his attitudes towards, and behavior over, his family. Her maternal grandfather, before his death, was also reputed to be "a bit like my father, he was the man of the house, and what he says go, it doesn't matter about you being the mother, you know...he was very loving, but he ruled the home."[93]

Edith Clarke argued that the incidence of marriage was closely correlated with class.[94] Economic stability (more likely to be found among the middle classes) provided the material conditions for marriage, and encouraged aspirations towards respectability. The lower down the socio-economic scale, the greater the incidence of concubinage and the lower the likelihood of marriage. In these three families, marriage was highly valued. Its meaning and practices, as we have seen, varied considerably, from a sequential stage after cohabitating to the *sine qua non* for creating children. Only in T's case was it also used to buttress male authority within the family, where its legitimation was undoubtedly to be found within a particular interpretation of the Bible. Paradoxically, however, this interpretation did not preclude T holding ambitions for all his children, regardless of gender, nor for encouraging his wife to work once the children ceased to be dependent on her. In other words, even in what may appear to be a deeply conservative, patriarchal family, elements can still be found of at least an economic autonomy for women, as well as men.

***

A number of features stand out in these family narratives. First, all emphazise "closeness" as a feature of their families, (see chapter 5 for further discussion on this in the language of transnationalism). Dawn, with her children and partner, lives with her parents, supported by siblings, cousins, uncles and aunts. She supports her children, and her children echo her sentiments of family, the "closeness," the love and trust. "Our family is very close." Said one of her children, "If I never had a family," said the other, "I wouldn't know what to do and *it makes me feel like someone*....People just stick up for me and they're very kind" (emphasis added).[95] Despite an absence of marital bonds, despite a variety of household types, despite multiple membership of nuclear families, both Dawn and Alana's family describe themselves as "very close," "rooted" together, and regard both family and family members as "important" Annie and Carmen similarly describe their families as close.

> As my Mum used to say, "we are the Ewings of Barbados!"...I don't think we have any nasty quarrels, but we do disagree with ideas and certain decisions. But it's something that's there and done, it's forgotten. And the worst thing, I think, you could ever do is, as an outsider,...interfere with one, then you're in for a lot of trouble...[because] you interfere with everybody...So, I mean, we are...like that, you know, very close.[96]

Linked with this is a positive avowal of African-Caribbean culture for, as Alana says, "I strongly believe that you should never forget your roots,"[97] an avowal which, in her case, is accompanied by a revival of traditional Jamaican cooking and home medicines, in Dawn's case by a job lecturing in black history, in Carmen's case by a desire to live in Barbados.[98] Dawn's son Mickey sees himself "like" his father, "I can see myself having more children...I've got two, three kids by two separate mothers. And I don't see myself stopping there. I'm too young."[99] Getting married and buying a house is not, he argues "how it is." And, echoing his mother, he argues that black people need to recognize that "everything they've brought here has been on their backs,"[100] and to find themselves, "for then you become larger than the society."[101]

All our informants continued to live close to one another. David Owen indicates that, despite the dispersal of black communities in British cities, there remain significant concentrations. Within that, populations from the different islands continue to be concentrated in particular boroughs or areas. Thus, for instance, in London, Barbadians are concentrated in Brent and Lambeth, Jamaicans in Lambeth, Lewisham, and Brent. Trinidadians tend to be concentrated north of the Thames, in Hammersmith and Fulham, Brent, Haringey and parts of Hackney. In the West Midlands, Barbadians are largely concentrated in central Birmingham, and the northeast quadrant of Coventry, although Jamaicans are widely distributed across the county, with concentrations in central Birmingham and Wolverhampton.[102]

The distribution of the black-other ethnic group is similar to that of African-Caribbean-born people, suggesting strongly that migrant children continue to live close to, or even with, parents and other kin and in areas that contain facilities (such as shops, community centers, supplementary schools, churches, restaurants and travel agents) that support the African-Caribbean and black-other community. As one (third generation) informant described it "instinctively we didn't want to go too far away from each other...you're all there, within reach of each other...it's as if we're carrying on a tradition that we're not even fully aware of."[103]

In thinking about the African-Caribbean family it is as well to remember that the conjugal relationship is but a passing moment in the history of the family. Far stronger, in the context of the Caribbean and its diaspora, are ties of consanguinity, affinity and lineage. Indeed, the importance of lineage—of whose continuity mothers and their children are living proof and where women, through their children, play a key role in linking kinship groups, including paternal kin—is a powerful directive within the Caribbean and may help explain both the occurrence of high levels of births outside of marriage, and the apparent tolerance of them by families.

The closeness and importance of kin may permit a high degree of autonomy for both men and women, and this too may be another factor behind the high incidence of serial parenting and/or the formation of mother-headed households, resulting in complicated kinship structures and considerable diversity of family form between and within families. Households do not necessarily or always equate with family and family members may consider themselves members of one or more households (and families). The diversity in living arrangements and family structure, and the apparent deviation from the British national norm, revealed by the 1991 census, can also be observed in the Caribbean suggesting a continuity, an inherited pattern, across the generations.[104]

Significantly, many mothers, whether single, married or cohabiting work to support their children, again replicating a pattern historically and contemporaneously noted for the Caribbean. All the women in these families combined a career with responsibilities for children. Equally, members of the wider kinship group are expected to take on caring responsibilities, and in this the kinship group includes not only the mother's family (as with Dawn) but also the father's, as with Alana. The involvement of the kinship group continues as an important aspect of family life. Carmen, for instance, was sent back to Barbados for extended periods, and Annie shared her childcare with her sister-in-law in England. Both Dawn and Alana were able to rely on the support of their mother. Family responsibilities stretch horizontally as well as vertically.

Families, indeed, make you "feel someone," and are an integral part of identity. Families are never static, but are reconfigured from generation to generation, in response to need, circumstance and convenience. At the same time, values proved by custom to be efficacious, and family models, which come in all shapes and sizes, are also part of the cultural capital transmitted, and transformed, across generations. It is the generation of this capital that is, perhaps, the most valuable function performed by families, providing the individual with a sense of value, and the community with a shared and distinctive culture and identity. It is, perhaps, the nature and transmission of this capital, rather than the haphazard formalities of family construction, that should direct family research, just as it drives family unity.

Notes

1. Mintz, Sidney *African-Caribbean Transformations*, (New York: Columbia University Press, 1989), 25.
2. For an excellent discussion of this see S. Mintz, and R. Price 1976, *An Anthropological Approach to the Afro-American Past: An African-Caribbean Perspective*, Philadelphia, Institute for the Study of Human Issues.
3. JD013 /2/1/1/7-13.
4. For family land see Edith Clarke, *My Mother who Fathered Me;* Jean Besson, "Family Land and Caribbean Society: Toward an Ethnography of Afro-Caribbean Peasantries" in *Perspectives on Caribbean Regional Identity*, ed. Elizabeth M. Thomas-Hope (Liverpool: Liverpool University Press, 1984), 57-83.
5. JD 012 1/1/1/8-9.
6. JD 012 1/1/1/9.
7. JD 012 1/1/1/17. The issue of domestic violence is addressed in chapter seven.
8. JI 028 2/1/1/7
9. See Klaus de Albuquerque and Sam Ruark " 'Men Day Done' ": Are Women Really Ascendant in the African-Caribbean?" in *African-Caribbean Portraits,* 1-13. The point here, of course, is that the continuities remain.
10. "Partnering," as it is known in Jamaica, is a form of informal saving where a group of people agree to contribute a weekly amount into a central pool, and the participants then take turns to receive the sum of the contributions each week. It is also known as a "meeting turn" in Barbados, and "sous-sous" in Trinidad.
11. JD012 1/1/2/35.
12. JD012 1/1/2/35.
13. JD012 1/1/2/33.
14. BK117 1/1/1/3.
15. Herskovits, *The Myth of the Negro Past.*
16. Mintz and Price, *An Anthropological Approach.*
17. Clark, Gracia 'Mothering, Work and Gender in Urban Asante Ideology and Practice' *American Anthropologist* 101,4, (2000):719.
18. JD 013 2/1/1/1.
19. JD013 2/1/1/3.
20. JD013 2/1/1/3.
21. JD013 2/1/1/4.
22. JD013 2/1/1/8.
23. JD013 2/1/2/24.
24. JD013 2/1/1/11.
25. JD013 2/1/1/6.
26. JD013 2/1/1/6.
27. JD013 2/1/2/28.
28. JD013 2/1/1/12.
29. JD013 2/1/2/23.
30. JD012 1/2/2/46.
31. Clarke, *My Mother Who Fathered Me.*
32. Besson, *Martha Brae,*17.
33. JD012 1/2/2/48
34. Note the continuity in patterns between the 1960s of the memories here, and recent data. Owen cites that in Britain 42.2 percent of the African-Caribbean community are lone parents. OPCS/GRO (Scotland)(1993) Country of Birth and Ethnic Origin. As cited in David Owen, "A Demographic Profile of African-Caribbean Households and Families in Great Britain," paper presented to a conference on

the African-Caribbean family and living arrangements in Britain and the Trans-Atlantic World, Cheltenham & Gloucester CHE, 27-29 March 1998). In Barbados, the proportion of female-headed households, which may or may not have had dependent children, was 43.5 percent, based on 1990 Census data. Godfrey ST Barnard, *Demographic Characteristics of Family and Living Arrangements in the Commonwealth African-Caribbean*, paper presented to a conference on the African-Caribbean family and living arrangements in Britain and the Trans-Atlantic World, Cheltenham & Gloucester CHE, 27-29 March 1998. Although the two categories are not interchangeable, nevertheless in practice most lone parents are women and are heads of households.

35. JD012 1/2/2/46.
36. Another informant explained the importance of education for social mobility, commenting how "when one get a break, the others will be better off." JL0351/1/7.
37. JD012 1/1/2/34.
38. JD012 1/3/1/50.
39. JD012 1/3/1/49.
40. JD012 1/3/1/48.
41. JD012 1/3/1/49.
42. JD012 1/3/1/51.
43. A. Giddens, "Problems of Action and Structure" in P. Cassells (ed.), The Giddens Reader (London: Macmillan 1993 124.
44. W. E. B. DuBois *The Souls of Black Folk* (New York: Signet, 1995 [1903]), 45. See also Paul Gilroy *The Black Atlantic. Modernity and Double Consciousness* (London: Verso, 1993); Mary Chamberlain, "George Lamming" in *West Indian Intellectuals in the Metropolis,* ed. Bill Schwarz (Manchester: Manchester University Press, 2003.
45. I am grateful to Constance Sutton for this insight on cultural code-switching, and for the links between DuBois and Giddens.
46. Herskovits, *The Myth of the Negro Past,* 298.
47. JD013/2/1/1/7.
48. JD013/2/1/1/7.
49. JD013/2/1/1/10.
50. JD013/2/1/1/7.
51. BK080/2/2/1/.
52. BB056/2/1/2/18.
53. JD013/2/1/2/27.
54. JB008/2 1/1/1.
55. Tariq Modood, R. Berthoud, J. Lakey, J. Nazroo, P. Smith, S. Virdee, S. Beishon, *Ethnic Minorities in Britain: Diversity and Disadvantage,* PSI Report 843 (London: Policy Studies Institute, 1997.) For the African-Caribbean, see Albuquerque, "Men Day Done."
56. JB008/2 1/2/9.
57. JB007/1 1/1/10.
58. JB007/1 1/1/5.
59. JB007/1 1/1/10.
60. JB007/1 1/1/12.
61. JB008/2 2/1/33.
62. JB008/2 2/1/35.
63. JB008/2 2/1/36.
64. JB008/2 1/1/5.
65. JB007/1 2/1/31.

66. BG120/1/1/1/1.
67. BG120/1/1/1/1.
68. BG120/1/1/1/3.
69. BG120/1/1/1/3.
70. BG120/1/2/1/28.
71. BG120/1/1/1/3.
72. BG070/2/1/1/1.
73. BG120/1/1/1/3.
74. BG070/2/1/1/4.
75. BG070/2/1/1/7.
76. BG070/2/1/1/7.
77. BG070/2/1/1/9.
78. BG070/2/1/1/17.
79. BG020/1/2/1/25.
80. BG020/1/2/1/31.
81. BG020/1/2/1/33.
82. BG020/1/2/1/33-34.
83. BG070/2/1/2/25-6.
84. BG091/3/1/1/9.
85. BG070/2/1//2/26.
86. BG070/2/1/2/26.
87. BG020/1/2/1/32.
88. BG070/2/2/1/37.
89. BG070/2/3/1/40.
90. BG091/3/1/1/3.
91. BG070/2/3/1/46.
92. Clarke, *My Mother Who Fathered Me*, 122.
93. BG070/2/1/2/17.
94. Clarke, *My Mother Who Fathered Me*.
95. JB009/3 1/1/6-7.
96. BG070/2/1/2/25.
97. JD013 2/1/2/34.
98. BG091/3/1/2/23.
99. JD014 3/1/1/9.
100. JD014 3/1/1/9.
101. JD014 3/1/1/9.
102. David Owen, "A profile of African-Caribbean Households and Families in Great Britain," in *African-Caribbean Families in Britain*.
103. JF022.
104. Godfrey ST Bernard, "Demographic Characteristics"; David Owen, "A profile of African-Caribbean households.'"

5

Transnational Narratives and National Belongings

"If I fly to Barbados tomorrow, I know that I can go at any one of my sisters, and I have a bed to sleep on...if I go to Toronto and I seek out my cousin, I know he's going to open the door to me. So I think that's where family links are very important."[1]

The contemporary Caribbean was founded on the migration of Africans and Europeans and, from 1838, Indians and Chinese, their numbers augmented by smaller migrations from free and liberated Africans, Portuguese and other Europeans, Syrians, Jews, and Lebanese. From 1838 Caribbeans of all races and ethnicities began to migrate to other parts of the Caribbean, and eventually to North, South and Central America. Approximately 45,000 Jamaicans and 42,000 Barbadians left Barbados for Panama between 1904 and 1914,[2] although Hilary Beckles estimates that for Barbados out-migration to Panama was as high as one in four of the population.[3] Many of those who left for Panama subsequently re-migrated.

By 1933, the Colonial Office had estimated that approximately 10,000 British West Indians were resident in Venezuela, "considerable numbers" in Guatemala, Honduras and Nicaragua, approximately 600 in Brazil, between 300 and 400 in Haiti, between 8,000 and 10,000 in the Dominican Republic and, of the 90,000 "negroes" resident still in Panama, approximately 50 percent were considered of British West Indian, mainly Jamaican, origin. In Cuba, there were sufficient British West Indians to constitute "a substantial problem."[4] Above all, West Indians went to the United States. By 1890, there were already 19,979 foreign-born black people in the United States, by far the majority of whom were West Indians, a figure which had risen to 73,808 by 1920 and 98,620 by 1930.[5] Yet between 1932 and 1937, more West Indians returned to the Caribbean than migrated to the United States.[6] Between the wars, migration from and within the region continued, albeit on a smaller scale, picking up again during the Second World War in response to the need for workers on U.S. bases in the Caribbean and for farm workers on the United States mainland. Aruba and Curaçao, Trinidad and St. Lucia entered (or re-entered) into the arena of destinations as a result of the Second World War, and, after the war, Canada and the United Kingdom.

As a response to the prevailing poverty in the British West Indies, and the demand for labor in the post-war reconstruction of Britain, West Indians began to migrate to the United Kingdom. By 1951, there were 17,218 West Indians in Britain, the majority of whom were Jamaican born. By 1961, the figure had risen to 173,659. The 1962 and 1966 Immigration Acts effectively halted migration from the West Indies (as elsewhere in the Commonwealth), although prior to both Acts there was a marked increase in the numbers arriving. By 1971, the Caribbean-born population of Britain stood at 304,070, and Ceri Peach estimates that the total Caribbean population in that year stood at 545,744. The Caribbean-born population at the beginning of the 1990s stood at 264,591.[7] The total Caribbean population now stands at 565,876.[8]

From the nineteenth and twentieth centuries, however, a number of characteristics emerged that distinguished Caribbean migration. While it may have been individuals who migrated, this migration was with, and for, the support of the family in the Caribbean. It was, in this sense, a family endeavor. For the most part, despite poor communications, nineteenth- and twentieth-century migrants maintained close links with family members across the oceans and the generations, through letters and remittances.[9] Many of the migrants (who included independent women as well as men) returned home to the Caribbean.[10] Those who remained in their host societies built new communities while retaining many of their cultural attributes and family contact with the Caribbean.[11] At the same time, contact between Caribbean migrant groups abroad helped to foster a broader political identity.[12] By the early decades of the twentieth century, out-migration had become an integral feature of the Caribbean, and an increasingly important component of the domestic and national economy.[13] As such, many families became increasingly to rely on the migration of its members for returning remittances, in cash or kind, and promoted or supported the migration of its members. Out-migration had become, in other words, an active ingredient in the culture of the region, each migration reinforcing its 'image' as a positive activity,[14] while family strategies evolved, and family structures accommodated, to encourage it. As a result, the Caribbean remained a constant feature in the lives of migrants, while for those who remained in the region, migration was seen as a link with 'foreign', not a severance from home, an opportunity to extend, not disrupt the family links.

For many individuals, therefore, the experience of migration was not new. Many of those who came to Britain had already been migrants themselves—within the Caribbean (to Aruba or Curaçao, for example) or to the United States on the farm workers "H-2" program (first instituted in 1942). Many had parents or grandparents who had migrated. Most had some family member or close family friend who had migrated. Migration, in other words, was a familiar (and familial) rather than an atypical experience. Indeed, the regularity of migration has led many scholars to argue that the Caribbean is characterized by cultures or traditions of migration,[15] an exemplar of globalization and transnationalism long before the terms were ever thought of.

***

Much of the growing literature on transnationalism has related to economic and political transnational transactions, or to occupational, religious or migratory transnational behaviors. There has, however, been relatively little that has examined the transnational practices in the most basic social unit: the family. A notable, recent exception is Deborah Bryceson and Ulla Vuorella (eds.), *The Transnational Family* (2002),[16] which contains a series of articles examining the shifting role and place of gender, home, and generations in transnational family experiences across a range of circumstances, cultures and time frames. Similarly, the special issue of the journal *Global Networks* (2004), guest edited by Selma Leydesdorff and myself, entitled "Transnational Families: Memories and Narratives."[17] attempted to draw out the specific contributions that life story and oral history methods could make in understanding the complexity of transnational families.

Yet the idea of transnationality as a feature of *Caribbean* families is not, of course, new. Rosina Brodber Wiltshire first coined the term —the transnational family—referring to those bifurcated networks that were a feature of Jamaican/North American families,[18] and has since been remarked upon by observers based both in the Caribbean and in North America, notably by Constance Sutton and Susan Makiesky Barrow, Paula Aymer, Linda Basch, Nina Glick Schiller and Christine Szanton Blanc (with their remarkable *Nations Unbound*), Nina Glick Schiller and George Fouron with their equally remarkable *Georges Woke Up Laughing,* Denis Conway and Karen Fog Olwig and Elizabeth Thomas Hope, to name a few.[19] In the United Kingdom, however, the focus on transnationalism and the Caribbean is more recent. Harry Goulbourne has already drawn attention to transnationalism in his contribution to Susan McRae (ed.) *Changing Britain. Families and Households in the 1990s*,[20] as well as, most recently, in his *Caribbean Transnational Experience.*[21] My own work has also drawn attention to transnationalism as a feature of African-Caribbean families (notably Barbados)[22] as does, more recently, the work by Paul Thompson and Elaine Bauer on Jamaican families.[23] For the most part, however, the role of Caribbean families in transnationalism in the U.K.-based literature is a relatively underexplored one.

But what is transnationalism? Transnationalism refers to actions that take place across, or have consequences across, national boundaries, where the actors involved have an active involvement, over time, in more than one nation state. How intense this involvement should be, of what nature, and for how long has focussed the attention of a number of theorists of transnationalism, for all of us are now exposed on a regular basis to some measures of activity that involves border crossings, whether through absorbing and consuming media and other products of global manufacture and economy,[24] engaging in foreign holidays, travelling abroad to work, finding work or being employed locally by a global company. What, then, distinguishes transnational behavior from the everyday consumption of global products, or from the practices of globalization?

Transnationalism needs to involve some measure of temporary or permanent migration, a movement of *peoples* across national borders. Yet Alejandro Portes, one of the earliest scholars to engage with transnationalism, cautioned against embracing all migrant activity within the umbrella of transnationalism, and thereby describing none in a meaningful way.[25] Rather, he highlighted many of the distinctive contemporary features of transnationalism, delineating its boundaries "to occupations and activities that require regular and sustained social contacts over time across national borders for their implementation." Excluded from this definition were the "occasional gifts of money and kind sent by immigrants to their kin and friends (not an occupation) or the one time purchase of a house or lot by an immigrant in his home country (not a regular activity)." While much transnational behavior involves regular and sustained contact, his definition excludes the kind of informal, irregular, and often emotional involvement that anthropologists such as Nina Glick Schiller have identified as the "transnational social field" that "transmigrants"—and their families—inhabit.[26] Pointing out that there is little agreement among scholars on the definitions of, and terminology used by, transnationalism, Deborah Bryceson and Ulla Vuorela offer a refinement to the debate in their development of the twin theoretical concepts of "frontiering" which "denotes the ways and means transnational family members use to create familiar space and network ties in terrain where affinal connections are relatively sparse" and "relativizing....to refer to the variety of ways individuals establish, maintain or curtail relational ties with specific family members."[27] While the ambition to clarify the ambiguity is laudable, the introduction of two additional terms seems to add little to the debate and, indeed, perhaps clouds it further by introducing terms with (in the case of "frontiering") a contentious and ambivalent pedigree, and (in the case of "relativising") a generality which does little to delineate the ebbs and flows of transnational family relations over the life cycle of the individual and the family.

I wish to take a broad understanding of transnational activity as involvement in social fields that cross national borders. In relation to families, this recognizes that the intensity and nature of the involvement may fluctuate according to the life cycle of the individual or the family, or to a range of social, political and economic conditions that may militate against regular or sustained contact with family members that would otherwise have been sustained. It is worth pointing out too, that it is possible for transnational activities to be also multinational, that is, to involve more than one nation state. They are also, necessarily, international for activities that cross borders must necessarily include activities between borders. However, although transnational activity is necessarily international, international activity is not necessarily transnational.

How does transnationalism mesh with the Caribbean? From the start the Caribbean was at the center of the global experiment, a region whose formation was, as Don Robotham has argued, "within the framework of global capitalism," and whose strength and livelihood was intimately bound up with the commercial, military and imperial ambitions of Europe.[28] Certainly for many of the wealthier Europeans from the seventeenth century, transnationalism was a central feature of their settlement as lives in the Caribbean became enmeshed with activities and ambitions (both professional and familial) in the metropolises of Europe, and vice versa.

The culture and society that emerged was inherently transnational, as successive waves of migrants (free, forced, or indentured) creolized the Caribbean,[29] developing languages, dialects and cultures replete with global vocabularies. In turn, as they migrated out, they creolized their new environments. The vagaries of migration as well as the family endeavour involved ensured that transnationalism was inherent in the Caribbean migration experience and built into the fabric of the Caribbean diasporic culture. The Caribbean became as much a state of mind as a geographic entity, characterized by what Susan Craig James described as its "intertwining roots and overlapping diasporas."[30] However imaginary that "home" may have become across time and space, at its heart remained the family, a complex and complicated network of kinship linked by lineage, consanguinity and affinity, and tied by values of loyalty and obligation. As one Jamaican abroad put it, "is them me get me blessing from."

In recent years, the trend to return—first noted for Britain by Ceri Peach[31] for the 1980s—has continued, and accelerated in the 1990s and beyond.[32] Returning residents, from Europe and North America, and 'new' migrants to the Caribbean (usually the overseas-born children of returning residents) were able to call on the support of Caribbean based kin to assist their settlement in the Caribbean. In some ways the "revolution" in communications has changed the shape of migration itself. As Nancy Foner[33] has indicated for the U.S.A., cheap flights have obviated the need to "return" permanently and have made possible a pattern of migratory "commuting," particularly for elderly African-Caribbeans. A comparable pattern is emerging with British based West Indians who either return to the Caribbean for protracted periods, or play host to Caribbean family members for up to six months (the legal maximum).[34] Many informants indicated a desire on retirement to alternate periods spent in Britain and the Caribbean.

This has important implications for families, enabling them to keep in close touch, and to replenish cultural contacts. Even without protracted visits, cheap communications allow both close and distant kin, in the Caribbean and in North America, to meet and keep in touch. Easy communications, and the possibility of dual nationality, also means that migrants are prepared to spend longer in their country of destination.

This means that links with new generations can be easily maintained or renewed, links which continue to replenish family values, models and behavior and enable a continuity across generations between family members in Britain, North America, the Caribbean and elsewhere. Aging parents in the Caribbean have heightened the emotional intensity felt by their children and grandchildren abroad, giving a fresh urgency to the frequency of contact and visits, and the desire to flesh out "roots" for younger British-born generations. Visits home, as one Trinidadian informant described, are "important, to see Mum and Dad regularly...[and] because I would like my kids to keep in touch with Trinidad and all the relatives there...to appreciate the other part of the culture....I think that makes them a better individual."[35]

Such patterns of migration and return are not, however, without pain and are marked, in both cases, by the absence of an older (grandparent) generation. One returnee's daughter felt that "now she's [mother] gone it's like losing my right arm."[36] Her mother, now settled in Trinidad, justified that "It's not far. It's just an eight hours journey to come, so [she] can always come along, or we can always come across."[37] But families, as we will see, are able to withstand the absence of members. The power of this linkage has roots within the family nexus that has been accommodated to migration, rather than disrupted by it, and should be recognized as a central element of African-Caribbean family culture.

Geographical distance has not been, therefore, a barrier to being a "close" family and informants stressed the importance of those links, the "tightness" of the emotional bonds, and the levels of "trust" expected of and experienced between family members. Such bonds contributed to the replenishment of Caribbean cultural influences and to a sense of identity based on family as much as location, or origins. Migration impacts, as we shall see, on the *gestalt* and the identity of the family, while the family provides a way of looking at, interpreting and organising the world—an example of what Sidney

Mintz and Richard Price term "cognitive orientations."[38] This is a key skill when family belongings extend beyond national boundaries, and when the world's resources can be utilized to further family ends. It contributes to the sense of well-being and identity of Caribbeans both in the Caribbean and in the diaspora, and to the continuing cultural links within the Caribbean and without. A migration culture, such as exists in the Caribbean, is manifested through its families, and to be a member of that culture, and of that family, is to maintain an emotional or material link with the Caribbean, regardless of natality. In this, memory (even when remembering what has never been known) helps maintain the links.

Let us turn now to four cases studies to explore how transnationalism operates as a dynamic within families, and how the narratives associated with transnationalism—in particular, the emphasis on "closeness" —become an identifying force for transnational families, and a directive in their composition and activities.

Hyacinth's Family

The first family migrated from Jamaica to Britain during the 1950s and 1960s. Lloyd migrated first in 1957 and was "received" into Britain by his wife's cousin. Two years later, he was joined by his wife, Hyacinth, who left their five children in Jamaica under the care of her sister and other kin. In time, those five children were brought over to join their parents and two more British-born siblings. Lloyd's migration to Britain paralleled other family members who migrated to the United States, Canada, and, unusually, Japan.

Hyacinth's mother, Lucretia, had married twice, and had four children from the first marriage, and two from her second. Hyacinth and her brother were from the second marriage, but their father died when she was two. Lucretia's first husband, a Chinese man (from China), had also died when his children were small. Lucretia supported all her children from her earnings as a laundress, and lived close to her mother (Hyacinth's grandmother) and her mother's six uncles and aunts (another uncle had migrated to Panama). This grandmother was a "beauty" who

> used to love me so much and love all the grandchildren. She would hold at least six, seven, eight of us on her knees. She used to be so good...she used to be so sweet. Everybody say I look like her sometimes. But her hair was like satin. Like satin. When you plait her hair, it just flicks up soft, soft, soft.[39]

Her maternal grandfather died when she was small, although she remembers that he "work hard" and "loved children, love his family."[40] She grew up "very, very. Very, very. Very, very close"[40] to her siblings, with no distinction made between fathers and, in this case, mixed race siblings. She remains close to all the family, "up to the fourth cousin," despite the fact that most of her siblings and cousins ("I've got cousins is no different from my sister" [42]) are now dispersed around the world. Indeed, she maintains regular contact with

> all the family, everywhere, everyone...because the way we grow up, our family was so loving and people know us to be so loving and kind and everything else. Why shouldn't you want to know them?[43]

Leaving her children behind in Jamaica, was, therefore, full of anguish.

> Can you believe it, when I said that I had to leave my children? I went bonkers! I tell you! But I never used to smoke and when I came here, and saw the situation, and it's so cold, and my children left behind. I know that they're well-looked after, but I couldn't bear to know that I have to leave them. And I start smoking. I smoke till I turn stupid. I smoked till all my lips stripped...I was dead. I was gone.[44]

She found work and saved hard and "in no time" had saved sufficient to bring four of her children to England to join her and her husband, and to send a fifth child, the eldest, to cousins in Canada. Her son, Jerry, was eleven when he joined his parents in 1966. He was six when his mother left, and although he lived with his aunt in a tenement yard in Kingston,

> the extended family that we came from, everybody shared in what we did, you know, we could stay with Uncle this or Auntie that, or what have you, so everybody had a responsibility to bring up everybody else's children. They weren't restricted to any one particular pair.[45]

The first and second-hand memories of his grandparents are strong. His paternal grandmother—with whom he lived for a year as a toddler—was, as he recalls "a very strong woman" and is still "in his memory." His paternal grandfather was equally "strong," but whereas his grandmother's "strength" refers in part to her disciplinarian character ("very strict"), that of his grandfather referred to his physical stature and his standing in the local community. Although Jerry never knew his maternal grandparents, from family stories his mother "has taken a lot from her, from the way she's spoken of by other members of the family."[46] In particular, the family legend recalls his grandmother as "such a strong woman." And one of the things she taught her kids was "Always be there for each other, no matter what."⁴⁷ Significantly, therefore, as Jerry stresses,

> ...The way that my mother has kept us all together...is identical...[to the] family unit there [in Jamaica]....That's the same sort of thing that my parents, especially my mother, has tried to maintain....So each of the siblings that's gone off, have...kept like the family thing going...it's so much instinctive....We're spiritual people...and our history is more of somebody telling you what's happened, and you never forget it. It's not a case of "Oh, I can't remember." It's there with you all the time...it's sort of passed down, which is good. It's nice because...especially living in this country, where there's a lot of pressures...especially because we're an ethnic minority, the family unit provides the type of solace, stability, that is needed to go ahead...we're always looking out, or thinking about the other one, or the two that's not here, or the three that's not here...it's as if we're carrying on a tradition that we're not even fully aware of.⁴⁸

As a result, in England, the family members—siblings, and cousins—live close to each other in South London.

When Jerry was sixteen, his mother went to the United States to visit her sister-in-law who was looking after three nieces from Jamaica, "keeping those children, school them and everything in America."⁴⁹ Hyacinth's mother-in-law, who suffered from diabetes and high blood pressure, was also staying in the United States with this sister. In the course of the visit, the sister-in-law became ill, and required hospitalization. Without hesitation, Hyacinth called her husband and informed him that she would be staying. She looked after the children, until her sister-in-law was better, then cared for her mother-in-law until her death, then, at her sister-in-law's suggestion, and with her help, got a job, while her husband took care of their children in England. She stayed for three years, sending over money and goods, and had planned to stay long enough to earn the right to live and work in the United States. However, she learned that her sixteen-year-old daughter was pregnant, and Jerry, too, aged nineteen, was fathering a child. She returned home immediately "after I spoke my piece, what could I do?.... but love them. Let them know that I'm their grandmother."⁵⁰

Hyacinth did more than love them. She allowed Jerry and his girlfriend to live in her home, until they were able to live independently, and helped bring up this grandchild along with her existing– and subsequent -grandchildren. She now has fifteen, and has played an active role in their upbringing. "I don't mind at all...if I only have the strength and the help that I need, financially, I don't mind at all. I love it."⁵¹ The help is both practical—and symbolic, as she recounts to them stories of Jamaica and their family, and acculturates them with their origins and values. As she says, "we are the grandparents, we know we are West Indians, we are not white English, so they have to have a background of their own."[52]

Significantly, however, it was not only Hyacinth who contributed to the care of Simon, Jerry's child. Simon's paternal grandfather was influential in his childhood, as was his maternal grandmother, from St. Vincent, who helped out in his childcare, as did Jerry's sisters. "The extended family" as Jerry described "that's been there. You know, if it wasn't my side, it was [my partner's], so, you know, it didn't really matter."[53] Simon, now aged twenty-two, lives with his maternal grandmother, in a neighborhood filled with both maternal and paternal kin—"we're a close knit family,"[54] and is as preoccupied with the importance of family as his father, and grandmother, travelling back to the Caribbean, Jamaica and St Vincent, and to North America to meet relatives. He has inherited a wide kinship network from his father and from his mother "another family tree. Very big....I went to Canada to visit my grandfather, my mum's dad,...and my auntie and uncle..."[55] this, he mirrors his father, who travelled regularly back to Jamaica and who insisted that Simon's mother revisit St. Vincent before he would marry her—"to be at peace with herself, settle some of the memories she had from home, instead of just thinking about it, the way I found whatever it was I was looking for at home...get to know her family...(and) her father's side of the family."[56] Jerry, however, has three sons, one of whom is an "outside" child."[57] Although Simon is not close to this brother, he's still mybrother...he's still part of me, he's still blood, at the end of the day, you know.[58]

In this family, the family values, which actively incorporated wider kin within the socialization of children, have been translated across the ocean and inherited through the generations. "What's helped [my sons] more than anything else," Jerry argues,

> is this network that we've got, the family network. It's given them stability, because they know they've got us to fall back on, should they fall by the wayside in any way.... Whatever happened to them out there may affect them more than it would have done, had they not had this.[59]

Thus Lucretia's dictum to stay together has been an ethos inherited across the generations or, as Jerry puts it, "I've got a saying: 'Your kids will always be your kids, but you can have an ex-wife and ex-girlfriends.'"[60] More particularly, the importance of the Caribbean, and of the family in the Caribbean, in providing a sense of identity is a further ethos that ran through the generations, and was well articulated by Jerry:

> I see myself as a human being first, and as a black person of African-Caribbean descent. I've become a British person through rules and regulations, but I can never be English. Not even my sons, who were born here. They might be English on paper, but they will not...be regarded as such. They will always be Afro-Caribbean, or West Indian.....And this is why I'm insistent about them learning about where their parents are from....I always thought that we've got this escape hatch in the back of our minds, those of us who are not born here, where we can always go back to. But those who are born here haven't got that, it's just stories to them, you know. But they're always being portrayed as being from somewhere else. Now, if you keep telling a young black kid that he's a West Indian, when he was born here, I mean, how does he feel? What sort of things are happening to his head all his life? To be apart from the society that he's grown up in?...The one thing they will feel, having gone back [to the Caribbean]...is that they realise, for the first time, that they are part of something...part of something else...[The Caribbean] will always be there for them as part of something that is their heritage.'[61]

Leonard's Family

Leonard came to Britain from Trinidad in 1950. He was the second youngest of seven surviving children (his mother gave birth to thirteen altogether). His mother was African-Caribbean, and migrated to Trinidad from Grenada as a young girl. His father was of Indian origin, whose grandfather had come to Trinidad from India in the nineteenth century. His parents had owned a small shop that had failed for

> ...in those days, life was very hard and people were extremely poor, everyone were very, very poor people...And my father and my mother... were such kind people...people couldn't afford to pay cash for the goods, they [parents] were allowing them to have credit all the while. And when time came for the creditors [meaning:debtors] to pay...my father use to turn around and say [to my mother] 'these people can't pay. They are very poor and they haven't got any money. Don't bother with them' and so on and eventually the business failed.[62]

The family, as a result, were left as poor as their debtors. Their parents survived from the produce they grew, and the livestock they reared on a small plot of land. Nevertheless, his mother "always taught us to share things, physically share everything we had."[63] In addition to sharing, the family fostered an ethos of caring. The older siblings were required to look after the younger ones, and the younger ones in turn were taught to respect and obey them. Indeed, this pattern of family behavior was extended beyond the family into the neighborhood, with a generic responsibility of caring on the one hand, and respect on the other. "All these were unwritten laws but it was something that was taken very seriously, and practice very, very strongly. I think it helped to shape our character and our behavior in later life. I'm sure it have some bearing on the way that we live now."[64] Family behavior may be seen as a metaphor or model for community life, with both respect and reciprocity, caring and sharing, as central values. It is a recurrent theme throughout the interviews and a central motif, and structuring principle, in Leonard's narrative. "I've always pledge to myself that as a result of my experience...that if I ever find myself in a position where I could help people, that is what I would do....that have helped...to make me a better person."[65] Despite their poverty and his mother's relative lack of education,

> she had a natural foresight of what life would be many years from the date she was born, the time that we were around. She for some reason realised that the whole way of life would change. And the process of which that life would change was through education.'[66]

She coordinated a family strategy which would prepare the family for change, and maximize its benefits. Despite Leonard's insistence that every member of the family was "regarded with the same concern and courtesy and kindness...is treated exactly the same,"[67] choices were made.

> My father and mother recognized that my sister was brilliant in her education...they decided that in order for her to increase that potential they will try to get her abroad so that she could. Now that is the period where they single the children, they began to sort them out. And they did manage to send my sister to the United States and as a result of that she is what she is today...after she left, they focused on me because they felt that I also showed signs of trying to achieve more than what could have been achieved in the little limited area that we were brought up in. And they did everything they possibly could to ensure that I too got to go abroad to see if I could increase myself.[68]

His sister was sent to stay with two aunts (who had migrated earlier) in the United States. The plan was for her to stay there, and for Leonard to join her later. His parents, as Leonard remarked, "couldn't have done it for all the children, but the two of us."[69] To do so, his parents sold everything they had, including the animals, to raise the money for the passage for Leonard and his sister. His sister's migration to the United States had, however, "a knock on effect. She then, when she achieved what she did achieve, she was in a position then to get my brothers to go to the United States and she looked after them there."[70] Only two of the seven children remained in Trinidad. In the event, Leonard changed his plans to go to America, and diverted his passage to the United Kingdom, arriving in Britain in 1950, penniless, and armed only with the belief that Birmingham, as the industrial center of Britain, was the place most likely to offer employment. "Now," he recalled, "was it madness or was it sheer ignorance or was it the folly of youth to arrive in a foreign land, having nowhere to go, without no money in your pocket and try to make a life?"[71]

Leonard found work, accommodation and, within two years, an English wife. (His sister in America sent the money for a honeymoon.) He also found discrimination. His original plan was to remigrate to the United States. England was merely "en route for what I wanted to achieve in my life"[72] He found the work was not highly paid,

> I realized that West Indian people like us were treated completely different...we were separated, you weren't normal people, you did the worst jobs, the most menial job, the filthy jobs...they didn't think that you could read and write and as a matter of fact people used to ask you, can you read or can you write?[73]

He was also sending money back regularly to his parents and family in Trinidad.

> When I start to work, and even when I got married, I send money regularly home. I always make sure...even though things were hard for us, my wife and I always use to send money for my father...and my mother when she was alive...he [father] would write us and say he want to buy a pig and tell us what the cost is and we rigged the money up and sent to him...we used to send him money regularly up to the time of his death.[74]

Nevertheless, in time Leonard and his wife bought their own home, and he secured a good job in management, before retiring a few years ago. He has one son by his wife, and a daughter (now deceased) from a previous relationship in Trinidad. Although they have no plans to return to Trinidad permanently, family obligations, in Britain and the Caribbean, continue to play a prominent role in their lives. Thus, in their retirement, he and his wife help care for his grandson, inspired partly by a desire to help the material well-being of his son's family, and partly by a deeply held sense of reciprocity,

> because this is the something that we could do to help the family...they cannot afford to put the child in nursery...and the both of them cannot afford not to work or else they would not be able to afford to pay the mortgage. Now we are at home...so we said it is something we could do for our grandson and to help our son and his wife. I would feel that this is the way that family should live.[75]

Most significantly, when Leonard's brother became seriously ill, they used up their retirement savings to pay for him to come to England for a series of operations for cancer,

> But we said it's a life and we couldn't let him die...we paid for everything....if my mother and my parents hadn't sent me to England I would not have been in the position to do what we have done. So it stems back from the original attitude of my parents, their unselfishness, the sacrifice they have made to send me here.[76]

Their son maintains close contact with family members in the Caribbean and North America, "We haven't got to...tell him. He regard the family abroad in exactly the same way."[77] Old age for Leonard holds no terror, "And the reason why I say that is the way family is made up and the caring way in which this family have lived and will continue to live."[78]

Leonard's life has been marked by a trajectory of upward mobility. But it is one which has its origins in a family strategy that benefited—and continues to benefit—kin in Trinidad as much as those in Britain. The decision of his parents to make strategic choices among their children and to promote the migration of two of their children, so that they, in turn, could help promote the life chances of their siblings, is an important story of transnational sibling support. Family decisions were made (from the initial move by his sister to kin in the United States, to his brother's medical visit to Britain) at a transnational level. This strategy involved sacrifices in the Caribbean, and in Britain, which could have resulted in a situation of economic stasis and did result in financial loss for Leonard and his wife in their retirement. Its genesis is to be found in the Caribbean, in the values of respect and reciprocity that were so deeply engrained in Leonard's upbringing. Any good fortune that came his way as a result of the sacrifices of others demanded return, and the sibling relationship proved a powerful binding force in the family. The site for mobility may have been Britain (or, in the case of his siblings, the United States) its causes and consequences were firmly located in Trinidad. And what makes it transnational is not merely the location of the ambition and the activities, but their nature, the sustained pattern of action across the years and the oceans that enabled Leonard, without a second thought, to help his brother, as if neither time, distance nor national boundaries existed, to care for his grandson, to know that in turn he will receive help in his time of need, and that his son maintains the same values of reciprocity and the same patterns of contact and closeness with his kin throughout the world.

Benson's Family

Benson was seventeen when he migrated from Jamaica to England in 1966 to join his parents and his other siblings who had been brought over before him. His father (now deceased) also had a number of "outside" children both before and after marriage to Benson's mother. These siblings were integral to Benson's definitions of family. Benson's family, like many in the Caribbean, was built on the migrations of successive generations. His maternal grandfather went to Panama, and then to Cuba (where he died), supporting the family, until his death, on the remittances returned. His father had migrated to the United States prior to re-migrating to England. Benson has one sister in Jamaica, two in Canada, and a brother in Germany. As a result, transnational kinship was an integral dynamic of this—and other—families, and the international network of kin in which the family was situated formed a continuing backdrop to Benson's perceptions of himself and his family. Benson's other siblings live close to each other in England.

Benson's father was in England for five years before Benson's mother joined him, leaving the older children in Jamaica to look after the younger ones, under the eye of her mother, her brother and a family friend. The family (including the "outside" siblings) lived in close proximity, and the neighborhood provided a context of both support and supervision. In time, Benson and his siblings joined their parents in England. Although much of his childhood was spent apart from his parents, family unity was a primary goal.

> To me, family is like a religion...you've got that belief...which is very important to you, in your life...it's something to pass onto the next generation...the children...see how everyone lives, so obviously they'll emulate them, try and do the same, try and be close knit, all stick together...blood is thicker than water, so families always come first...we share and share...that's the way I was brought up...[79]

The sharing of resources is integral to this sense of family.

> If you can't keep in touch with your family...then who can you?...If you can't be friendly with your family, who can you be friendly with? So it's very important. We share and share you all...that's the way I was brought up...[80]

Identity, and family, are of far greater significance to Benson than the accumulation of material wealth or social status. "I'm not that kind of a person."[81] Blood, as he says, is thicker than water, a belief created partly from his upbringing, and partly from his own experience of long separation from his parents "I didn't want that to happen to my children."[82] He has been married twice, and has two children from each marriage. Bringing up children in Britain, however, has been a hazardous undertaking,

> It's very hard, very different. I don't know if it's the change of times...I mean, they have a lot of things which we didn't have...plus the society which you live in...there's two different societies. I mean, in Jamaica...if I done something wrong, anybody would give me a good beating and my school, if I done anything, I dare not go home and tell my parents, 'cause if I do that, I'm going to get another beating on top of it. But now it's not like that and I notice that today you...don't have much control over you kids....I don't know if all kids are like that, but most West Indians find it...you've got to be a saint to bring up kids in this society.[83]

In contrast to his own childhood in the Caribbean, which afforded him a relative freedom, with his own children he insists on firm control:

> I don't allow them to go on the street and play....If they want to go, they ask...if I think it's necessary then I'll let them go. If not, I'll say no...I want to know where they are. They don't just run out as they like. You see, at this age, you've got to have some control.[84]

Ironically, however, he argues that he has given them "more freedom":

> My parents was maybe strict, what little of them I know because...in the early part, my mum left, my dad first, then my mum...I would say I bring them up better, much better than the way my parents brought me up, if that makes sense to you...cos...I've seen what's going on around and I've...take note...that I can pass on a little knowledge. If I seen anyone on the wrong road, I can, you know, can try and correct them. I would say...I know better than my mum and dad. And I know...the change in circumstances and all that, so I would say I'm a bit wiser in today's society than what they were in those days.[85]

His first wife subsequently had a third child, although she no longer lives with the father of that child. Nevertheless, according to his eldest daughter, Juliette (from this first marriage) Benson does not discriminate between his children and their half-sibling. Equally, Juliette "gets on fine" with her former step-father. "Something that my dad's always told me, you know, friends are for, like, now, but family's forever...my family's always been important to me, and always will be."[86] Juliette is equally close to her maternal kin, particularly her maternal grandmother, whom she calls "Nan," and her maternal step-grandfather "my nan's husband is the only grandfather that I know."[87]

This grandfather has family living in America, the Cayman Islands, and the Virgin Islands and "likes to go on holidays, at least once a year, to visit them and keep in contact."[88] It is behavior that

Juliette lauds. Equally, she is close to her brother, her half-brother and her two half-sisters and

> my little brother's father, he's got two daughters as well, two older daughters...and my mum said they're my sisters, even though they're half sisters or whatever, so I've got a very extended family...we're very close.'[89]

Accordingly, family played a significant part in her childhood,

> Every weekend we'd go to somebody's house...we still do it now, we take it in turns...not so much my mum's side, but my dad's side. We still do it now, like one week we'll go to one aunt's house, next time another auntie, and then my uncle's house, and then they'll come to my dad's house and we'll all go to his house...every weekend we'd be down to somebody's house for dinner, or whatever...play with my cousins, something like that.[90]

—as did members in her parent's friendship networks. "My godparents...in a way...were my aunt and uncle...[this] uncle was my uncle's wife's brother, that's why he was my uncle by marriage...there was my mum's cousin...and then there was this family that lived a couple of doors away...I'm always down there, at least twice a week, maybe it's more than that."[91]

She does not feel disadvantaged by her parent's divorce. On the contrary, her half-brother's father was a constant presence in her childhood, as was her own father. This half-brother she and her brother regard as "just our little brother, at the end of the day"[92] Godparents and family friends were also brought into the ambit of "family" replicating as far as possible her father's concept of neighborhood family, which he cherished from his childhood in Jamaica. Benson considered it of primary importance to impart to all his children a sense of their history and culture, taking them to Jamaica (and Canada) to meet their family and their culture.

> I want them to know a bit their history, where they're coming from...not just Jamaican, but black culture...we haven't got a lot of role models, so when I see role models that really set example....I can turn to my kids and say 'That's what I would like you to be, like that person'...it's very important, me telling them my background and things like that...[and] it's good to know that family keep in touch. And they should know who their cousins are, aunties are, whoever.[93]

It was this aspect of Jamaica that Juliette, on one of her visits to the island, found so appealing. It made her feel

> comfortable. Everybody was so friendly, and they'd walk past you and say "Good morning" The people just don't do that here...if you walked past them and you said "hello" or "good morning" they'd look at you as if you were crazy. [It was] just the sheer friendliness of it.[94]

As a result, if the opportunity arose, she would settle in Jamaica, "I would. I'd definitely go." Her cousin had already settled there a few years ago. In terms of identity, Juliette considers herself both British and Jamaican, although "the only connection I've got with being British is that fact that I was born here and grew up here, but all of the time (I felt I was) Jamaican."[95]

Juliette's experience and her model of family is extensive and inclusive, embracing kin on equal terms regardless of locality or genealogy. The inclusive definition of family and the strength of kinship ties may be seen as both cause and effect of this transnational African-Caribbean family. Like her father, Juliette feels that it is of vital importance to maintain the links with her family in Jamaica as well as in North America, and would wish to transmit that inheritance to her own children in time, "definitely, definitely. It's really important...[for] the family's here forever, whereas friends come and go."[96] Benson, in time, plans to return to the Caribbean where the direct links with another generation will begin and the cycle continue.

Jim's Family

Jim migrated to Britain in 1961. He was twenty-nine years old, and had migrated previously to Canada, staying there for five years before returning to Trinidad. Jim and his wife returned permanently to Trinidad nine years ago. His mother's family had migrated to Trinidad from Barbados, his father originated from Monserrat. From the nineteenth century, Trinidad had been the locus of much of the inter-island migration, attracting, in particular, migrants from the Eastern Caribbean and many of our Trinidadian informants (like Leonard, earlier) had grandparents who had originated elsewhere in the Caribbean. Jim arrived in London, staying first with a friend, then renting a room, and then a flat, which he learned about on the Trinidadian grapevine. After a few years, Jim (who by now had married another Trinidadian) bought a house on mortgage.

Jim had served an apprenticeship in Trinidad as a diesel mechanic and secured work in Britain as a mechanic, although "it took me some leather beating on the pavements."[97] It was, however, poorly paid and through a contact (another Trinidadian), he left this employment to work with British Rail as a fitter. Although the money was better, the hours were difficult. By then Jim and his wife had a child. His wife was working as a nurse. They managed to care for the child through alternating their shifts. The situation was not satisfactory, and Jim changed his job and took employment as a technician in a school. He then retrained as a teacher because "I found a lot of the black kids were having a raw deal...most of the teachers couldn't understand the black child...that was one of my main reasons for going into teaching, to see what help I could offer those kids."[98] The family lived on his wife's salary and his grant which "wasn't much...it was only about £600 for the year. You had to pay mortgage, water rate, lights, gas...so you had to prepare for that."[99] Jim continued in his career as a teacher, rising to Head of Department before taking early retirement in 1990.

While caring and sharing was a structuring theme in Leonard's narrative, preparation was the central theme of Jim's narrative. He prepared for life as a student by saving when he was employed. Indeed, with the exception of the mortgage on the house, he has never taken on a loan, or bought goods on hire purchase, preferring to save, rather than go into debt. From early on, he decided to return to Trinidad—"my attitude to Trinidad never left me...no matter where I go, I had to come back here."[100] The move was carefully prepared. In order to save, Jim taught two extra evening classes a week. He never bought a new car. Every year he had saved sufficient to return to Trinidad, and to return with savings that he banked in Trinidad. "And my colleagues want to find out 'How could you do that every year?' And they're smoking a pack, or two packs of cigarettes every day...they couldn't understand it. You see, I don't smoke....That's how I can save my money and travel every year."[101] The purchase of property in Trinidad was not made until there was sufficient saving—and the time was right. The oil boom in the 1980s had inflated the price of property in Trinidad. Jim bided his time until prices began to fall. In 1987 he took early retirement ("a lot of teachers end up with stress and heart attacks and die, you know. I want to enjoy some of my retirement, which I am doing right now. I'm on happy hill."[102]), and then worked as a supply teacher until 1990 when he returned to Trinidad and purchased a house for cash.

The planning did not stop there. The house was rented out, providing an income. In the meantime, his wife had inherited her mother's house in Trinidad. Jim moved into this house, renovating and extending it, and renting out rooms to visitors. With the rental from the first property, he bought a small estate in the countryside. He cleared the land, and has planted citrus, mango and is cultivating other rotating crops. "It has to be a going concern, eventually...next four or five years, this garden has to be paying for itself."[103] He is currently building his own house on the property, large enough to incorporate two apartments to let to visitors.

He still owns a house in London (lived in by his son) and before leaving helped his daughter (who studied biochemistry at university and is now a teacher) to buy her own home. His pension is paid into his English bank account, which his daughter draws for him when needed.[104] While Jim's career has, like Leonard's, displayed evidence of upward mobility, moving from the ranks of a skilled worker into those of the lower professionals, the extent of this mobility is unlikely to emerge on any statistical indicator. While not a wealthy man, Jim owns four substantial properties. Three of them, however, are in Trinidad. His savings were (and are) in Trinidad. He has substantial collateral that can be used to raise cash in any emergency. The trajectory of his life has been orientated not toward Britain, but to the Caribbean. To this end, he also kept up with both friends and family in Trinidad. Return was not therefore the social dislocation that it can be for some returning nationals. His children and grandchildren remain in England and for them Jim's return extends the direct links with the Caribbean for another generation.

***

The case studies here have articulated both the symbolic and the practical, discourses of transnational family narratives. All were families in which, as Jerry described it, "There's always somebody going abroad to foreign." In Leonard's case, his parents made a strategic choice among their children to send abroad those most likely to benefit from the experience so that they, in turn, could benefit the family at home. In many ways, the family demonstrated an almost classic example of "chain migration" as first one child was sent to kin abroad and, in turn, assisted other kin to move. In Hyacinth's and Benson's case, the migration patterns seemed less strategic and more general, as parents, uncles, cousins and siblings regularly traveled back and forth to the Caribbean. In Leonard's case, the strategy was accompanied by a vision in which the world's resources could be utilized to pursue the betterment of the family, and where a clearly accepted value of reciprocity ensured that it succeeded. While such a vision was less clear in the case of Jim, he nevertheless calculated carefully in order to maximize his opportunities within a global context. The vision was also more opaque in the case of Benson and Hyacinth and their families, but nevertheless a global context was part of the everyday milieu in which these families operated, and the benefits resulting were considered there for the reaping—Canada, the United States, Europe or Japan, St. Vincent or Jamaica. National borders were no barrier to family connectedness, while the idea of family as a Caribbean family centered the sense of identity of family members.

African-Caribbean family narratives focus on the celebratory, rather than the problematic, aspects of their relationships.[105] Thus the language of the family stresses its closeness and linked with these "close" family narratives is a positive avowal of Caribbean culture for, as Alana argued in chapter 4, "I strongly believe that you should never forget your roots."[106] It seems that the British-born (or brought-up) generation of African-Caribbeans have a clear sense of the difference of the African-Caribbean family, and a pride not only in individual members, but in the system as a whole. As another British-born woman described it "The sense of family, the sense of unity, was much stronger (than English families)....I'm actually really proud of Caribbean families, that was something that we will always retain."[107] Over and over in our study we heard stories of pride taken in the family, of its importance for both support and solace, identity and differentiation.

The emphasis on closeness extends the meaning of the narratives, by encoding values and prescriptions for loyalty, love, and "living good." They are particular ways of talking about particular relationships. These narratives link families across the oceans and the generations. They strengthen family membership and ties that have very practical implications in enabling migration, and facilitating return. But they are also increasingly powerful as expression of, and foci for, a Caribbean cultural identity abroad, and in the Caribbean. As African-Caribbean family patterns in Britain continue to conform to those identified in the Caribbean, and as transnational links continue to affirm the influence of the Caribbean, the idea of family and the meanings attached to it have emerged as key elements in the narratives of belonging and identity. It is not just that you come from Jamaica (or Trinidad or Barbados) but that you come from a particular Jamaican (Trinidadian, Barbadian) *family* that stands for identifiable beliefs and values, and that represents a formidable network of kin whose loyalty—as members of a shared lineage—can be taken on trust.

we have a family reunion now...New York...Two years ago ...(it was) in Canada...the one before that was in Jamaica ...Every two years, yes...every year it become bigger...a few hundred I would say....How many tables it was? About 30![108]

Indeed, as Sutton has argued, family reunions, as rituals, provide a public expression of what is normally considered a private world and are visible affirmations of family identity that override all other affiliations.[108] What links the family is kinship and lineage, neither of which relies on place for meaning. The longevity of migration as a feature of Caribbean life has arguably reinforced the sense of kinship and lineage as unifying features of family life and as a distinguishing feature of Caribbean diasporic communities.

But if the language of families is symbolic, it also contains practical elements. Loyalty, as members of a shared lineage, can be assumed and trust guaranteed. Members of a transnational family, of close transnational networks, are provided with opportunities to utilize them to enhance their material or occupational world, to broaden their experience, or to provide support when required. Hyacinth flew across the Atlantic to support her sister-in-law and she, in turn, provided her with employment in America as recompense. This employment, in turn, helped her children in England. Leonard's brother flew to England to take advantage of medical care.

While individuals may not be characterized by wealth accumulation, the social capital invested in and created by families is often considered more significant. For all the families here the ties of consanguinity and affinity—across a complex kinship pattern which spread across the world—were given the highest priority. Indeed, the capital generated by good family relations was considered a finer value, and of more practical use, than material success.

Membership of a transnational family contains within it a "transnational imagination." With a family dynamic and a family culture built on transnational links, and close family networks that stretch around the world, family members are provided with opportunities to utilize those networks to further their own employment or career profile, to broaden their experience base, and to strengthen family resources. The links and networks are both multinational as well as transnational. Indeed, the spreading or dispersal of material and emotional resources throughout the diasporic trajectory of each family provides diversity and security, strength and opportunity. Family members provide important points of contact, facilitating migration, re-migration and, of course, return. When the family is both the source of belonging and the resource for survival, then identity is both portable and secure.

It is precisely the flexibility of the African-Caribbean family at home and abroad that provided it with the means to survive and to support the high levels of migration that accompany it. For African-Caribbean migrants the borders of the nation may, like the family, be emotional rather than geographic, political identities and belongings shaped by the networks of transnational kin, citizenship contingent on a diasporic imperative. For these African-Caribbean families are also black families. They hold a peculiar and precarious position in the grand narratives of globalization that brought them to the New World and in the narratives of citizenship, nationhood and national identity that subsequently emerged. "I am," as one informant said, "a citizen of the world." "I belong," said another, "to whoever wants me." From a metropolitan perspective, the objective in any policy on immigrants may be to synthesize a national identity. For the migrant, transnationalism may become, or already be, their synthesizing identity.

Notes

1. BB056/2/2/2/41.
2. Velma Newton, *The Silver Men. West Indian Labor Migration to Panama 1850-1914* (Kingston, University of the West Indies, Institute of Social and Economic Research, 1987).
3. Hilary Beckles, *A History of Barbados* (Cambridge: Cambridge University Press, 1990).
4. BDA. GH4/52, Colonial Office paper on position of British West Indians in Central and South American countries, n.d. but presumably 1933. See also Howard Johnson, "Barbadian Migrants in the Putumayo District of the Amazon, 1904-1911" in *Caribbean Migration, Globalised Identities,* ed. Mary Chamberlain (London: Routledge, 1998); Sidney Greenfield, "Barbadians in the Brazilian Amazon," *Luso-Brazilian Review,* 20, 1 (1983), 4-64.
5. Philip Kasinitz, *Caribbean New York: Black Immigrants and the Politics of Race* (Ithaca: Cornell University Press, 1992).
6. Philip Kasinitz, *Caribbean New York.*
7. Ceri Peach, "The Caribbean in Europe: Contrasting Patterns of Migration and Settlement in Britain, France and the Netherlands," Research Paper in Ethnic Relations No. 15 (Coventry: Centre for Research in Ethnic Relations, University of Warwick, 1991). Also, see Owen, *A Profile of Caribbean Households.*
8. www.statistics.gov.uk/census2001.
9. George W. Roberts, "Emigration from the Island of Barbados," *Social and Economic Studies,* 4, 3, (1955). Bonham Richardson, *Caribbean Migrants. Environment and Human Survival on St. Kitts and Nevis* (Knoxville: University of Tennessee Press, 1983); Bonham Richardson, *Panama Money in Barbados 1900-1920* (Knoxville: University of Tennessee Press, 1985).
10. Roberts, "Emigration"; Richardson, *Caribbean Migrants* and *Panama Money*; Kasinitz, *Caribbean New York.*

11. Kasinitz, *Caribbean New York*; Linda Basch et al, *Nations Unbound*.
12. There is an insightful passage in George Lamming's *In the Castle of My Skin* (1953) when Trumper returns to Barbados after his sojourn in the United States, full of "new" political ideas.
    "You know the voice?" Trumper asked. He was very serious now.
    I tried to recall whether I might have heard it. I couldn't.
    "Paul Robeson," he said. "One o' the greatest o' my people."
    "What people?" I asked. I was a bit puzzled.
    "My people," said Trumper. [...] "The Negro race."
13. Richardson, *Caribbean Migrants*; A. Segal, "The Caribbean Exodus in a Global Context: Comparative Migration Experiences" in *The Caribbean Exodus* ed. B. Levine (New York: Praeger,1987); Robin Cohen,*Global Diasporas. An Introduction* (London: UCL Press, 1997), Elizabeth Thomas-Hope, *Explanation in Caribbean Migration* (London: Macmillan, 1992).
14. Thomas-Hope, *Explanation in Caribbean Migration*.
15. Richardson, *Caribbean Migrants;* Thomas-Hope, *Explanation in Caribbean Migration*; Mary Chamberlain, *Narratives of Exile and Return* (London, Macmillan, 1997).
16. Deborah Bryceson and Ulla Vuorela, eds., *The Transnational Family. New European Frontiers and Global Networks.* (Oxford: Berg, 2002).
17. *Global Networks. A Journal of Transnational Affairs*, Special Issue, "Transnational families: memories and narratives" 4, 3 (2004).
18. Rosina Brodber Wiltshire, "The Caribbean Transnational Family," paper presented to UNESCO/ISER Eastern Caribbean Sub-regional Seminar, University of the West Indies, Cave Hill, (1988).
19. Constance Sutton and Susan Markiesky Barrow "Migration and West Indian Racial and Ethnic Consciousness" in *Caribbean Life in New York City: Sociocultural Dimension,s* eds. Constance R. Sutton and Elsa M. Chaney (New York: Center for Migration Studies of New York Inc.,1994); Constance Sutton, "Celebrating Ourselves: The Family Reunion Rituals of African Caribbean Transnational Families" *Global Networks. A Journal of Transnational Affairs*, Special Issue, "Transnational Families: Memories and Narratives" 4, 3 (2004), 243-259. Paula Aymer, *Uprooted Women. Migrant Domestics in the Caribbean* (Westport:. Praeger,1997); Linda Basch, et al. *Nations Unbound* (1994); Nina Glick Schiller and Georges Fouron *Georges Woke Up Laughing: Long Distance Nationalism and the Search for Home* (Durham: Duke University Press, 2001); Denis Conway, "Conceptualising Contemporary Patterns of Caribbean International Mobility," *Caribbean Geography*, 2,3 (1988); Karen Fog Olwig, 'Constructing Lives: Migration Narratives and Life Stories Among Nevisians,' in Chamberlain, ed., in *Caribbean Migration*. Thomas Hope, *Explanation in Caribbean Migration*.
20. Harry Goulbourne, "The Transnational Character of Caribbean Kinship in Britain" in *Changing Britain. Families and Households in the 1990s,* ed. Susan McRae (Oxford: Oxford University Press, 1999).
21. Harry Goulbourne, *Caribbean Transnational Experience* (London: Pluto Press, 2002).
22. Chamberlain, *Narratives*.
23. Paul Thompson and Elaine Bauer, "Recapturing Distant Caribbean Childhoods and Communities: The Shaping of Memory in the Testimonies of Jamaican Migrants in Britain and North America" *Oral History* 30, 2 (2002): 49-59. Paul Thompson and Elaine Bauer "Jamaican Transnational Families: Points of Pain and Sources of Resilience," *Wadapagi*: a Journal of the Caribbean and its Diaspora (Summer/Fall 2000): 1-37. See also Bauer and Thompson *Jamaican Hands Across the Atlantic* (Kingston : Ian Randle 2006 forthcoming).

114   Family Love in the Diaspora

24. A. Appadurai, *Modernity at Large: Cultural Dimensions of Globalisation* (Minnesota: University of Minnesota Press, 1996); Ulf Hannerz, *Transnational Connections: Culture, People, Places* (London: Routledge, 1996); Giddens, *Modernity and Self Identity.*
25. Alejandro Portes, Luis E. Guarnizo, Patricia Landolt, "The Study of Transnationalism: Pitfalls and Promises of an Emergent Research Field' *Ethnic and Racial Studies* 22, 2, (1999): 217-237.
26. Glick-Schiller and Fouron, *Georges Woke Up Laughing.*
27. Bryceson and Ulla Vuorela, eds., *The Transnational Family.*11, 14.
28. Don Robotham, "Transnationalism in the Caribbean: Formal and Informal," AES distinguished lecture, *American Ethnologist* 25,2, (1996):307-321.
29. Brathwaite, *The Development of Creole Society.*
30. Susan Craig James, "Intertwining Roots" *Journal of Caribbean History*, 25:2 (1992): 216-228.
31. Peach, *The Caribbean in Europe.*
32. Goulbourne, *Caribbean Transnational Experience.*
33. Nancy Foner "West Indians in New York City and London: A Comparative Analysis" in Sutton and Chaney, eds. in *Caribbean Life in New York City;* Nancy Foner, "Towards a Comparative Perspective on Caribbean Migration" in *Caribbean Migration;* Basch et al. *Nations Unbound.* See also Carol Boyce-Davis, *Black Women, Writing and Identity. Migrations of the Subject* (London and New York: Routledge, 1994).
34. Dwaine Plaza, "Frequent Flyer Grannies," paper presented to the Caribbean Studies Association, (1996).
35. TB018.
36. TR038.
37. TR097.
38. Mintz and Price, *An Anthropological Approach,*14.
39. JF020/1/1/1/13.
40. JF020/1/1/2/16.
41. JF020/1/1/2/17.
42. JF020/1/1/18.
43. JF020/1/1/18.
44. JF020/1/1/1/10.
45. JF022/2/1/1/6.
46. JF022/2/1/1/6.
47. JF022/2/1/1/15.
48. JF022/2/1/1/10-11.
49. JF020/1/2/31.
50. JF020/1/2/1/38.
51. JF020/1/1/2/26.
52. JF020/1/2/1/42.
53. JF022/2/2/2/32.
54. JF021/1/1/6.
55. JF021/1/1/10-11.
56. JF022/1/2/36-37.
57. "Outside children," and "outside woman" refer to relationships and families maintained outside the permanent or "inside" relationship.
58. JF021/1/2/1.
59. JF022/2/2/41.
60. JF022/2/2/40.
61. JF022/2/2/42-43.

Transnational Narratives and National Belongings 115

62. TJ073/2/1/1/12.
63. TJ073/2/1/1/10.
64. TJ073/2/1/1/19.
65. TJ073/2/1/1/23.
66. TJ073/2/1/1/10. For a discussion of women with a "global" vision, see Elaine Bauer and Paul Thompson "She's always the person with a very global vision: The Gender Dynamics of Migration, Narration, Interpretation and the Care of Jamaican Transnational Families" *Gender and History* 16(2) 2004, 334-375.
67. TJ073/2/1/2/15.
68. TJ073/2/1/2/17.
69. Ibid.
70. Ibid
71. TJ073/2/2/1/27.
72. TJ073/2/2/2/31.
73. TJ073/2/2/2/30.
74. TJ073/2/2/2/31.
75. TJ073/2/3/2/53.
76. TJ073/2/3/2/55.
77. TJ073/2/3/2/56.
78. TJ073/2/3/2/56.
79. JG025/2/1/1/11.
80. JG025/2/1/1/12.
81. JG025/2/1/2/20.
82. JG025/2/1/2/32.
83. JG025/2/1/232.
84. JG025/2/2/1/38.
85. JG025/2/2/1/40.
86. JG023/3/1/1/6.
87. JG023/3/1/1/13.
88. JG023/3/1/1/14.
89. Ibid.
90. JG023/3/1/1/6.
91. JG023/3/1/1/16.
92. JG023/3/1/1/5.
93. JG025/2/2/1/43.
94. JG023/3/1/2/26.
95. JG023/3/2/1/33.
96. JG023/3/2/1/35.
97. TQ109/2/1/1/4.
98. TQ109/2/1/1/7.
99. TQ109/2/1/1/8.
100. TQ109/2/1/2/14.
101. Ibid.
102. TQ109/2/1/2/15.
103. TQ109/2/1/2/17.
104. Only Barbados and Jamaica have arranged for their returning nationals to retain index-linked pensions. Returning nationals elsewhere in the Caribbean may continue to draw their pensions, but without the index-linked payments. This anomaly is a source of discontent for many returning nationals in the Eastern Caribbean. Jim, by having his pension paid into his UK bank account, is thereby able to retain its index linking.

105. Constance Sutton, "Celebrating Ourselves: Keeping Kin Connections Alive. Family Reunions in the Afro-Caribbean Diaspora." Gender and Transnational Families Conference, Amsterdam, May/June (2002.); idem, "Celebrating Ourselves."
106. JD013 2/1/2/34.
107. JC011.
108. JL0351b.
109. Sutton, "Celebrating Ourselves."

Part 3

Families through the Narratives of...

6

The Wider Household: Grandparents and Other Kin

> "...amongst all the 270 families...studied in Jamaica, not a single one consisted only of parents and their children. Every family included additional children and adults variously described as nephews, grandsons, stepsons, cousins, 'aunties' and 'grannies.'"[1]

In memories of childhood, grandparents—and grandmothers in particular—loom large. Growing up in the Caribbean for the majority of informants meant growing up in close proximity to a grandparent or two. Indeed, for many, it was the grandparents (or an older female relative) who were primarily responsible for their care, either because one or both parents was absent through work or migration, or because a grandparent (or another female relative) chose to foster —and a parent to relinquish—one or more children. Yet despite the prevalence in the scholarly literature of references to "aunties" and, in particular, "grannies," and despite the descriptions and observations relating to the widespread practice of child-shifting (the temporary or permanent fostering of the child by kinfolk, usually a grandmother, aunt or a close family friend) there has been surprisingly little focus on the role of grandparents except in relation to their function as surrogate parents, a function interpreted variously as a standby position resulting from the absence of the biological parent(s), and/or as a dependency feature characteristic of lower-class families. In this, the grandmother or maternal family is

> so-called because the grandmother or some female relative, perhaps a sister, usurps the function of the father and at times that of the mother. Such a family can originate through the girl becoming pregnant while still living at home. The household may consist of her mother, her mother's sister, and the girl's siblings. The girl may remain at home and look after her child, but in many cases she leaves and the child is brought up by its grandmother. The girl's child is treated in the same way as the other children in the household, no distinctions are made. If the girl's father lives in the house he will act towards his grandchild as if it were his own child.[2]

And, as Henriques observed, in this type of family "the usual period of maternal dependence is enlarged from that of childhood to include the greater part of adult life...daughter can look for protection and care for herself and her children to the latter group."[3]

For Henriques, as for other scholars, the primary explanation for both the prevalence of grandparents in the upbringing of children and for what appears to be an extended period of dependency lay in economics. Poverty was the overriding imperative driving the sharing of childrearing activities, initiated by the mother as a response to the need for childcare to support her extra-domestic activities in the absence of a husband or male breadwinner and willingly condoned by the grandmother. Indeed, in Henriques view, the introduction of the grandmother or other relative into the care of the child emerges as a casual consequence of the daughter's fecklessness (tinged with patriarchal disapproval for the women who have "usurped" the male authority). Once there, however, the daughter has an obligation to support not only her child but the household in which she lives. What seems to be lacking in such a perspective is a human and a cultural response: the desire of all parties to be engaged in the rearing of children, regardless of economic demands.

In the context of African-Caribbean migrant families, the role of grandparents in the rearing of the children of parents absent through migration is necessarily brought into profile. Interviewing across the generations however, revealed that the role and importance of grandparents in contributing to the upbringing of grandchildren was not solely dependent on an absent parent but is evident, to a greater or lesser degree, in many families regardless of economic circumstance, and regardless of the generation or period. Thus, while many of the children of the migrants who came to Britain between 1948 and 1966 were brought up by their grandparents for part or all of their lives, their parents recounted similar family profiles. While this profile has revealed the importance of an older generation in the care and rearing of children, the narratives employed in these descriptions raise issues that extend beyond a base definition of financial or social convenience. That grandparents—and grandmothers in particular—could be relied upon to provide practical support in childcare and fostering suggests at minimum a cultural disposition toward assuming this role. But the role itself is multifaceted, embracing a broader disposition toward childcare as a family, even a communal, responsibility. This, in turn, raises issues on the nature, purpose and practice of networks, and extends interpretation beyond the physical nature of support into metaphysical concerns over the nature and meaning of family and lineage, and within that, on the nature and meaning of the mother and the child. Equally, the presumption that the grandmother role is solely occupied with childcare obscures not only the complex meanings behind such roles, but obscures the role that grandfathers may play in family and kinship relations—in much the same way as a concern with mother-headed households has obscured the role of fathers within the household and family.[4] Thus, the multifaceted nature and gender differentiated aspects of these roles may be seen not only through the practical help in childcare/fostering and support, but equally in the communicative role in linking family members and retaining (and extending) kinship networks within and between families, the symbolic role in providing continuity through the generations (including ancestors), and a socializing and "community" role. Conversely, grandchildren often have close relationships with, and responsibility toward, grandparents, extending what Brodber described as their "perceptual" field of family, and generating a sense of "emotional expansiveness" although, in her view, while this may create a greater sense of independence, it may also lead to feelings of dislocation and anomie.[5]

Claudine's Family

"My grandmother...she was, she is, a blessing, she's sweet, she is so sweet"[6]

Two images of grandmothers recur throughout the narratives. Grandmothers are invariably described in terms of endearment, frequently couched (as noted in chapter 3) in spiritual metaphors. In parallel with these images are notions of strength. Grandmothers are as frequently described in terms of being a "strong woman," a "hard worker."

Claudine, whose description of her grandmother is cited above, was born in 1956. She and her two (Jamaican-born) younger siblings were brought up by their maternal grandmother, Beth, when their mother migrated to Britain in 1960. Claudine's parents were not married, and each of her Jamaican born siblings had a different father. Claudine's mother subsequently married in England, and had two more British born children by this husband. Beth had ten children, six of whom died in infancy. Although she was married, (this occurred late in her life), to the father of her two youngest children,

Beth lived on family land in Jamaica, close to her parents (Claudine's great-grandparents).

Claudine's description of her grandmother is bound up with the image of strength and hard work, her contribution measured as much by the quantity of hours expended as by the qualitative nature of, and produce from, her labors. Children rarely differentiated between the housework and homework performed by their grandmothers, seeing the two as an integrated whole. Indeed, many informants, when asked if their grandmothers worked, replied in the negative, only later to explain in some detail how their grandmothers made ends meet through a variety of strategies that could generate either income or goods for home consumption. Beth worked some ten acres of farm land, travelling to market each week to sell the produce. As Claudine recalled,

> I can't remember a day when we were…ever hungry…my sister was reminding me 'you know, we never used to, like, go to school bare-footed, or anything like that. We never wear, like, torn clothes.' Because she used to go to market and…she used to bring either a piece of material, or a little dress, or a little pair of shoes or something. She'd always bring something back for us and we would look forward to it, and always waited for her every Saturday night when she gets back. And on Sundays, she was very, very strict…we never missed Church, we have to go to Sunday School. So every Saturday night she's home, the first thing she does, she'll just come into our bedroom and she'll look, she'll want to see the dress you're wearing to church, the shoes, the socks, the ribbon, everything she needs to see…if anything was dirty…you have to wash it over…but she was really…really good…And from school, you get home, you have to do your homework, and she sits and she helps you to do your homework. And after that, you'll have to read to her and then you get ready and you go to bed.[7]

In descriptions of growing up in the Caribbean, there was a clear recognition that the means of economic survival were integral to socialization, and that children needed to be trained in the practicalities of life. Grandchildren, as with the case of Claudine, were implicated in the activities of the family.

> You can't stay in bed late, you always have a little something to do, always have your chores from very early…you know, she made us responsible from such an early age…[8]

In this, her brother was treated equally with herself and her sister; all were given chores necessary to the smooth operation of the farm and the home. (See also chapter 7). Although in many other instances these chores were differentiated by gender, with the boys given a primary responsibility outside the home, on the land and in the yard, while the chores given to girls were concentrated within the domestic activities involved in running the home, memories of gender-equality also recur in the narratives. Indeed, in households where boys predominated, they were by no means exempt from routine domestic chores such as cleaning, cooking and even childcare. Clearly, in a context—such as the rural Caribbean—where labor was not only central to a family's survival but also equated with capital, the contribution of children to sustaining that resource was central and the penalties for squandering were severe. Discipline—often harsh—may be seen as related not merely to beliefs about child-rearing and the importance of instilling authority, hierarchy and respect, but as functional to survival. For much the same reason, it could be argued that Henriques' notion of extended dependency had a functional source: to keep the labor and/or wages of adult children (and grandchildren) for as long as possible.

While the notion of "blessing" may be seen as an epithet of endearment, it also recognized a wider community role. Beth was also a "blessed person," taking in, and bringing up, in addition to her three grandchildren, nine nephews and nieces, and six other non-kin children such as Tyrell, who "came from a different parish, and he was like, in the area, and his dad was…doing little bits and pieces for her, following her to get…oranges when she was going to market and then, all of a sudden, he was living there!"[9]

The occurrence of child fostering or child-shifting is a feature recognized in many African-Caribbean households,[10] with varying degrees of stability and success and with a variety of explanations for its cultural origins and social causes, whether out of benevolence, duty, or as a form of exchange. In Beth's case, it appears to be a combination of motives. Her grandchildren were living with her when their mother migrated. Claudine's mother had never set up home independently, nor cohabited with any of the fathers of her children. Beth's nine nephews and nieces lived in the house opposite hers when their parents migrated. Beth took the youngest two to live with her, while the remaining seven slept in their own home, under Beth's vigilant eye. Beth was requested to care for the other, non-kin, children. Three features are significant about Beth's role. Her willingness to rear the next generation enabled her own children and her siblings to migrate, to Britain and to the United States. Indeed, in this family, as in many African-Caribbean families, there was a long and continuing tradition of migration. Beth's father, and her husband had both migrated for periods to North America. In her father's absence, Beth lived with her mother in her grandmother's house. The family model was one that implicated the grandmother in the rearing of children and featured as an unquestioned dynamic in family organization. Many scholars have argued that such practices were the result of male absence, serving as an explanation of the high incidence of single-mother-headed households and the subsequent heightened authority and power of women (what was referred to in chapter 3 as the power by "default" thesis[11]) and as evidence of the singular adaptability of the African-Caribbean family to adverse circumstances. The corollary, however, may suggest that this family formation preceded the migration movements of the nineteenth and twentieth centuries[12] (in which, incidentally, women as well as men migrated[13]) and was the enabling factor in, rather than the consequence of, migration.

Second, while child-shifting has been a regular feature of African-Caribbean families, Beth clearly became a pivotal figure in the community to whom parents—and children—could turn for help in this key area. Such a status could not arise in a vacuum, but from a reputation transmitted through networks of contact and support and through an acceptance that children could be as adequately reared by another as by their own kin or mother. Tyrell, after all, came from another parish. The other children came as a result of requests: regarding one for instance, "his mum had three of them and she was only young and she couldn't take care of them"[14] and so asked Beth to take care of one. Finally, the result for Beth was an incorporation into her family of other members who brought with them, as children, a share of and contribution to the human capital of the household. One child, for instance, a boy called Clifton,"helped her to run the house, she sent him to school, and he was there for about six or seven years."[15] Clifton would act as babysitter during Beth's two-day visits to the market.

> We got up early. We'd do what we had to do, because we couldn't make any mistakes and Clifton was there…Clifton was like a lady! My goodness, if you clean that, because he used to do all the cleaning and the washing and stuff at that time, when we were maybe like six, seven, growing up. And if we did something and it wasn't cleaned right, we had to do it over. And if we refused…the first thing when my grandmother come, he will tell her that…and we would really get a hiding…so we'd just do what we had to do, and make sure that we do it good…Clifton was very good with us. The only thing I think he couldn't do, he couldn't comb our hair…so early morning we had to go by [a neighbor]…and she would do it.[16]

As adults, her "investment" has reaped dividends. The son of one of the nephews she raised now lives with Beth in her advanced years.

All the children she brought up—including those like Clifton who were not kin—continue to help support her:

> she's always happy, because...every now and then she'll get a letter from someone who she actually brought up and if...they're still in Jamaica, they'll drive up and give her little bits and pieces and stay for the day and what have you. So she's well loved in the district.[17]

Indeed, as Claudine observed,

> She has got everything she wants now. She's got her nice fridge, she's got a freezer, she's got everything. It's amazing though, because whatever she wants, she would go for it and she would start it on her own. If she get stuck, if the money is, like too much for her, she would ask, she would send to me or my other sister, saying she's doing this, or she's doing that, can you help?...And we'll always help her. We'll buy curtains for the house, we'll pay bits and pieces, we send her toiletries, all sorts of stuff. So she really doesn't have to...buy anything as such.[18]

The element of instrumentality inherent in this behavior may be seen as a form of trade, perhaps akin to (but by no means the equivalent of) the trade in works of art, "a trade in things which have no price [which] belongs to the class of practices in which the logic of pre-capitalist economy lives on (as it does, in another sphere, in the economy of exchanges between the generations)."[19] What gives such trade its value is the accumulation of what Bourdieu calls symbolic capital. 'Symbolic capital' is to be understood as economic or political capital that is disavowed, misrecognised and thereby recognized, hence legitimate, a "credit" which, under certain conditions, and always in the long run, guarantees "economic" profits.'[20]

Yet the element of instrumentality should not obscure other, supplementary, interpretations. Indeed, an emphasis on economic instrumentality and reductionism, reduces behavior to a trade-off and puts a price on practices that, in essence, have no price. At the same time, value—through reputation—is accrued. Thus, caring for children may in later years produce rewards that can be measured in economic terms, through direct financial support in the supply of material goods, and indirect support in the supply of care and other services.

Beth's role as a surrogate parent clearly involved a degree of instrumentality and exchange that may have been one motive behind the actions which she, and many other grandmothers or women (particularly those who had been childless) in the sample, followed. This was within a cultural context that expected and approved such activity, and that thereby extended kinship and surrogate kinship bonds and networks.

As an ancillary, the value in the return extends beyond the children into the neighborhood. Beth, for instance, regularly fed passers-by and acted host to a range of visitors. After her husband died, help with the heavy work involved in agriculture was received from the community.

> [if] ...they're going...to dig the yam hills...they tell people in the area that they're going to have a party...so sometimes they have like ten, or fifteen, sometimes as much as twenty men, and ...my grandmother ...will have to cook for all those people. So she'll get her women friends...and they cook a big pot...and we'd have to take it...all the way to the field....She still does that sometimes.[21]

And, in her old age, has the support of both kin, adoptive kin, and the neighborhood.

Relatedly, many of our informants stressed the importance of the parenting role performed by the community or neighborhood, often using, as has already been noted, metaphors of the family or kinship titles (such as "aunty," "uncle," "cousin") to describe both status and expected behavior of neighborhood relations. Godparents, in particular, played an active part in childrearing. "My godparents" as Claudine recalled,

> ...had you under their wings, and they'd teach you things, and you'd learn a lot of things from those people because they would steer you in the right direction...you could really discuss things with them...they would...talk to you about family values...and stuff like that. And they would talk to you about the church...and manners..."Manners" she used to say "carries you through the world...regardless of how rich or how poor, or ugly or good-looking you are, if you haven't got manners, you're not going to reach anywhere"...and she would say "make sure...respect, you should have respect, to even the baby that was born last night". And that is how we were brought up.[22]

Part of the explanation for this active incorporation into parenting must lie in the "open" structures of kin membership,[23] and one of the recurring features in this research has been the strength of kinship and the importance of kinship networks in sustaining the emotional and the material support of its members. Yet none of this arises in a vacuum. The "adaptive" arguments as explanation of African-Caribbean family formation and kinship may have a compelling rationale in terms of maximizing scarce economic resources and as responses to poverty, and may be corroborated by other studies, which appear to demonstrate that the formation of powerful mother figures and extended kinship links is a modern response to poverty with parallels among the Irish community,[24] or in London's East End.[25] Such explanations do not, however, take into account the importance of both history and culture in the shaping of contemporary behavior.

Indeed, as we have seen, such patterns can also be discerned among middle-class African-Caribbean families, and among African-Caribbean migrant communities abroad, suggesting that culture may be a more enduring ingredient in family formation than (unstable) economic constraints.

There remains, however, another important consideration relating to wealth. While the symbolic capital accumulated by a woman may in the long term be translated into crude dollars, the symbolism itself has not been dissipated. While "making" a child "for" its father may be seen as a ritualistic entry into adulthood, children are regarded as the inheritors of a lineage, as evidence of continuity and, in turn, conduits of that continuity. This may also involve the inheritance of family land.[26] As Constance Sutton has pointed out, there are important parallels between these beliefs and those held by the Yoruba, who

> consider children their most important form of wealth...a woman's ability to produce this form of wealth, that is, her procreative power, was regarded as a critical immanent power that women—referred to frequently as "our mothers" possessed...continuity was inscribed in the culturally constructed meanings of life, death, and rebirth of genealogically connected humans. New born children represented reborn ancestors, recent and distant. They in turn give birth to the future, and after their death become ancestors waiting to be reborn.[27]

The repetitions and commonality in the language used by women to describe their mothers and grandmothers suggests the existence of widely held beliefs relating to lineage and continuity. Lineage becomes the logic that conveys the meaning of family; the "pull" of the ancestors is reflected in a strong sense of "carrying" previous generations, in a belief that ancestors have the power to "take" a child into their thrall, and an equally powerful language suggesting a reconstitution if not a rebirth in the generations. "I am a nice woman," another informant said "I am *from* my mother" (emphasis added).[28] Descent is, finally, the only immutable inheritance (though disputable when carried through the male line). It is both actual and symbolic, carries responsibilities as well as privileges. Mothers and mother substitutes, such as grandmothers, have to be sufficiently strong to carry out the physical labor of childrearing (and bearing), as well as bear the spiritual or symbolic responsibilities as carriers of lineage.[29] Part of those responsibilities are to ensure that the children in the line can mature to respect and continue it, and as women mature into old age and grandparenthood, those responsibilities increase and extend over their grandchildren, and over those of others who cannot shoulder the responsibility. It is, therefore, significant that such women are described both as "blessed," for their symbolic capital has been extended, and they are "strong," "hardworking" women.

***

While such behavior may generate what Brodber described as an "emotional expansiveness," it is not without risks. Claudine, for instance, failed to establish a close relationship with her mother. She was four years old when her mother migrated to Britain, and regular contact was not created until Claudine herself came to England in 1989. The subsequent relationship has been stormy and spasmodic. Other informants also recounted difficulties in re-establishing (or establishing) relationships with mothers after periods of absence.[30] Yet the symbolic link remained. Claudine refused to deny her mother or ignore her existence. At the same time, when Claudine gave birth to her son in 1978, she chose to "shift" him not to her grandmother but to her son's paternal great-aunt, who had no children. The arrangement permitted Claudine to work and, ultimately, to migrate to Britain. It also helped redistribute the wealth inherited in and through children, to divest some of the symbolic capital into a branch of the family where it was lacking, and to return the child, a son, to the paternal line.

The emphasis on the maternal grandmother should not obscure the role of the father's family in the sense and meaning of family. Claudine's father had migrated to Britain shortly after she was born. She did not meet him until she herself migrated to Britain, although she was aware that he took an interest in her progress, and maintained contact with her family and, to a lesser extent, her mother. Claudine knew her father's mother, although she never knew his father. Her mother's father (her grandfather) lived close to her grandmother and, although married to another woman, visited weekly, and was part of the cohort of neighbors who could be called upon to help on the land. Indeed, Claudine included in her concept of close family her mother's (half) brothers and sisters, recalling how "we used to, like, on our way home from school, we used to go round there and get...[at] my uncle's, lunch...and my uncles...we had good relations with all of them."[31] The grandfather she was closest to, however, was her grandmother's husband, and it was for him that she reserved the familial endearment of "a very hard-working man." He co-farmed the land with her grandmother, and "he was so nice," acting on occasions as mediator between her grandmother and herself. He died when Claudine was nineteen.

Although none of her grandfathers featured as significant figures in Claudine's account of her childhood, they and their families were nevertheless actively present, and included within the broader definition of family and kin. Indeed, it was through them that her own kinship network was extended. They clearly assumed a paternal and grandpaternal role toward all children brought within the umbrella of Beth's household. Relatedly, and significantly, Claudine's maternal uncle played an equally active role in her upbringing, contributing help in cash and kind, and fostering her when she went to secondary school in Kingston. "My whole life," she said, "revolved around them."[32] It would, therefore, be mistaken to assume that the male members of the family—from all sides—were marginal figures. Indeed, when her son was born, it was to his father's family that she turned for support. Her son, Gregor, lived as a young child with his father and stepmother who, in turn, lived with his parents, until Gregor's father migrated to the United States. It was at that point that his paternal aunt took over his care, and as he says, "taught me everything I knew. And when it wasn't her, it was my grandfather."[33]

Indeed, this aunt lived close to his paternal grandparents, and they played an active part in his upbringing. "I grew up with them," he says, "and now I've been apart from them...it's just your family man, they're just not here, so you miss them."[34] This grandmother travels to North America, to visit and help out her children there, with such frequency that, as Gregor joked "I think she's got her own(airplane) seat!"[35] He did not meet his maternal grandparents until he came to Britain to join his mother as a teenager and, largely as a result, is not close to either of them.

It would, equally, be mistaken to equate the expansive family exclusively with lower-class values and lifestyles. Although Beth was a small farmer and higgler, all the children in her care—including Claudine received secondary and in many cases tertiary education. Claudine herself is a professional woman, as is her uncle. Gregor's paternal grandfather was a businessman, his maternal grandmother a teacher before working in the family business. Nevertheless, across both sides of the family, there was an assumption that childcare was, when necessary, a family affair and an equally powerful assumption that all consanguineal kin, regardless of which side of the conjugal bed they originated, and which line of the family they most favored, shared an equality of family membership. These were values that Claudine clearly recognized in her grandparents and Gregor saw in his, and which became an integral feature of both of their socialization. "The family," as Gregor concluded,

> is the greatest thing on earth. It can also be the most troublesome, but the family is, I don't know how to put it better than blood over water. It's part of you. There's no way you can escape from it. Absolutely no way. You're tied to them for life, *and beyond*.[36] (emphasis added)

The role of grandparents and other elderly relatives in the care of children necessarily extends the influence of the generations and the cross-generational link, providing a longitudinal or vertical integration into the family, and its values. Grandparents ensure also horizontal links both within generations, for instance, between cousins, and between families, between "inside" and "outside" family members, and stepfamilies.

Alma and Her Family

Not all families are, however, as expansive as Claudine's, and the lack of kinship support can be an issue. Alma "never meet a husband. I'm still a single person. I never have any children, but I grow my niece." Alma left school at fifteen, and at seventeen migrated to Kingston from St. Anne to learn dressmaking. The wages, however, were low and she found a job in a sweet factory in 1948, where she stayed until migrating to Britain in 1960. Once in England, she sent for her niece to join her "I used to love her, from she was a baby at home, and I used to send things for her, you know. And as I didn't have any children...her mother was poor."[37]

The choice to "grow" this child is significant. Alma was born in 1926 in Jamaica. Her father, a stevedore, died when she was four years old. She was raised initially by her paternal grandparents, "my father loved me so much, you know, that he wanted me, and my grandparents loved me so much that they wanted me and then, you know, in the West Indies, them days, people don't fight against...you can't have the child...you just go to them."[38] Her grandfather (also a stevedore) died when she was six, and her grandmother when she was eight years old. Then, "my mother take me over."[39] Alma was the eldest of her mother's three children. She was not married to

Alma's father, and Alma's two siblings (one of whom died) were from a subsequent relationship. Their father, however, acted as a father to her: "he was kind," she recalled, "he look after the two of us. Christmas time, whatever he got, I get it. There was no difference. You know, there was no difference."[40] Alma's own childhood had been punctuated by a series of child-shifting arrangements.

The niece she "grew" was her brother's child, looking after her from birth. Her status as a single, childless aunt, and her love of the child, was sufficient to enable her to claim the baby as her own, in much the same way that her own grandparents had claimed her. Alma migrated to Britain in 1960, sending for this brother in 1962 and, in 1965, her niece, Marvetta. Alma's brother was not married to Marvetta's mother, and they had never lived together. Marvetta's mother worked as a child attendant for a "higher status" family in Kingston, and while her memories of her mother are "warm," they are "limited":

> I then came to England...I kept in touch with her through post but ...I wouldn't say she was illiterate, but she wasn't good at writing letters...Over the years it dwindled, but we kept in touch...There wasn't much that my mum was able to do for me, really.[41]

In this case, Marvetta did not know her mother's parents, nor her mother's two sons, nor her father's other son. She was brought up by Alma, who lived in what she describes as the "tenement yard," with her paternal grandmother (she never knew her paternal grandfather, who died before she was born) and other kin in close proximity. "It was warm, it was like a big family really"[42] Her grandmother, like others, was "a hard worker" but it was of her aunt, who had no children of her own and never married, that she reserved the notion of "strong,"

> Looking back, really, I suppose she's been a mother and aunt! She was there for me before I was born, and she's always been there. She's a very independent woman...taking on the role as a mother, my aunt has helped stabilized...the family unit, because she looked after me when she herself was in Jamaica. When she left and went to England...she then helped send for my Dad which, in turn, both of them sent for me...she was the one who basically was the order of the day...And she's very dominant...just being a strong black woman has helped kept the family together and has helped put me on the right road, so to speak. She's given me all the things, really, that my mum and dad should have.[43]

Unlike many families, this family is small. Marvetta's siblings are strangers. Marvetta's mother had one brother who survived to adulthood. Marvetta did not know him as a child. Her father had only one sister, her aunt. Her grandmother, however, had a number of brothers, so great-uncles featured in her childhood although many of them, and their children, had migrated. The family, as she described it, while "not really small [was] distant, very far apart...there's no strong link between anyone,"[44] a circumstance which Marvetta attributes to slavery (sic) and migration, "so over the years you find that communication breaks down. So I put my family down to that."[45] After her aunt migrated to Britain, Marvetta (like her aunt) was "shifted" between her mother, her paternal grandmother, and "going back to that kinship thing then, you'll find that within the tenement yard, you'll find other people able to look after kids...knitting together as a family."[46] In 1965, when she was nine she was sent for by her aunt to join her and her father in England. She lived with her aunt until she left home at eighteen. At twenty-one, Marvetta had her first child. She now has three children, by the same man, from whom she lives apart. She supports her children alone. "I'm basically back into that circle again, as my mother, my aunt, you know. With my mother, there was no support from the male. I'm now in that position."[47] Indeed, she sees herself as a replica of her aunt "I'm a bit in her shadow...a lot of her has been instilled in me."[48] Marvetta works as a clerk and, despite attempts to improve her education and skills through evening classes, "what's held me back in life is that I've had my children, and *I haven't got family support*"[49] (emphasis added).

The limited circumference of the kinship circle has left Marvetta bereft of family help, and the experience of two generations of child-shifting has created a determination not to replicate the patterns with her own children. Nevertheless, despite her experiences, she argues, "I am a black West Indian woman, living in England, trying very hard to achieve certain goals, for the benefit of myself and my family, and to one day return back to my homeland...the links in the Caribbean for my children are not very strong...I hope, by the end of the year or next year, that I can take all three boys out to meet what family I do have out there...and through meeting...to keep that link."[50]

Ermal's Family

Our final family illustrates how the practice of child-shifting has retained its importance in Britain, although it also illustrates the pressures on British-based families. Ermal's mother came to Britain in the 1950s as a young woman in her early twenties, leaving her four young children with her mother in Jamaica. Ermal was only a few months old. She sent first for her five siblings, one by one, before finally bringing her children over to join her, starting with the eldest. Ermal was the third child to come out. He was eleven years old. He barely knew his father, who did not live with his mother, and once in England, Ermal lost touch with him altogether, although he keeps in contact with some of his paternal uncles, who keep him in touch with news about his father. He is his father's oldest child, and has two half-siblings whom he has never met, but would like to

> very much. It's something that I sit down and think about daily. Really, I would like to get to know them, and meet that side of the family. It's like something missing, really.[51]

His mother, the eldest of fourteen children, did not share paternity with her thirteen younger siblings. In addition to bringing up her own children, and Ermal and his siblings, his grandmother also looked after other grandchildren, cousins, nephews, and nieces, numbering,

> ...about 26, 27, she had a lot of responsibility, and she had to really prepare...and make sure everything was alright. She was very hard-working, a very hard-working woman.[52]

It was his elder sister, though, with whom Ermal was particularly close.

> She was living at my grandmother as well...she spend a lot of time with me, really, when I was growing up. She would fend for me...she was always looking out for me...she take her home responsibility from when she was very young...she grow up into a woman even before she was the age of a woman.[53]

His mother returned regular remittances to his grandmother, as well as parcels of clothes and toys for her children. Her family owned and, for the most part, lived on family land, and Ermal lived in Jamaica in a neighborhood surrounded by kin. His grandfather was a builder and cabinet maker, as well as a farmer. Like many others, he was brought up to help "you have to help out somewhere along the line. It doesn't matter what."[54] Coming to England was a shock, and

> it takes me a while to settle in, because when I... was in Jamaica, I remember seeing one and two English people but when I come here and start see a lot, they terrify me. I was scared. Seriously! I was really scared, because I had never seen so many.[55]

His mother, however, had bought a large house in London, working hard at a variety of jobs—sewing, cake making, hairdressing-saving hard, and raising the rest through a "partner."[56] Some of the house was rented out for a while. She had also married. Arriving in England meant adjusting not only to a new country and climate, but to his siblings, to his mother, whom he had not seen for eleven years, and to a stepfather. His siblings delighted in showing him off, his reunion with his mother was good, and he got on well with his stepfather. The neighborhood, moreover, was populated by many other Caribbean families and

> we all used to get on together. I think we used to stick together, it doesn't matter where you come from. We had people maybe from Trinidad...We've got people from St. Lucia...we'd got people from St. Vincent...We have people from Guyana. We all get on together.[57]

The difficulty was not with the neighborhood, but with the British authorities. When Ermal arrived in England, aged twelve, he was given an intelligence test,

> giving me bricks and all these things to set up, like puzzles and all these things...and basically what they did after that, they said I weren't capable of going to a proper school, they send me to a backward school. Well, I didn't feel backward...that kind of world hold me down, and hold me back, to a level that I didn't even get to achieve in the education that I was supposed to have...That's what they used to do to a lot of kids who were coming from the West Indies in the sixties, and I happened to fall in that group.[58]

Ermal experienced racism in the school, "on the street...all over the place." He left school with no qualifications, and worked in a variety of semi-skilled jobs until he got into trouble with the police and was put on remand for six weeks. The accusations were, however, never proved, "they...just dismissed the case...they [police] just pick me up and tell a lot of bloody lies."[59] This proved to be the first of several such incidents. On another occasion, he was accused of stealing a purse but released after eight hours in the cell, and on a further occasion, he was charged with assaulting a police officer after a fight at a funfare. According to Ermal,

> some big massive ones [police officers] are coming in and they grab around the neck...they lift me up in the air, man...about four or five...and then when they bring me now, they lift me and they strangle me. I could hardly breathe, till this woman said to them "Can't you see you're killing the guy? Can't you see that? Ease the pressure off his neck a bit"...then he ease the pressure a bit, or else I would have suffocate to death, because I was lusting for air...They start beating me...and they were saying "You black bastard. Giving us this trouble." Bam. Start beating and beating and beating and beat me. And they tell lots of lies. One of them said I bite him on his ear...they had me up on lots of different charges...and when I got to the station, they punched me up as well, my back, my face...after they already done beating me in the park.[60]

The case was brought before the Crown Court, and Ermal won. "The judge said, 'To be quite frank...somebody of Mr. X's structure, he's so small, I can't see him beating up four trained police officer'...And the jury came back and they say not guilty.'[61]

Not surprisingly, these experiences have marked his attitudes both toward England and toward his family. Ermal maintains contact with his large family in Jamaica (as well as those who came to Britain) and considers it important to do so -partly because they are a "close" family and partly as a precaution against difficulties.

> At any stage or any time of your life...when you're fed up or want a change, or you want to move or you want to go somewhere else, so it's very important to keep connection with your family and get to know them well. That is very important. It's like anything [happen] and you want somewhere to run to, or you need to flee and go somewhere and you don't know nobody, then you're doomed. So that's best to know and keep in contact, then you say, you can write, or you phone and you say 'Listen, it's hell going on in England' you know, 'I'm coming home. I cannot stay here one more year'...So in that sense, it's good to keep in contact, you know?'[62]

One of the major difficulties facing many African-Caribbean migrants in the early years was the reality of bringing up children without the support of an extended kin network. Most West Indian women, including mothers, worked in Britain, continuing a pattern that was familiar from the West Indies. Establishing adequate childcare was, therefore not only a major but an unfamiliar problem. Children born in the Caribbean were, as we have seen, often left with grandparents or other family members. Those born in Britain could be, and sometimes were, sent back to grandparents if alternative suitable arrangements could not be made. Ermal and his partner, with whom he lives but has not married, have five children. Ermal was adamant that no stranger would care for his children. His partner therefore cared for the children when they were small because

> I always worry when I leave my kids, therefore their mother takes care of them till them big enough. Nobody has looked after our kids...I'm just very afraid of people ill-treating my kids...that wish is a sacrifice my missus have to make at the same time. And she was doing like part-time jobs so I like, fill in, and do my part and look after them and so forth.[63]

At the same time, his own mother in England, like her mother before her in Jamaica, also looked after children, as Ermal's daughter, Tracy, explains

> she used to look after a lot of children...one of them's my friend...my friend's mum wanted my gran to foster her, like adopt her but she said no because she...thought that the mum would come back and took her...because she was starting to love the child.[64]

Part of the practice in child-shifting was the apparent fluidity with which children would be able to move between their parent(s) and their carer, although clearly at times this was easier said than done. Nevertheless, whatever the emotional bonds that could develop between a child and a carer, the natural parent had the prerogative to reclaim the child. As Erna Brodber explained it:

> The children who enter the units in this way were treated as blood relatives and the surrogate parents, despite what emotional attachments might have developed between themselves and their 'taken' children, were easily able to pass them on to other adults or back to the parents themselves. This act was looked upon as one carried out "through love."[65]

Significantly, and like his mother and grandmother, Ermal and his partner also foster another child (the son of a friend and a distant relative) who "is part of the family...growing up with my children."[66]

For his daughter, Tracy, the family expansiveness has been illustrated by her parents, grandmother, and great grandmother, and she is only recently coming to appreciate the extensiveness of her family networks, particularly those from her paternal grandmother. Her mother's kin she is less close to. Her maternal uncles, in particular, she disapproves of, for they all have white partners and this

> messes up the family...why people have to act different because they're going out with white girls, like, especially my gran...I could be in her house, right, and then you play a tape, and if it's reggae "Oh, turn it off', like just to suit the white woman, like, why?"[67]

In addition, she considers their children "spoilt" and "not used to black people...when...my uncle's daughter was small...she couldn't believe she had black cousins."[68] Tracy's school career, like that of her father, was punctuated with instances of racism and discrimination. She left school with poor qualifications, although she has since improved them through evening classes, and is now taking a professional training. Her experiences of growing up in Britain have been for the most part negative and she is critical of "the system, everything. It's just everything's rubbish."[69] She feels she has no stake in Britain and would like to live in Jamaica when she has completed her education, just as her father and mother, in turn, wish to return once they have a secure financial footing. And on this, Ermal hopes his mother and father will be in a position to help him for "nobody else can help me. Even if I'm trying to graft hard, the system is so, in such a way that everything that you take out, you have to put back in. So you find it very difficult."[70] Under the circumstances, the expansiveness of the family may prove invaluable.

***

The origins of how the role of grandmothers and of older women in participating in the "growing" of children remain both tantalizing and speculative. Yet, as the case studies show, such practices and beliefs in the importance of this role, even when the kinship circle is thin, have endured across the generations and through the migration process. Social necessity or utility provides one explanation for its continuing practice, and, as with many useful social practices, it adapts to meet changing circumstances. Practicality may not be the sole explanation, however, for such practices are accompanied by an elaborate system of values, and a compelling and abiding logic of kinship and descent that recognizes the role of kin in "growing" children. Indeed, the language of childbearing and childrearing and childhood is surprisingly pro-active and self-conscious.[71] Children are not "had by," but "made for." Children are "grown." Childhood memories begin when an individual "first knew him/herself," while the family memory extends across the generations. The oldest participant in the family may be the one who harbors the family memory, and is closest to the family ancestors. While the maternal line may be the most familiar, the paternal line, as we have seen, is far from excluded in the distribution of ancestors and in the sharing of children. In all of this, it is the family history, and its past, that shapes contemporary responses. The grandparents of today may have experienced childhood in the Caribbean, but they are willing conduits for these memories to pass to their grandchildren, and with that, the values that surround and support the importance of kin as both a practical element of family life, and of a symbolic element of belonging. Furthermore, the centrifugal tendencies of African-Caribbean kinship formation increase, rather than diminish, the importance of lineage. "Blood over water," as Gregor argued, "... you're tied to them for life, *and beyond.*"[72]

Notes

1. Simey, *Welfare,* 84.
2. Henriques, *Family and Colour,* 110.
3. Henriques, *Family and Colour,* 163.
4. For a discussion on the role of fathers in parenting among the African-Caribbean community in Britain, see Tracey Reynolds, "Caribbean Fathers in Family Lives in Britain," in *Caribbean Families in Britain and the Trans-Atlantic World.*
5. Erna Brodber, "Afro-Jamaican Women at the turn of the Century,"*Social and Economic Studies,* 35:3 (1986):23-50.
6. JK030/2/1/1/9.
7. JK030/2/1/10.
8. JK030/2/1/1/10.

138 Family Love in the Diaspora

9. JK 030/2/1/2/15.
10. See, for instance, Olive Senior, *Working Miracles. Women's Lives in the English Speaking Caribbean* (London: James Currey/Bloomington and Indianapolis: Indiana University Press, 1991),12-18; Dorian Powell, "Caribbean Women and Their Response to Familial Experiences," *Social and Economic Studies,* 35:2 (1986), 83-130.
11. Constance Sutton, introduction to Virginia Kerns, *Women and the Ancestors: Black Carib Kinship and Ritual* (Urbana and Chicago: University of Illionois Press, 1997), ix.
12. Higman, *Slave Populations.*
13. See Chamberlain *Narratives of Exile and Return.*
14. JK030/2/1/2/11.
15. JK030/2/1/2/11.
16. JK0302/1/2/19.
17. JK030/2/1/2/11.
18. JK030/2/1/2/17-18.
19. Pierre Bourdieu "The Production of Belief: Contribution to an Economy of Symbolic Goods" in *The Field of Cultural Production* (London: Polity Press, 1993), 74.
20. Bourdieu, "Production," 75.
21. JK030/2/1/2/12.
22. JK 030/2/1/2/16.
23. R.T.Smith *The Negro Family in British Guiana* (London: Routledge and Kegan Paul, 1956), 157, 164. Hyman Rodman *Lower Class Families: The Culture of Poverty in Negro Trinidad,*101.
24. Elizabeth Bott, *Family and Social Networks: Roles, Norms and External Relations in Ordinary Urban Families* (London: Tavistock Publications, 1957).
25. Michael Young and Peter Wilmott, *Family and Kinship in East London* (Harmondsworth: Penguin, 1957).
26. In the context of the Caribbean, family land is often inherited by all descendants through both the mother's and/or father's line. No one family member can claim superiority based on age, gender, legitimacy etc. As a result, ownership of shares in such land is often symbolic, but powerful. For a full explanation and discussion of family land, see Jean Besson "Family Land and Caribbean Society: Toward an Ethnography of Afro-Caribbean Peasantries" in *Perspectives on Caribbean Regional Identity,* ed. Elizabeth M. Thomas-Hope (Liverpool: Liverpool University Press, 1984), 57-83 and Jean Besson, *Martha Brae's Two Histories. European Expansion and Caribbean Culture-Building in Jamaica* (Chapel Hill and London: University of North Carolina Press 2002).
27. Constance Sutton "Motherhood is Powerful": Embodied Knowledge from Evolving Field-Based Experiences' *Anthropology and Humanism* 23:2 (1998): 143-44.
28. JH141/1/1/1.
29. Sutton "Motherhood is Powerful."
30. See for instance Samuel's story in chapter 7.
31. JK030/2/1/1/11.
32. JK030/2/2/2/34.
33. JK031/3/1/1/8.
34. JK031/3/1/2/18.
35. JK031/3/1/2/17.
36. JK031/3/2/1/45.
37. JP061/2/1/1/8.

38. JP061/2/1/1/11.
39. JP061/2/1/1/2.
40. JP061/2/1/1/10.
41. JP052/3/1/1/3.
42. JP052/3/1/1/4.
43. JP052/3/1/1/7.
44. JP052/3/1/1/9.
45. JP052/3/1/1/10.
46. JP052/3/1/1/10.
47. JP052/3/1/2/17.
48. JP052/3/1/2/21.
49. JP052/3/1/2/17.
50. JP052/3/1/25.
51. JN049/2/1/1/5.
52. JN049/2/1/1/6.
53. JN049/2/1/1/11.
54. JN049/2/1/2/20.
55. JN049/2/1/2/23.
56. Also known in Barbados as a "Meeting Turn," in Trinidad as "Sou-Sou," it is an informal savings scheme whereby a group of trusted friends contribute an agreed amount each week, and take it in turns to collect the weekly total.
57. JN049/2/1/2/28.
58. JN049/2/1/2/30.
59. JN049/2/1/2/37.
60. JN049/2/1/2/39.
61. JN049/2/1/2/39.
62. JN049/2/2/2/52.
63. JN049/2/2/2/44.
64. JN057/3/1/1/17.
65. Erna Brodber "Afro-Jamaican Women," 26.
66. JN049/2/2/2/44.
67. JN057/3/1/2/25.
68. JN057/3/1/2/29.
69. JN057/3/2/2/56.
70. JN049/2/2/2/51.
71. Sutton, "Motherhood is Powerful."
72. JK031/3/2/1/45.

7

Small Worlds: Families and Children

"You know, I think this thing run in families, the way you were brought up, you brought up your children the same way, and it goes on. I think so, you know."[1]

This chapter is about children and childhood in the Caribbean and Britain. It is about what values are taught to children, and how; it is about resources, resilience and adaptation. In chapter 6 we looked at the practice of child-shifting, or fostering, as a variant of family formation and child care. In this chapter, the focus is on the child. It is as much about the memories, practices, and inheritance of childhood as the ideologies that informed it.

Attitudes toward children vary historically and culturally, and how a society treats its children—defines what is a child and provides protection for them—may be seen as a barometer of social progress[2] while attitudes to children, childcare, and childrearing reveal many of the values and philosophies that underpin social organization, social provision and economic opportunity. Exploring families from the perspective of the child and childhood may be a fruitful way of exploring these social values. It is especially fruitful in terms of a migrant population because it is often through the children that tensions and conflict surface between the generation holding to the values and practices of the "old" country and the young, who have been exposed to those of the "new."[3] Equally, it is the children who represent a major interface between a community and representatives of the state—its schools, police, social services and welfare. If children may be seen as a barometer of social progress, attitudes to children and childrearing may also be seen as a measure of change and adaptation, and of the robustness of a family system.

Recollections of childhood are, however, notoriously unstable. Childhood memories have a design imposed on them by the adult life story, by conventions of recall, and by nostalgia. The importance of childhood and childhood memories in adult (Western) autobiographies has, for instance, been noted as the link that explains, excuses or exonerates adult behavior and, as such, has a long and interesting pedigree.[4] But from sources as diverse as psychoanalysis,[5] South American *testimonio,* or working-class autobiography emerge accounts of childhood which—despite variations in content and form- remain, as a *corpus,* as highly stylized. The rose-tinted accounts of childhood can, therefore, be seen as part of a particular genre of childhood, and one that has an almost universal appeal. Childhood hardship may be equally conditioned by type. This does not mean that such accounts are invalid, but rather that their purpose and context be taken into account in any analysis. They may, for instance, be interpreted as an ideology, prescriptions denoting ideal rather than actual childhoods, or (as in autobiography) as a lesson or exoneration of subsequent behavior. As such, how people recount childhood reflects not only their experiences, but also the assumptions and attitudes to children and childhood that they have inherited or acquired in their adult lives.

Despite variation in the composition of childhood homes and in the relationship of the adult(s) primarily responsible for the care of children, most informants who grew up in the Caribbean emphasized the communitarian basis for childcare and childrearing which included and permitted a high level of fostering, enabling mobility and flexibility for adults. As we saw in chapter 3, this may be interpreted as a metaphor, a language of prescription in which appropriate social values were embedded and transmitted. The behavior exhibited in the public arena embodied practices and skills essential for "living good," and for the successful socialization of the young into adulthood. It was a powerfully wrought ideology, and the notion that the community assumed a "parenting responsibility" was a theme, as we have seen, that recurred throughout the islands. Mrs B., born in Barbados in 1937, recalled, for instance, how "...neighbors around... sort of keep an eye, you weren't their children, but... *you were their responsibility."*[6]

In practice, what did this mean? Five principles can be identified that suggest an ideology of childhood. First, adults had the right, and duty, to reprimand children. Any child caught misbehaving could be, and was, corrected, and the child's parent(s) appropriately informed,

If they saw you doing something that you shouldn't be doing, they would say, "Well, I'm going to tell your mother or your father," and you knew, well, definitely they will tell them, and it's lashes for you. So you had to be careful, even ... although you were away, out of your parents' sight, you know, there were still people there sort of keeping an eye to make sure that you didn't do anything that you shouldn't be.[7]

Another informant from Trinidad described it thus:

You hardly could have misbehaved really long ago... family, and the neighbors, you are friends....If they see you talking to anybody that they know ...[is] a loose person...they would ...tell you, "Listen, you must not keep that person's company, because they would lead you astray." And you frightened because you don't want them to go home and tell your parents you was talking to such a person. You have to go in front and tell your parents.... You have to talk the truth, you understand. That's how well they brought us up... you have to tell them the truth, you have to respect everybody, that's about it.[8]

Implicit in the deterrent and corrective effects of neighborly behavior were wider social lessons of concern, reciprocity and respect. Children were not only taught to pay (and return) concern and respect for others; they also learned that others had a deep concern for them. Neither fear nor danger were recalled. "There was no child abuse... no rapes and all of that, we didn't hear of that."[9] "At the time anybody see a child walking, where are you going?' I'm going to such and such a place.' I will come.' At least nobody could interfere with that child because they are going to carry that child to the house."[10] While adults may have been owed respect on the grounds of seniority, and while seniority bestowed authority, it also implied protection. Children may not have been regarded as equals in a community, but they were aware that they were important, had a place in that community, and were valued as members of it.

Second, children were taught principles of sharing and exchange. Again, informants recall how

... friends and family always there, you know. And I know when we... like, when the old man... things were in land... he bring them in, and we've got to... to take them this body...and this body, and all the different people, you know. ...And that's how it go on, you know.[11]

It was a caring community.... So, a lot of giving was done. If you know that Mrs. Bloggs down the road has a daughter in America, and is living on her own, when my father came home from the fields with provisions and food, Mrs. Bloggs could have a little basket. And if Miss Brown across the road had just had a baby, and the father hadn't, wasn't supporting her, Miss Brown had a little package of stuff, or a couple of eggs for the baby. And there was this sharing, caring, cohesive community, which I believe is almost lost now.[12]

All kind of people, and anything we give. If they go on a hunt, they get a ...a deer, you know, these thing, they make sure, when they kill it, that...this part...is for Mr. Joe, this is for this body ...when they bake long time ...they always handing it...(to those) less fortunate, and they have less to give their children...there's so much in this giving, that even you have, and they have something, they will still send something to give, you know. You know, people used to live nice a long time.[13]

Such practices had an instrumental value: exchange was a necessary part of the sharing equation, cementing good will and insuring reciprocity.

The third principle—respect—was at the core of the system. "you have to respect everybody, that's about it."[14] "As I say, like, we grow up, one thing I will say, you learn respect, you know..."[15] Respect contained within it two seemingly contradictory notions: first, respect or honor due to the position within a hierarchy, on seniority (of age, rank, or position); and second, an essential egalitarianism that commanded honor and civility regardless of rank, age, or position. While children were commanded to pay respect to others, and particularly to their elders (even among siblings), respect was paid to them even though it might assume a corrective, and at times, punitive character. Children could not expect equal treatment with adults; but they could expect adult concern, care and interest. Equally, children grew up to expect respect for their adult status from those "coming up" below, and in turn to convey it to those over whom they now held a respectful seniority. Values of respect and mutual responsibility that were taught in the home reinforced shared community values, and were reinforced by them. As Beryl recalled,

> She [mother] was strict about good manners, respect. We had to...greet everyone...we had to respect everyone, even if they were poor, and those who were invalid ...who were beggars. We were not allowed to pass them unnoticed, we had to greet them too. She taught us about caring, that to share whatever we had...We were taught ... justice... And swearing was not allowed...they gave us very sound, moral code, I feel, on which to, on which to live, and I thought that was really good.[16]

Relatedly, children were also taught to take a part in (and responsibility for) family chores, and taught a fourth principle—self reliance—so that

> you have to do everything for yourself, because, I mean, they're not encouraging you that they will have you sleeping, and coming to wake you up to take your breakfast. You had to get up. You have work to do. You have to sweep, you have to see after your fowl, or your goat, or whatever it is. And we, we used to enjoy that.[17]

> We had some cows and sheep and goat and thing, look after them,... in the morning you've got to... pick meat for the rabbits and so on, and take ... take [sheep] out and graze them, and tie them out and so on and thing. And then in the evening, go and fetch them, and all such like.[18]

> We were certainly ... encouraged to be self-reliant, to say not to rely on anybody to feed and clothe you, you've got to work for yourself, and this is where the education came in, you see, if you are educated, you'd have all of that automatically. [19]

Not all children regarded such chores as enjoyable, particularly if they were not shared equitably. Beryl, for instance, was encouraged to study and *her* social development and self-reliance were harnessed toward the achievement of a professional training, a goal realizable only away from home. She was therefore exempted from household chores,

> and that's what's caused the problem within my family and myself. I was seen as someone who was always studying, therefore I wasn't allowed to do very much around the house. We had chores we had to do, like washing up the dishes after breakfast, and sweeping up the back yard, and cleaning the house. I was often let off from that. 'You go and do your studying. You go and read your books and do your studying', and my sister had to do that, and that's where the resentment and the anger started.[20]

It was not necessarily favoritism that singled Beryl out from her siblings. The family may well have calculated that she would be most likely to repay such "investment" in her education, much as Leonard (see chapter five) and his sister had also been singled out for special treatment within the family. Given the strong collective sense of family, this would have been interpreted as a sound policy for improving the life chances not only of the individual son or daughter, but by extension, of other family members.

Indeed, economic and social mobility were seen as values and goals that many families strove to inculcate in their children, notably through geographic mobility and migration. It was the willingness of family members (and even neighbors) to support each other that enabled people to engage in the highly modern activity of solo or individual migration. At the same time, family members abroad were expected to reciprocate by returning remittances that helped support, and in some cases improve, the quality of life for those left behind.

From a child's perspective, growing up in a family characterized by migration would mean witnessing individual (male and female) choice and activity, but learning also that individualism did not equate with autonomy, nor that migration signalled the end of active family membership. On the contrary, particularly for the children of a migrant, the choice exercised would have been for the benefit of the family, an individual choice made (and made meaningful) in a social context. For the most part, the relative (or parent) absent through migration retained contact and returned remittances, while the wider family cared for the children left behind. Furthermore, notions of travel, distance and absence would have been part of the family rhetoric, along with the corollaries of return and reunion. Distance was not a barrier to family unity, and family unity was a principle taught and endorsed in childhood.

> I was the letter-writer for the family—Beryl recalled—and for my grandparents too, because [relatives] went abroad...to Panama, Cuba, the United States...I recall her [grandmother] getting lots of letters with money from Panama and the United States....One of my uncles, Uncle Vincent, was in the United States. ...my mother's brother....My father had relatives in Cuba...I remember my cousins with strange names like Alfonso, Ejida, Fredimando, and we used to have a good laugh, and think, 'What strange names!' But, of course, they're Cuban names, they were all born in Cuba.[21]

Yet absence was not without its pain, particularly for a child.[22] Sometimes, the adult migrant neither returned nor kept in contact, particularly when communications were difficult and expensive, and when illiteracy was high. Even where migration was not a feature of family life, nevertheless men and women exercised individual choice despite—or because—of a notion of collective family life. The final principle, then, relates to individuation. That individual choice came with responsibility was a necessary part of the equation. Thus, for instance, men and women chose sexual partners freely, but both considered they had a responsibility to support (materially or otherwise) the children of any such partnership, and/or their partner's children from previous relationship(s). As a result, stepfathers (and mothers) supplemented and sometimes substituted for biological fathers (and mothers). One Trinidadian informant explained how her father assumed responsibility for her mother's children from an earlier marriage:

> They was like his children. He, he never make no distinction with them. He always love them, treat them the same way, and all this sort of thing, yes, you know. Well, I don't know about now, but long ago, the people took children and all this kind of thing, they used to treat as their own, you know. They didn't have no family, you know, "That's my children, and this is yours." Theys treat everybody as one. Yes. Yes, he used to treat them good, and they were very ... were loved by him, and they were, you know, and he loved them very much.[23]

Beryl did not share paternity with her eldest brother, her mother's first child. Nevertheless, her father assumed responsibility for him and,

> he grew up as part of the family, because, again, this is the order of the day. And so, in all, our parents had eight children, and we all grew up in a lovely, loving household.

Mum and Dad were always there. . His seven children were all with my mother....Had he had any [outside children], it would have been accepted, because that, again, was the order of the day. They would have been part of the family and visited, and we'd have known about them.[24]

As a result, many children grew up as members of shared, and different, families and replication (or multiplication) of kin. Most children were brought up aware that their family was as one young British-born informant described it, "more than my brothers and sisters." Avis, for instance, recalled that as a child,

I didn't sort of appreciate the importance of the family tree. [But] my mum used to make us know every cousin, brother, uncle, distant, whether it was fourth, third, sixth. She used to tell us who had what, who had how many sons, what daughters, what children, who they were, where they lived. And she used to visit as well....She used to tell us all those things. ...I can still remember all the generations. I mean, I might not know the children if I see them, but I knew of them, and naturally, like the children now and their children, I wouldn't know, but I still ring my uncles every now and then, to make sure I speak to people before they die![25]

The prevalence of the practice of the community participation in the socialization of children, linked with wider family responsibilities for their welfare, suggests that it was contrived rather than coincidental, that it was a desired way of bringing children up, rather than a system arrived at by default. As Erna Brodber argues "For a pattern of behavior to become traditional, it must not only be performed consistently, but be seen to be right."[26]

As noted in chapter 6, not only did this practice contribute to an "emotional expansiveness" but the language of childrearing was characterised by the active, rather than passive, verb. It was language and behavior that suggested that children were considered as emergent (if unequal) adults, with a measure of self-reliance and responsibility. It was a very different model from that which sees children as individuals to be protected and to some extent isolated, as a *tabula rasa* upon which values and behavior must be inscribed before they are entitled to enter into adult society. In this sense, it is part of the philosophical approach that underpins Caribbean social organization, in which adult individuality, independence and autonomy are valued as the best ways to contribute to the collective good, and which is reflected in the values taught, and the resources developed, in the processes of socialisation.

Such principles clearly had widespread endorsement. Nevertheless, while the ideology endorsed broad communitarian principles at the same time as it encouraged independence, there remained a potential for tension and/or slippage between the two, particularly when migration over long distances, and for long periods of time, was involved. Some accounts of childhood, as Samuel's story (below) suggests contain pain—separation from one or both parents was on occasion traumatic, and not always resolved by reunion; the relationship with biological or social fathers was not always smooth, fathers were not always known, acknowledged or permitted. The trauma associated with absent parents, even if reunion was eventually achieved, may be a contributory factor in the high levels of schizophrenia recorded in Britain for second-generation African-Caribbeans males—precisely those left with grandparents while their parents established themselves in Britain.[27] Since the rates of schizophrenia among African-Caribbean in Britain are not congruent with those in the Caribbean, the explanations point to social and environmental factors—of which separation from parents may be one, (along with stress caused as a result of high levels of both institutional and personal racism, low employment levels, poor housing, and loss of cultural identity.)[28]

Poverty could, on occasion, lead to neglect and abuse. All children reported that their parents, and parent substitutes, firmly believed in not sparing the rod lest the child be spoiled and it was not always clear whether corporal punishment meted out to children may have merged into what, by contemporary standards, would now be considered abuse.[29] Experience of childhood abuse is now recognized as a key contributory factor in adult abusers. Research by Elsie Le Franc et al., on domestic violence in contemporary Jamaica, indicated that, while "the structure of the family of origin had no predictive nor explanatory power," for men, "the only factor that was significantly and independently associated with the use of violent conflict resolution tactics was the incidence of severe childhood punishment."[30] There were, however, as the research indicated, other circumstances associated with adult abusers that could aggravate or exacerbate (though not necessarily cause) the situation in which adult abuse was likely to occur. For both men and women—just as likely to be perpetrators of violence as the victims—household instability, unemployment (particularly for men), and an instrumental or "market" approach to partnerships (where women in particular chose partners most likely to provide) were also linked with domestic violence and child abuse (which also may well have been the case earlier in the twentieth century), suggesting, as Le Franc concludes, that in order to try to reduce incidences of domestic abuse "it may be more useful to focus attention not so much on the formal form of the family structure, as on the character and quality of gender relationships, on the process of managing and establishing the 'market-type relationships,' as well as on the capacity to manage and negotiate them."[31] Nevertheless, while domestic abuse may be associated with severe childhood punishment, this is not to suggest that it is more likely to occur among the African-Caribbean population than among other communities in the Caribbean or elsewhere. On the contrary, among the African-Caribbean community in Britain it is no higher than in other ethnic groups.[32]

***

It remains to be seen whether a general endorsement of the principles of childrearing emerged in particular material and physical conditions—small, rural localities with few social disparities- and could survive displacement. Let us now turn to some families to explore the patterns and process of childrearing, and to see how those broad values—of caring, sharing and respect, of responsibility and self-reliance, of individuation and family unity- have played out over the generations and in Britain.

David's Family

David was born in Britain in 1954, the eldest of five children. His parents had arrived in Britain from Jamaica in 1952, and had married the same year he was born. According to David, his father was one of the first West Indians to buy a house in Britain, and was able to do so through "throwing a partner," by adapting a cultural practice from one environment to another. "It was a lot of money," David recalled, "but he saved, throw a partner…put a deposit on that house and I think paid off the rest fairly soon."[33] This house then became the hub for newly arrived migrants from the West Indies, and for other family members who followed his parents to Britain and who "came through the same house."[34]

> A lot of people, in them days, used to come, stop at that house. Most of the West Indians that came in the early sixties, stopped at my old man's house for a time, and then moved on and got their own house.[35]

As a child, therefore, David grew up in a household which had a wide, if relatively itinerant, membership within the young West Indian community in Birmingham. His childhood, however, echoed the Caribbean. "We were" he said,

> very respectful, with that type of respect. If we was a young boy, it was the same in Jamaica, with big people, you see, you've got to have manners, and you swore to them, then they'd clip you round the ears and when you got home, you'd have another clip from your parents. Them types of values we had in them days. Very different then, you know, we had respect for people, you know, it was always the manners.[36]

Like his peers in Jamaica, he and his siblings were required to help in the house. As children "we all had our chores...somebody did the hoovering, somebody wash the plates...you had to do chores before you went to school."[37] Although David did not travel back to Jamaica as a child, nevertheless neither distance nor absence have been an impediment to family sentiment: "we are a close knit family."[38] Although he has never met his grandparents (who died when he was young, or before he was born), his maternal grandmother, by repute, was

> a loving woman...everybody comes to her for their problems, you know, and everybody comes to find out how she is...my grandmother grew up kids, you know, the Jamaican system.[39]

The proof of family loyalty and support came, unfortunately, early. David's father died when David was fifteen. As a result, he had to leave school and start work to help support his mother and younger sisters, becoming in effect a surrogate father,"...in a sort of way, for a while. Send my sister through college, and my youngest sister, because my youngest sister...didn't really know my father."[40] Other family members also stepped in. His maternal uncle and his wife kept a watchful eye, as did aunts. His mother had not worked when the children were small:

> she had five kids to look after, so she was more or less the housewife. She kept everything. She was a strong woman, yeah she was a strong woman....well, when you have five kids, and you go through them days, you've got to be strong in that situation... most West Indian families, you know, the women are the strong people. Men are the ones who take chances, They're usually hardworking, too, but the women were the backbone.[41]

As a widow, however, she needed to support them and accordingly went out to work for the first time. The family was close anyway, ("we live as one, you know,") and continues to be so. Despite growing up in Birmingham, much of David's childhood was replicated from Jamaica, including the language and imagery with which he describes his family members. His mother was "strict. And we grew up strict, and valued education very strongly...especially with the girls."[42] Above all,

> My father and mother didn't have to show me that they loved me. I think the people who have to play with their kids, they've got a problem, because they have to show... they have to prove to their kids that they love them...the child should automatically know that you love him...Like my mother, she never have to tell us that she love us. If you have to tell your kids that you love them, then there's doubt...you know Jamaica, you can ask a Jamaican, and the first thing he'll talk about is his mother. ...I knows that my mother love me. And sometimes she wouldn't eat, make sure you eat, and yet she don't eat...sometimes Christmastime, we often said to my mother 'Don't buy me nothing, man, buy yourself a frock...that's why certain things in this society, I think they're lost, I don't think they understand the word 'love'. Here, they'll love today and hate tomorrow...don't care what me does she's there, you know what I mean?[43]

As a result, David considered that his family gave him considerable social strength, particularly in being able to combat racism, "we're strong," he says, "mentally and physically, and we've got a strength that they can't understand."[44] Indeed, David is a forceful advocate of Jamaican culture and argues that the traditional values are being jettisoned in Britain:

> We're mixed up with our culture...we've adopted a culture that is now our culture...the way of life, greed, television has destroyed the kids...they have this competition between man and woman, that's been destroyed, the relationships have been destroyed by society. You can't even discipline your own child, with telling them what's right from wrong, because they're portraying theirself as God, telling you how to live, basically, their way is right, and your way is wrong...a lot of it is single parents, single families, bringing up kids on their own, has a lot to do with it...you need two to have the balance...the kid has got to see you, that father figure...if he don't see, he's going to go wild...[45]

He speaks with a strong Jamaican accent, even though he has only been to Jamaica twice.

> People always say that Jamaicans speak with an accent, but Scottish people don't speak with an accent...that's why I say I want my kid to grow, to know so well he's got some heritage...show him the division between black and white, and show him where he's coming from, and that, not to be made to look like you're nobody...if you feel you're just as good as that man, you will try as hard as that man...your confidence is most important...I want to give him the positive vibes...tell him you are a black person, but you can be like that person.[46]

And feels strongly on the need for role models:

> We need somebody...that we can follow...that's why a lot of our boys are not doing so well, there's no black role models out there that they can emulate, you know...look at sportsmen, sports this, sports that, we want somebody academic, to come out through the ranks, that still holds his blackness, and not has to turn traitor to it...that's what we need, and there's not a black man, literally, or a black woman...that's why I say we need a role model.[47]

David's contacts with Jamaica are still strong and, through his mother, he sends money to family members there and, in time, would like to live there. But his advocacy of Jamaican culture is partly linked with a national pride, and partly with broader experiences of race, racism, and exclusion. He has travelled widely in Europe, and can tell when the welcome is "artificial and plastic, and they smile because it's polite," in contrast to when

> you go to a black person, they will welcome you, they want to know about you. And if he's any relation to you, of if there's anybody who he may know, so you know that it's genuine, you know, from the heart. But you haven't got, really, basically, nothing in common in Europe, with the Europeans, so they're not going to talk about history, and ask you "You know about Marley?"...Yeah, what are you going to talk about after that?...So the artificial life I don't really want to know. I want to be, live with the people I choose to live with, and we can talk and you can say what you feel, you know?[48]

Indeed, for David, the blot on family closeness comes from his sister's marriage to a white man, of which David does not approve. He is, as he says, "black-orientated" and offers some general advice, "I always say 'Hold your blackness, man, because it's the only thing they can't take away from you.'"[49]

David has a small son with the woman, of Jamaican heritage, with whom he has lived for five years. She has two other children by an earlier relationship, the oldest of whom is Faria, a girl of thirteen. For the last five years David has assumed responsibility for these children, and acted as stepfather. Faria calls David "Dad," and describes him as "just loving and caring, he's great, he's always there. He's just there. He's Dad."[50] Indeed, in her view, David is "more better" than her own father who she still sees, though with less frequency after David moved in to live with her mother. Her biological father also has another son by an earlier relationship with whom, now, she is losing contact. It is David's family which has entered into, and supplemented, her kin orbit. "She calls David's mother 'Gran' and I say to a lot of my friends that she's my granny."[51] This grandmother cares for her grandson (Faria's youngest brother) while Faria's mother works, and Faria sees this grandmother every day and feels close towards her. While David's family network may have extended Faria's paternal kin, she is also deeply involved with her mother's family. Her maternal grandmother she describes as "nice and caring and loving." Her mother was one of seven children, six of whom are in the United Kingdom, one of whom is in Germany. She insists that they are all very close as a family, and she in particular is close to one aunt who lives in the same street, and to her cousins from that aunt. The networks, however, extend to her mother's friends and, as in the Caribbean, the concept of family is inclusive. Thus "like family" includes, for instance, her brother's godmother, plus a close friend of her mother's who is "like my mum, really, she's loving and caring and she's got a daughter called Sandra, ...and me and Sandra we're definitely like cousins."[52] More particularly, many of her family, and family friends live in the neighborhood that has other African-Caribbean neighbors and, as a result, other family members take part in disciplining her. If she was caught misbehaving, they would "tell my mum," who would then take the necessary action. David, moreover, takes an active part in her upbringing, reinforcing, for instance, his (and her mother's) belief in education, and the need to inculcate responsibility. The children are, therefore, required to help around the house, for "he'd rather us learn to do it for when we grow up and we've got our responsibilities."[53]

Yet despite the closeness of the relationship, Faria would still like them to get married.

> It makes me feel that we're a proper family. I can't explain it...the actual marriage would make it more special...Do you know what I mean? They're more strong. That's the ideal family, where you've got the mum, the dad and the children.[54]

In many ways, therefore, Faria's childhood in Birmingham contains many features which would be recognizable from the Caribbean, and are clearly part of the continuities in cultural practice. Indeed, although Faria is now a third generation African-Caribbean, and has never visited Jamaica, she still argues, like David, that it is important to retain contact with the Caribbean, and to impart to children, in particular, the values—of sharing, caring and respect—relevant to successful family life.

Avis' Family

The second family demonstrates a very different ethos and outcome. Samuel was born in Barbados in 1952, and came to Britain with his younger sister in 1968 to join his mother, Avis, her husband, and his four younger (British-born) siblings. He had not seen his mother for twelve years; he had never met his stepfather or his siblings. "I want," he said, "to give you a true picture, which would identify with the research that you want."[55] During his mother's absence, he and his sister had been looked after by her mother. Samuel's grandmother had twelve children now dispersed "all over the world." Individual family members who went abroad could rely on communal family care for the children left behind. As a consequence, Samuel's grandmother had, as she put it, "reared enough grands." Avis returned remittances regularly to her mother to support her children and contribute to the domestic economy of her family.

Avis was the second oldest of her mother's twelve children and had migrated in 1956. Her memories of her mother were vivid. She was a "wonderful woman."

> I remember her as being very beautiful and with long hair and we always used to be sitting down playing with it, you know. For some reason, she doesn't really like long hair and we used to plait it over the ears...and she's always be poking it back, poking it back.[56]

Her maternal grandfather was one of seventeen sons, her mother the only daughter in a family of ten. The family was musical. Her grandfather invented the foot harp and "they were all into the music" either as instrumentalists or, like her mother, as singers. This grandfather was a mason who travelled considerably, her father a carpenter/joiner who also had part-shares in a fishing boat. The family lived well on the fish and the produce from the land, and food and sharing were also part of the leit motif of this family, "I remember her always sharing whatever she had."[57] When Avis left for England, her mother continued to send food packages of sweet potato, cassava, corn meal and hot pepper sauce. It was a way of retaining both family connections and a potent reminder of the culture and its values of support and sharing. There was, in the words of Walter Benjamin, a "compressed fullness"[58] in those packages. The exchange was not confined to food. One uncle, who had no children, and who lived in Trinidad, fostered Avis's eldest sister. Avis was as close to her grandparents as to her parents, her uncles and cousins, to her brothers, childcare and support crossed generations and transversed kin. Thus individual family members who went abroad could rely on communal family care for the children left behind, bounded within a neighborhood of friends, godparents and kin. Its topography was, as Avis says, "a map of my childhood."[59]

When Avis was eighteen she "had a boyfriend and a son."[60] A few years later she had a daughter, by a different man. Her parents were, at the time, "bitter" but nevertheless stepped in to help her so that when, in 1956, she left to join her then boyfriend in Britain, she was able to leave her children confidently in the care of her family, the loss minimized by a history of affection. "My love was with me, so that was a comfort in itself."[61] (Many informants talk of the loss and absence of family in similar terms, conveying an abiding emotional presence. "I carry my family within me" was how another informant described it.) Twelve years later, when her son was sixteen and her daughter fourteen, she sent for them both to join her and (new) husband in England. The reunion was "wonderful" but marred by the discovery that her son had difficulty reading and writing. "I don't know why...it could have been the disturbance at losing the Mum."[62] Once discovered, he was sent to a special school but after four years in England, he was returned to Barbados.

> He was being...rebellious. We don't know for what reason. Who knows what goes through children's heads?...Sometimes children see themselves suffer, they see things that you don't see...but...deep down, he's a very nice chap and we have a good relationship.[63]

Samuel now has a successful business in Barbados and Avis is "proud" of his achievements, as indeed those of all her children. As a mother, she had insisted that her professional life (she was a nurse) was organized around their needs, that they were always fully supported, that time was always allocated to them, and their friends always welcome,

> Once I said to [my son], I said 'I don't understand it. Why would your friends from these love homes, rich, wealthy backgrounds, want to come and kip on my floor?' And he say "Because this is a home, and theirs is a house." Big difference.[64]

Like her mother, she has always laid stress on the family lineages and links, and maintained close family contact with her siblings and cousins across time and the world. "It's important," she argues "(family) is part of one's identity...I want to keep in touch with all my older family, whether they're here or there, they're mine." There is, however, another reason for insuring that family members know each other. She is divorced from her husband, who now has three more children by various girlfriends.

> Where my children are concerned, with their new family from their father, we round them all up, my daughter and my son does that, and make sure that they're in touch with these children from other families, because they're all similar ages. Our greatest fear is that they will end up...loving each other...in the wrong way. So they're maintaining the contact, so they get to know each other, so if they acknowledge each other as sisters, or families and brothers, then that kind of love will not come to mind...so every chance...we get them together...It's important that families know each other because...in the West Indies, people often say "Oh, you look like so and so, ah! You Princie's daughter? You know, you're my cousin!" you get a lot of that in the West Indies. You might not know

a person, but they recognize you from sixth cousin. Therefore that...sexual relationship doesn't come into it. In this country, where people are scattered, you meet someone, you like them, you get involved...before you know it, they could be married to their cousins, and we don't want that...you see, any genetic problems will carry on. So it's important that people know who their families are.[65]

This was Avis's story. Her son, Samuel, wanted to give a "true picture." "I love my Mum," he said, but,

if I tell you my whole life story, I'll cry. And what I'm saying to you, I'm not telling you anything out of any kind of hurt and revenge or animosity for my mum. I love my mum.[66]

As Avis's story overflowed with love and inclusion, Samuel's was its mirror image, characterized by absence and loss. Samuel has no memory of his mother. He can only "pick up" from when he went to Britain at the age of sixteen. His adjustment to Britain, the family, and his mother was hard, and was compounded by his mother's "hurtful" reaction to his learning difficulties. As soon as he left school,

I was placed on an aeroplane back to Barbados...I didn't get the opportunity...like the rest of my brothers and sisters. Everything that I had and they wanted, it would be taken from me and given to them.[67]

Samuel's agenda was a catalogue of maternal neglect and exclusion, culminating in his peremptory return to his grandmother in Barbados. His narrative moves through cycles of explanation: his mother's memory of him was a "still memory" and he had changed; his learning disability proved "hurtful" to her, he failed to understand how someone could be so cruel: "How can a mother love a son, how can a mother do this kind of thing?"[68]

Finally, his analysis comes full circle. Samuel never knew his father. He had been told he was dead. It was only on returning to Barbados and a curiosity to discover his roots that he made enquiries, discovered his father and established a relationship with him. His father had not known of Samuel's existence.

She (mother) didn't want anyone to know that she had any contact with him. Up to this day, she's still denying the fact that he is my father. Her would not say who my father is.[69]

On one occasion, when his mother was visiting Barbados, she saw Samuel with his father. She responded angrily,

...and everything clicked in my mind. I went back to England, and all the years that I spend in England, up to that particular time, last year, I wonder how it is that my mother, when she see me, she feel so excited about me, she talks...even in England, she speaks highly of me, she's proud of me. And what is it that my mother treat me the way she treat me? And I thought, in my mind, that it was because I could not read. But it clicked then. It was nothing to do with I not being able to read. It was that I was growing up in[to] the splitting image of the man that she was denying.[70]

Avis had glossed over Samuel's conception and birth: "I had a boyfriend and then I had a son." As Gorell Barnes et al. remind us:

> Intergenerational patterns are often invisible guidelines to family life which appear to indicate the way a family regulates its present interactions in response to what has gone before...The recognition of avoidance or reversal as a form of intergenerational influence is particularly important.[71]

Samuel attributes his success in Barbados to a desire to prove himself to his mother, and to seek her approval. His narrative is punctuated by the question he never dares pose to her, "why are you hiding? Why are you still, after forty years, why are you still trying to hide?"[72] His mother, however, remains "in denial,"

> [But] it has to be finished. It needs to be finished. She need to come and speak the truth. She need to tell me who it is...I want to know the truth. He tell the truth. But I haven't heard her say.[73]

While he waits for her answer, his response takes the form of a public exposition. He is an active and articulate proponent of the rights of fathers in paternity and parenting; he argues vehemently for the recognition of "roots." He actively and positively maintains contact with all his family in Barbados, as well as those in Britain and North America; he is active in the education and school life of his daughter. On the surface, his public persona is in the image of his mother, a committed family man with a strong sense of civic duty. But, as he says, "I take it and turn it all around."[74]

Jill's Family

A theme of self-sufficiency runs through the final family. Jon was born in England in 1973, the eldest of two children. His parents, Jill and Jeremy, were both born in Trinidad, but met, and married, in England. They had both left Trinidad when they were eighteen, Jill to train as a nurse, Jeremy to join his mother who had left some six years earlier. Jill was born in 1945, the fourth of her parents' five children. Her father, a school teacher, died when Jill was seven and Jill's mother—who up until then had not worked—began to take in home work to support her children. She was also given some financial support from her father who was "quite well off...owned a lot of land,"[75] and some practical support from her aunt and sister. In addition, there were a number of relatives who lived close by. But, as Jill explains, her mother was a "proud woman...my mother wouldn't accept help...she would help (other people) but she didn't like to accept help of any sort."[76]

The family did not mix much with their relatives (with the exception of her maternal grandfather), and as a result there were many family members whom she has not met, or did not meet until she was an adult.

> One cousin I met here...I'd never met her while I was growing up...when she came she said, "Your mother was such a proud woman. She wouldn't let you mix with anybody...I should have met you when you were a child!"...There are lots of regrets, because I think I led a very sheltered life. I don't know all my relatives, that's why I allow the children to go to Trinidad, and they explore with their cousins.[77]

Jill's upbringing was strict. Her mother commanded obedience, insisted that domestic chores be shared and completed, homework done and,

> then when we became teenagers, she was very strict about, and very selective in, who we fraternised with, or went out with, or boyfriends and things... now that I reflect, there were so many girls who went to school with me who became pregnant...and I look back and think 'that's what my mother was trying to protect me from.'[78]

Jill won a scholarship to secondary school, and from there went to England to train as a nurse, to join an elder brother and sister already studying there.

Jeremy's mother, Correyne, (born in 1924) commuted with her family between Grenada and Trinidad and it was on one extended stay that she met Jeremy's father (also a Grenadian) who was working in the oil industry in Trinidad to save sufficient money to go to the United States to study dentistry. According to Jeremy,

> she was very bitter towards him, for some strange reason... He took me out somewhere once, and I can remember him taking me back home. He had me in his arms and I can remember him taking me back home...He left, and that was that, you know. We never made contact until recently.[79]

As a result, Correyne brought Jeremy up with no financial help from his father although "he tried to, but she refused. That's a case of her defiance...she was very independent...But he did try."[80] When Jeremy was eight, Correyne married Johnny, the father of her second child, Selwyn, and took in and helped bring up Eddie, Johnny's son by another woman. Indeed, Eddie "was part of the family...we were all brothers."[81] When Jeremy was twelve, Correyne and her husband migrated to Britain, leaving Selwyn and Eddie in the care of Johnny's mother, and Jeremy in the care of Correyne's aunt. But prior to and after Correyne's migration Jeremy was surrounded by a wide circle of maternal kin, all of whom lived in the same village that had become a Grenadian enclave in southern Trinidad.

Like Jill's mother, Correyne was strict about the company Jeremy kept, keeping him away from those children whom she felt would be a "bad influence...drifting, you know, about the village...the poorer children did that...there were kids with not a lot of parental control."[82] Jeremy left Trinidad when he was eighteen to join his mother and stepfather in Britain, a decision precipitated by the company he began to keep.

> I got into steel bands, when I was about fourteen, fifteen...in those days, steel band men had a reputation of being...bad men...I was beginning to rebel a bit...and they couldn't really control me because I used to do what I wanted to do. I left school [at fifteen] and they didn't like it. [My aunt] said "Look, I'm going to send you to your mother, because I can't take this responsibility. You're getting out of hand." And before I knew it...I was on a plane...I landed in England, and that's it. But I didn't want to come here. No.[83]

Correyne, in turn, had also been brought up strictly, with firm control over the company she kept, by her maternal grandmother, after her own mother had died in childbirth. Moreover, "*her* mama, I heard, was very strict as well, that's why she was such a strict old lady."[84] Despite this, Correyne loved her dearly and when she died "I dreamt of her time and time and time, and cry and cry, till one of my aunties said 'if you go on like that your grandmother is going to take you...stop crying, child, your grandmother's going to take you.'"[85] Correyne's parents had not been married, but she nevertheless knew her paternal grandmother who "couldn't talk very good English, and they said she was from Africa...I used to say to me next granny, which is the one I grew with, 'Is she from Africa, mama?' She used to say 'Child, is a story.' Because she had a brother...with her and people say again that he did fly away."[86]

The family was large, and socialized regularly, as her aunts and grandmother "used to tell us lots of stories...the Nancy stories they used to talk about is frightening when you're a little girl or so!"[87] Correyne became pregnant when she was twenty. Her grandmother "made a fuss, but then afterwards, she cooled off."[88] Correyne and her grandmother went back to Grenada where Correyne gave birth to Jeremy, returning to Trinidad three weeks later. Her grandmother and her aunt (who subsequently cared for Jeremy) adored him, "spoilt" him. After her grandmother died, Correyne provided for him with the help of her uncles, and with what work she could find, but "things was ever so cheap. Cheap as hell (excuse me!)."[89]

Her grandmother "teach me a little bit of everything, how to cook, how to look after washing clothes, cleaning the house, the yard, the little bit of everything."[90] Correyne made sure, in turn, that she brought her own children up "in the right way, and they both come out all right."[91] She left Jeremy when he was eleven, and Selwyn when he was three. Leaving the children was hard "they was on my mind, on my mind, on my mind. On and on and on and on. Children, children, children... I was really, really, really, how must I put it? In a state, when I left them at that age."[92]

The reunion with Jeremy six years later prompted her to buy a house but shortly after he came to England, she returned to Trinidad for the first time, returning for an extended stay later when Jon was born. As Jill recalled, "the first grandchild. She came to tell me how to bring him up, which I wasn't having!"[93] Nevertheless, difficulties in securing childcare (Jill continued to work as a nurse) meant that Jon was sent to stay with Correyne in Trinidad. He has few memories of those years—only "snatches"—and when he returned Jill was able to put him into the creche in the hospital where she worked. After her second son was born, she and Jeremy boxed and coxed with shift work for a while and then engaged au pairs to help with childcare. Jon's parents had a circle of West Indian friends with whom they used to socialize, and from time to time relatives from Trinidad would stay for extended periods. When Jill's sister in Trinidad died seven years ago, Jill and Jeremy sent for her only daughter (then aged ten) to live with them. With the exception of the short period when Jon was in Trinidad, Jill and Jeremy brought the children up alone, without the help of relatives and friends—a conscious choice on Jill's behalf as she

> didn't really want relatives and friends...I knew they were growing up in British society and I wanted them to be able to adapt...I'm not being disloyal to my country, but a lot of the attitudes that some of the older Trinidadians [had], I didn't want them to have to [put] up with all of that...I felt things like reading to them and playing to them were much more important than hoovering the stairs...I know how important it is for 0-5s to be able to play and explore and learn, and make mistakes and learn. And I didn't want any West Indian person coming and saying "Oh, he's five and he can't count," or "he's four and he can't spell his name." He won't be able to spell his name, but he might have lots of other experiences that other children did not, so I didn't want them involved. So I did it my way.[94]

In much the same way, Jeremy carved out a parenting role. While Jill worked a night shift, he took care of Jon and

> it never bothered me. Although my father wasn't around...that more or less fatherly role that I gave to my kids, no man ever gave that to me, because my stepfather and I was never close. So I more or less made my own decision, you know, without a man to support me.[95]

In many ways, Jill's decision to bring up her children "the British way" echoes her own childhood, and her mother's determination to bring up her family alone. She admits she has "boundaries, rather than being strict. They know what they can and cannot do...my husband had an extremely strict...mother. His mother was even worse than mine and because of that he is very relaxed...but at the end of the day, we agree."[96] From Jon's perspective, his father "is strict, but he isn't as strict as my mum. He's more...relaxed...(but) he's got defined ideas...no stealing, no drugs, don't get your girlfriend pregnant before you can afford to look after her and just don't...I was going to say a prat...but don't generally...be unpleasant in life."[97] Yet Jon saw marked contrasts between his upbringing and those of his white British friends:

> I was always amazed...some of my friends used to swear a lot in front of their parents, and call them this and call them that, and get away with murder as far as I could see, whereas if I did that...I'd be dead! And they always seemed much more comfortable and prosperous, more well-off, more spoilt, to be honest...They took everything for granted, they were very blasé about the possessions they had...and their parents...were very tolerant of their bad behavior.[98]

The significant difference in the context in which Jill and Jeremy bring up their children is that of racism. Both Jill and Jeremy placed the highest priority on education.

> I was passing a school and I just didn't like the state of the children, you know?...and I looked back at myself at the school that I went to, the Roman Catholic School. It was fee paying and they were pretty strict. We had to be pretty clean and wear a tie and all those things...I just didn't like the behavior of the kids in the school yard and how they were looking...I said "I want my kids to go to a school like I went to"...And we chose private, and that was it.[99]

Jon won a scholarship to an independent school (the youngest children attend grant-maintained schools). He "always wanted to do well at school...plus my mother always used to say to me, 'You know, you have to do twice as well as anybody else, because you're black'... (but) I was always quite politically, socially, racially aware...I was always, to be honest, very proud...to be a black person in that school, and I was always trying to push it."[100] Jon has now graduated from University, and is taking a second degree. Although most of his friends (including his girlfriend) were and are white, he was conscious of being in a minority at school, with the teachers "being quite nervous in dealing with me...they were uncomfortable in dealing with me."[101] (Jill herself on occasion complained to the school over a racist text set for an examination). He felt "different" at school

> It's quite hard to articulate...you just know you're different, you feel you're different...their whole way of behaving was English white way of behaving...when I go home it's always reinforced that you're black and Trinidadian, West Indian.[102]

At University, he felt patronized by "people who didn't see me...they used to make a bee line for me and when they found out I didn't...deal in drugs and I wasn't a DJ they ...went the other way, because I didn't fit their stereotype."[103] This sense of difference and awareness of stereotype continues, when,

> people assume things about you...you do get names called, and you get funny looks... the police do stare at me quite a lot...Sometimes it just gets on my nerves, because I'm not the type of person who wants to be picked out of the crowd to be stared at, and yet people will stare at you and it just annoys you, intensely sometimes...sometimes you put your head down and you want to hide, and sometimes you just ignore it and carry on...[my parents] said "You have to remember...what you are, and you have to be proud of what you are, and if people are staring or saying things...they're ignorant...you can't let their stupidity bother you."[104]

Despite Jill's recognition of the differences between African-Caribbean and British childrearing practices and her attempts to adapt the former to the latter, the pressures of living in what Jon describes as "two cultures" are, he argues, intense for all young black people.

> It's difficult to get on in England...you find yourself having to divide your mind... you're working...and living in a white environment, and then you find yourself in a black environment with your family and friends so that creates...a lot of pressure for people...They're not accepted in the white community, fully, I mean, they are accepted but there's always the odd slight, or the odd patronising remark, or outright discrimination. And in the black community, there's people who...retreat into the bunker to cope with the problems in Britain....It's difficult for black people, because they have to...get on in the white environment, because those are the people who control everything in Britain, but at the same time...you have to stay true to your roots, so that creates a big pressure...I don't think it's just me. I think it's a lot of young black people.[105]

***

In all three families, the central principles that underline African-Caribbean attitudes toward children and childrearing can be seen, in varying degrees. For some families, moving to Britain made the collective childcare—a feature of their own childhoods—problematic, as family and friends were necessarily dispersed, or absent, and the urban British neighborhood did not offer the same protection or shared values; for others, such as Jill, it afforded an opportunity to break away from some child-rearing practices and pressures considered inappropriate. In either case, however, it has not been the practical aspects that are remembered and recreated, but the values such a system represented, with its emphasizes on concern, respect, and its buttress for family life. Indeed, all families reiterate their unity and, in the case of the final family, reconstruct it in Britain.

While the stern upbringing of the Caribbean necessarily contrasts with what is perceived as lax British practices, the young people here appear to endorse their upbringing, recognizing that its differences represent a cultural marker, and recognizing the significance of that in a context where difference is emphasized and often negatively connoted. Indeed, the importance of family becomes a point of pride and an important strength in any struggle against racism. For the older generation, the attitudes to children, childcare and childrearing reveal social principles that are essentially egalitarian, and a social world characterized by order and respect. They reveal, in other words, many of the values and philosophies that underpin social organization and provision, while the sense of pride with which West Indians described their childhoods and the family and neighborhood that structured them may be seen as one of the bedrocks of social esteem and even a contributory element of West Indian nationalism.[106] Significantly, the family has retained its hold as a rallying point among the young generation and has become a central element of contemporary identities in the diaspora. Indeed, the robustness of the family system may be measured by its political symbolism and the ways in which it was retained its core values in an often hostile context.[107]

Notes

1. JL035/2/1/1/11.
2. "How a society treats its children has much to say about its charitable quality and its rational organization." Stein Ringen, *Citizens, Families, and Reform* (Oxford: Oxford University Press, 1997), 56. See also Anna Davin, *Growing Up Poor* (London: Rivers Oram Press, 1996).
3. Stuart Hall rightly points out that it is also possible for the young to support the values of their parents *and* subscribe to an alternative view. "You may say this is like having your cake and eating it and I do believe that is what it is. We witness the situation of communities that are not simply isolated, atomistic individuals,

nor are they well-bounded, singular separated communities. We are in that open space that requires a kind of vernacular cosmopolitanism, that is to say a cosmopolitanism that is aware of the limitations of any culture or any one identity and that is radically aware of its insufficiency in governing a wider society, but which nevertheless is not prepared to rescind its claim to the traces of difference, which make its life important.'" Stuart Hall, "Political Belonging in a World of Multiple Identities" in *Conceiving Cosmopolitanism. Theory, Context and Practice* eds. Steven Vertovec and Robin Cohen (Oxford: Oxford University Press, 2002), 30.

4. David Vincent, *Bread, Knowledge and Freedom. A Study of Nineteenth Century Working Class Autobiography* (London: Methuen, 1981); Philippe Lejeune *On Autobiography*, ed. Paul John Eakin, trans. K. Leary (Minneapolis: University of Minnesota Press, 1989). For a brief discussion see also Mary Chamberlain and Paul Thompson, Introduction to Chamberlain and Thompson (eds.), *Narrative and Genre*.
5. For a fascinating account and use of psychoanalysis in recollections of childhood see Ronald Fraser, *In Search of a Past* (London: Verso, 1984).
6. BK080/1/A/8.
7. BK080/1/A/8.
8. TM098/1/A/9.
9. JI028/1/b.
10. BK117.
11. BK080/2/A/43-44.
12. JI028/1/A/8.
13. TM098/1/A/13.
14. BK080/1/A/8.
15. BK080/2/A/43-44.
16. JI028/1/B/25.
17. TM098/1/A/10.
18. BK080/2/1/42-43.
19. JI028/1/B/25.
20. JI028/1/B/24.
21. JI028/1/A/6-14.
22. It has also been attributed as an ingredient cause in clinical depression among African-Caribbeans in Britain. See Rosemarie Mallett, Julian Leff, Dinesh Bhugra, Dong Pang, Jing Hua Zhao, "Social Environment, Ethnicity and Schizophrenia: A Case-Control Study" *Social Psychiatry and Psychiatric Epidemiology*, 37:7 (July 2002), 329-335.
23. TM098/1/A/17.
24. JI028/1/A/5.
25. BF069/1/A/18.
26. Erna Brodber "Afro-Jamaican Women at the turn of the Century."
27. Mallett et al., "Social Environment, Ethnicity and Schizophrenia."
28. D. Bhugra "Migration and schizophrenia" in *Acta Psychiatrica Scandanavia* 102 (suppl. 407), 2000, 68-73. At the same time, African-Caribbeans with mental health problems are more likely to be detained in institutions, more likely to be treated with drugs, and less likely to be offered psychotherapy. See Kamaldeep Bhui's editorial, *British Medical Journal*, 329, 7462, 2004, 363-364.
29. For a full discussion see Elsa Leo-Rhynie *The Jamaican Family: Continuity and Change* (Kingston: Institute of Jamaica, 1993).
30. Elsie Le Franc, Don Simeon, and Gail Wyatt, "Family structures and domestic conflict in Jamaica" in *Caribbean Families in Britain,*199.

31. Le Franc et al. "Family Structures," 203.
32. Jon Simmons and colleagues *Crime in England and Wales 2001/2* (www.homeoffice.gov.uk/rds/crimeew1/html). Roanna Gopaul and Paula Morgan, "Spousal Violence. Spiralling patterns in Trinidad and Tobago," proceedings of a workshop (Kingston: Institute of Social and Economic Research, 1997) suggest that there has been a rise in domestic violence in Trinidad and Tobago, pointing to a broadly based acceptance of a culture of violence which tolerates this. At the same time, they argue that there is an increasing awareness of domestic violence as a crime, an increasing resistance by women to its toleration (including a willingness to strike back) and as a result a rise in the incidence of domestic crime reporting and convictions.
33. JE017/2/1/3.
34. JE017/2/1/1/4.
35. JE017/2/1/3.
36. JE016/2/1/1/14.
37. JE017/2/1/1/15.
38. JE017/2/1/1/6.
39. JE017/2/1/1/6.
40. JE017/2/1/1/11.
41. JE017/2/1/1/4.
42. JE017/2/1/1/2. The comment on the value of education for girls is significant, given the higher levels of education and employment achieved by African-Caribbean women in the Caribbean and in the U.K.
43. JE017/2/1/2/16-17.
44. JE017/2/1/1/5.
45. JE017/2/1/1/14.
46. JE017/2/1/2/18.
47. JE017/2/1/2/22.
48. JE017/2/1/2/26.
49. JE017/2/1/2/27.
50. JE016/3/1/2/30.
51. JE016/3/1/1/12.
52. JE016/3/1/1/16.
53. JE016/3/1/1/8.
54. JE016/3/1/2/30-31.
55. BF123/2/1/1/2.
56. BF069/2/1/1/1.
57. BF069/2/1/1/2.
58. Walter Benjamin, *One Way Street* (London: Verso, 1997 [1979]).
59. BF069/2/2/2/32.
60. BF069/2/2/2/4.
61. BF069/2/2/2/9.
62. BF069/2/3/1/5.
63. BF069/2/3/2/4.
64. BF069/2/3/2/1.
65. BF069/2/3/1/5.
66. BF123/3/1/1/2.
67. BF123/3/1/1/2.
68. BF123/3/1/1/9.
69. BF123/3/1/1/9.
70. BF123/3/1/1/9.

71. Gorell Barnes et al. *Growing Up in Step Families.*(Oxford: Clarendon Press, 1998).
72. BF123/3/1/1/15.
73. BF123/3/1/1/11.
74. BF123/3/2/1/33.
75. TA001/1/1/2.
76. TA001/1/1/2.
77. TA001/1/15-6.
78. TA001/1/1/5.
79. TA004/1/1/4.
80. TA004/1/1/4.
81. TA004/1/1/6.
82. TA004/1/2/14. It is, of course, striking that children with little parental control always belonged to other families!
83. TA004/1/2/15-17.
84. TA095/1/1/4.
85. TA095/1/1/3.
86. TA095/1/1/4. The story of "flying Africans" has a long and important history. See Lorna McDaniel, *The Big Drum Ritual of Carriacou.*
87. TA095/1/1/8.
88. TA095/1/1/11.
89. TA095/1/1/13.
90. TA095/1/1/1.
91. TA095/1/1/8.
92. TA095/1/1/17.
93. TA001/1/2/25.
94. TA001/1/2/26.
95. TA004/1/2/28.
96. TA001/1/2/27.
97. TA015/1/1/3.
98. TA015/1/2/15.
99. TA004/1/2/28.
100. TA015/1/2/15.
101. TA015/1/1/10.
102. TA015/1/2/16.
103. TA015/1/1/11.
104. TA015/1/2/17.
105. TA015/1/1/13.
106. See Mary Chamberlain, "Small Worlds: Childhood and Empire" *Journal of Family History,* 27:2, (2002).
107. There is an important corollary that relates to the above average numbers of African Caribbean heritage children taken into care, and the longer than average duration of their stay in care. See Ravinder Barn "Caribbean Families and the Child Welfare System in Britain" in *Caribbean Families in Britain and the Transatlantic World'* eds. Harry Goulbourne and Mary Chamberlain *(London: Macmillan, 2001),* 204-218.

8

Brothers and Sisters, Uncles and Aunts

> *"It has only been in the last quarter of the twentieth century that our culture-bound notion of kinship has begun to be recognized, and 'kinship structure' to be acknowledged in the manner in which a pattern of physical relationships (however these are conceived) is made use of for social purposes. It is not really the 'reality' of physical relatedness but what is added to it, omitted from it, and distanced from it which becomes the actual stuff of kinship."*[1]

While kinship has and continues to feature in studies of the African-Caribbean family, the peculiar role of siblings has, curiously, often been neglected except in a few studies of migration that focus on families and networks as an integral process of migration.[2] Indeed, the study of siblings has rarely featured even in other studies on families. The ESRC's program on population and household change in Britain[3] did not feature one study on siblings, and there are no references to siblings in *Changing Britain*, the book resulting from the program.[4] The importance of siblings in the shaping of the family, spatially and emotionally, has, for the most part, taken a back seat to the more predominant role of one or both parents. In this, sociology echoes psychoanalysis where, as Leonore Davidoff et al.. have pointed out, "despite the clinical details about the importance of other members of the household and outsiders in the development of the child, it is the central triad of small (male) child, mother and father which predominates."[5]

Yet today's sibling is tomorrow's kin and the number of siblings, as well as the quality of the sibling relationship, will have repercussions in terms of family membership, roles and sentiments that can recur for several generations. This chapter will focus on the role of siblings—brothers and sisters, uncles and aunts—and on migration, the roles of family members (and memories) located elsewhere, the importance and nature of families dispersed transnationally, and the use, once again, of family as a metaphor for social behavior.

There are, of course, problems in any studies of siblings. In general, they raise definitional problems that are short-circuited in other family relationships. The relationship of a husband and wife, parent and child, is, on the whole, relatively clear cut, albeit dependent on cultural circumstances and historical moments. Beyond the conjugal, (or social) ties, it is assumed that particular functions, rights, and responsibilities relate to these roles and relationships, and failure to perform or conform is, in both social and legal terms, measurable. But who is a sibling raises all manner of definitional problems. While children who share a biological parentage are related as brothers and sisters, the definitions from there on begin to shade into degrees. Siblings may share full parenthood, but not necessarily. "Half" siblings will share only one biological parent, "step" siblings will share none. Siblings may, therefore, claim membership simultaneously in several (parent/child and extended) families, through either one of their parents and/or stepparents, particularly in the context of the Caribbean where, as we have seen, both men and women have children by different partners, and often assume parenthood over their partner's previous children. Children may not always know their siblings, or indeed, know who they are. "Outside" siblings may be rejected by their "inside" counterparts, or may be accepted as full members of the family. They may not be aware of each other's existence. There is, relatedly, a problem over location, and identification. It is assumed that siblings share a common experience of parenthood and childhood, and common structures of identification such as race, ethnicity, class, and social status, and that, gender aside, they will be broadly equal. Such assumptions, as Leonore Davidoff indicates,[6] assume a two-parent norm, an experience not necessarily relevant to a West Indian context where, as we have seen, half-and stepsiblings and membership in multiple nuclear families is not uncommon, and where children may be brought up for part or all of their lives by a foster parent, which may involve separation from their siblings.

The sibling relationship itself is, moreover, often fraught. It may change over the life cycle of the family and of the individual, it may imply competition and exclusion as much as, or as well as, cooperation and inclusion, and the status, nature and meaning of a sibling relationship may well, in due course, influence the relationship of siblings' children, and among cousins. Birth order and color can also affect the nature of the relationship between siblings, and the direction of family resources and can, and often does, result in fierce rivalry and even estrangement, as well as determining individual life chances. Indeed, the passions evoked by sibling rivalry can often mold the attitudes and behavior and personality development, and may in many ways, be a more powerful force than parental influence. The sibling relationship itself has, therefore, few of the formal social and legal constraints that characterized the parental relationship, although there are powerful informal social pressures that control expected behavior, and that, as we shall argue, have entered into the public imagination as a guide to and a metaphor for social relations in general.

While most of those interviewed sent or received remittances from children or parents abroad, they also sent or received remittances from siblings and other kin who played an equally important role in enabling the migrant and/or supporting dependants. If we look at the family as a centrifugal, rather than a centripetal form, some of the mechanisms that support and encourage migration and transnational families begin to emerge. Lloyd and Hyacinth, who feature in chapter 5, migrated to Britain along tried and tested lines, where the structures of support were, for the most part, provided by siblings and other kin peers. Lloyd, for instance, was "received" into Britain by his wife's cousin. Their brothers and sisters (and uncles and aunts) who had settled in North America retained emotional and material contact with their kin in Jamaica, along with other families and generations in migration, a perception which continues to echo. A Barbadian woman described it:

> We love each other a lot...although I love being with my family, there is a feeling I cannot explain, when I'm among my brothers and sisters...there's something that just, like, bonds you together, like you feel you don't want to part...I love my children, but I love my brothers and sisters so much. [7]

Siblings (and affines) are for the most part peers, and always part of a cohort that will embrace both kinship and friendship networks. Stories from family members migrating to Panama, Cuba, or North America recount joining siblings, cousins, uncles and aunts, much as the cohort who arrived in Britain in the 1950s and 1960s. On arrival the metaphor of this relationship embraced friends and former neighbors, replicating the neighborhood families of their childhood. The importance of kin as a powerful social metaphor is revealed over and over in the recollections of African-Caribbean childhood, and may be regarded as one of the principles that guide behavior in the villages and neighborhoods of the Caribbean which, in many cases, metamorphosed into the networks of migration and the models of settlement. Telling phrases such as living "like family" in the shared residencies that many experienced on arrival, friendships "like sisters," support "like brothers," indicate the importance of such roles in the early stages of migration, while the use of these metaphors suggests the vitality of family models, and in particular that of sibling relationships, in the shaping of networks. "We help each other out" was a common comment, we "trust." Networks were put to work to survive in a context of social and racial exclusion, integrating material help, social support and cultural identity. But they did so in a particular way, through the relationships of lateral kin and friendships and through a language of collectivity.

Indeed, a response to the experience of exclusion and disconnection that many West Indians experienced on first arriving in Britain was to pool individuality into a shared experience, a collective specialness, where the sense of individual, social, and cultural self could become reconnected,

> If you see a black face, well, you felt as though he was your brother...whether he was from Jamaica, or Trinidad, or Guyana, or whatever, you greeted him as a brother.[8]

This sense of solidarity helped resist the city with its indifferent and racialized gaze, which both picked out the individual and collectivized him or her,

> You worked with white guys and...on the trains...you would...exchange a cup of tea...but outside of that there was no socializing....And quite often these guys would...see you in the road outside of the working hours and would walk past as though you were not standing there...it is as if they couldn't allow their other white colleagues or white people to see them talking with a black person. It was not the done thing to be seen talking to a black person.[9]

It also reinforced itself every Saturday night at a dance or party, or every Sunday in church, and gradually evolved into, on the one hand, formal representations in the various island associations, or, on the other, into pan-Caribbean organizations such as West Indians disregarding their island differences and pooling their resources in the fight against racial exclusion.[10] It also became articulated in a program of conscious cultural revival.

> (We) formed (a) social club...to teach them our principles and our standards...we're going to form this group where we will call it a family club and we encourage the elderly, whatever age. If you have young children, you can bring them if you wish...we decided that we would have the principles that we grew up with in the West Indies.[11]

The networks and group cohesiveness transformed not only the fabric of life in England, but the imaginary framework of the migrants' being, reinforcing a sense of identity. These were not simply West Indians in exile; they had extended and reinscribed the space of the Caribbean so that the national boundaries extended within and beyond the region; "the frontiers," in Susan Craig's terms, became living rather than geographical.[12]

Now demographic change may have an impact on the role and position of siblings. This means first that the move from larger to smaller families means that individuals have fewer brothers and sisters, and the subsequent generation will have a smaller number of uncles, aunts and cousins. The kinship networks will in time become smaller, and this may have a bearing on how families perceive themselves. Many families, for instance, see their extensive and increasingly transnational family networks as providing an important part of their Caribbean cultural identity. Second, migration initially reduced the physical presence of siblings, although their role as providers may not necessarily have been diminished. For migrants, and in particular for their children, the day-to-day influence of brothers and sisters, uncles and aunts may not be as powerful a factor as it was for their parents' generation, although over time this is changing. Third, rural and urban neighborhoods in the West Indies survived and functioned according to a sibling model of the family, as adults assumed an avuncular and quasi-parenting role, and children, in turn, learn to defer to their "natural" authority. This idea of a neighborhood, modelled on the family emphasized trusteeship and respect, and became translated into survival strategies of migration (both for the migrants and those left behind) and continues to be transmitted to subsequent generations of migrant families.

Beryl's Family

Beryl (whom we met briefly in chapter 7) was born in 1935 in Mandeville, Jamaica, the first daughter but the fifth child of her mother's eight children. Her father was an "agriculturer,"farming rented land, her mother a "higgler." Beryl shared paternity with seven of her siblings. Her eldest brother, George, her mother's first son, was the child of a white man, distinguished from his (half) siblings by color. Nevertheless, he "grew up as part of the family." George migrated to the United States and from there "was responsible for paying for my education...in all ways, *he was my parent, really, in a sense*. And to this day, he is special. Very, very special to me... he shaped a lot of my thinking..."[13] The role George played was similar to that performed by her parents' siblings on both sides who had also migrated, to Panama, Cuba and the United States, "sending back" both money and clothes to help support those left behind. These remittances were an essential ingredient of the family economy. The pattern of sibling support in, and through, migration, and the importance of sibling networks for the migrant, has been an established feature of Caribbean migration. At the same time, through the return of remittances, migrant family members retained their claim to family, and in particular, sibling membership, for it was that relationship which held the promise of long term reciprocal support, particularly on return. In family chronology, siblings can expect to survive the parents.

The neighborhood in Mandeville was peppered with relatives who were in close and regular contact, and "would sort of make sure that we were looked out for,"[14] providing physical shelter, financial support and moral guidance. "My (childhood) was shaped by a lot of these people." But the classification of "sibling" itself became a powerful metaphor within the neighborhood, and governed the roles of parental peers—godparents, friends and neighbors—who became, in essence, fictive siblings. It governed, equally, the behavior and attitudes of children toward these adults.

Of the eight children, Beryl was the one, as she saw it, to be privileged. She was "cherished," "let off" family chores to pursue an education. This preferential status was confirmed and reinforced by her parents' peers in the community who, "nurtured me too and *wanted me to become a special young woman*. In other words, I was a role model and didn't even know it" (emphasis added).[15] Her father mortgaged the house to raise the money to send her to England to train as a nurse. It is not clear why Beryl was singled out within the family for preferential treatment. It may have been related to her position as the first daughter, or to an estimation within the family that she would benefit most from education, or to her relationship with her eldest brother whose color, and links with his white paternal family, privileged him in a society where class, race and color were broadly coterminous. The favoritism, however caused "resentment and anger" among her siblings who "did not have access to education like I did...my sister and myself are estranged almost totally. I see my (other) brother sometimes, but... we're not close."[16] This estrangement has repercussions for her own daughter, Laura.

For many West Indian migrants, coming to England meant that day-to-day contact with siblings in the Caribbean or elsewhere was reduced for themselves and, particularly, for their children, although many families continue to retain vibrant and supportive links with kin abroad. Beryl married a Trinidadian, one of thirteen children, most of whom migrated to North America. Laura and her brother had relatively little contact with their grandparents which, as Laura says "is really sad. I think it's one of the sad things about West Indian parents, or West Indians coming to Britain, because I've never really known my grandparents, not on a daily basis."[17] Laura also grew up distanced from regular contact with her father's siblings through geography, and from those of her mother's siblings in England as a result of "this family politics."

In marked contrast to her mother, whose "counsel" was provided by aunts and other significant female members of the neighborhood, and who was singled out as a role model, "to be a special young woman," there was no such "counsel" available for Laura, nor was she held up or expected to be a role model. As the eldest of only two children, sibling experience and support was limited. Equally, the family was isolated in the predominantly white neighborhood in which they lived, and from the daily influence of other family members and even family friends who may have provided additional or alternative guidance and models.

Laura describes her father as "Victorian" in his views on women, "I was a female and, you know, there's a whole thing about protecting your girl children and not wanting to get pregnant and the whole of that... my brother didn't have all that stress and aggravation....Inequality, yeah."[18] Laura became a nurse, like her mother but, unlike her mother, left after six years, went to Italy where she worked (as an au pair, and then an English teacher) for two years, and on her return, secured a place at university to study languages. She is married, to a man of mixed Guyanese/Jamaican parentage, and plans, in due course, to have her own family. Laura's trajectory, in England, was in many ways far more autonomous and self-defined than that of her mother from Jamaica, and the concept of family that she espoused far more numerically limited and nuclear. Her mother had been earmarked for upward social mobility. Laura had no such collective direction or confirmation in her life choices, and no favorite sibling to "cherish" her sense of self. Laura has become a born again Christian, and this has also been an influence in how she imagines and will institute family. She disapproves of her brother, who lives with his girlfriend and their child, and is critical also of her father who has an "outside" child in Trinidad, whose existence she did not discover until her teens.

Arianne's Family

Arianne was born in Trinidad in 1931, the eldest of five children who also had "quite a lot of half-sisters" originating in the first marriages of both her parents. Arianne's grandmother came from Venezuela, trading goods in Trinidad until eventually settling there. Arianne's father was born in Trinidad, of (African) Venezuelan parents although her family was ethnically diverse, "...pure, pure [Amer]Indian...we grow with them...on the father's side, we have Chinese...we have Assyrian...we're all kind of people in our family...oh, it was....colorful."[19]

Her mother, though born in Venezuela, was brought up in Trinidad (while *her* mother was travelling), by her elder siblings, in particular, "the eldest....[who] used to see after the smaller ones. So my mother stay here and she went to school here in Trinidad."[20] The parenting role of siblings in this family continued across the generations. Arianne grew up with her seven siblings, including two from her mother's first marriage, and a cousin "like sisters." Her father died when Arianne was fifteen and her mother when she was eighteen and her aunt, who was also her godmother, assumed the role of parent, looking after Arianne, her brothers and sisters, and by this time another nephew. The family was surrounded by aunts and uncles and, as with Beryl's experience, the metaphor of family extended throughout the neighborhood, from material support to control.

Moral and practical guidance in sexual matters was assumed to be the provenance of older women in the neighborhood: "I always have older people friend...my mother hadn't any course to tell us anything, but she used to tell us...everything. Everything....What to do, what not to do, what we mustn't do, what to expect..."[21] Arianne became pregnant when she was twenty and gave birth to her only child, Clarissa, in 1951. She did not marry Clarissa's father and although he supported Clarissa when he could, Arianne had to work to keep them both, moving from the country to a suburb of Port-of-Spain in order to do so. Arianne's siblings remained in Rio Claro. Although Arianne was not the oldest in the family (her half siblings preceded her) she was the eldest girl and was "always... responsible for everybody...everyone turned to her....If they had problems...anything at all, it's 'Auntie Ari would sort it out.'"[22]

As a child Clarissa spent her holidays with her grandparents who owned a cocoa plantation and her aunts and uncles where "all the children would be growing up together." Her grandfather played the quatro in a Parang (traditional music) band and "we would go round with him as well, to all the houses...he liked all his grandchildren."[23] Clarissa describes her father as a "lady's man." It was not until she was in her teens that Clarissa discovered that she had eight other brothers and sisters and "last year, I found I had another one."

Clarissa was her mother's only child although, in addition to her siblings through her father, Clarissa also had a number of stepsiblings, the children of the man with whom her mother eventually lived during Clarissa's adolescence. Prior to that, however, Arianne shared a household with another family in Lavantille, replicating here her "siblings" left behind. It was there that Clarissa spent her formative years as a singleton child.

> We grew up together...we were never alone. We were either with Aunty Iris, as I call her, or Mum was there, and Mum would have the two girls, or Auntie Iris would be looking after us...They're in America at the moment. They're all married with their families in America...[we are] like sisters... we had people like Aunt Iris and friends who had their own families and who were...sort of like sisters... they were that close... it was like having aunties, really... you felt as part of the family...I was always treated like one of the family...I really had a lot of influences from the families. And basically, you know, had a lot of family life.[24]

Arianne's "way of life" incorporated not only the creation of substitute families, but within that, replicated the role of elder sister, "...my mother...was always being called upon to do something for everyone, and so I've had loads of aunts and uncles, by virtue of being friends of hers...there have always been people around."[25] Clarissa came to England to train as a nurse, and had a child by a Barbadian "who turned out just like my father, really." She did not marry him and, like her mother, found herself having to work and bring up a child alone, removed (like her mother) from broader family networks. It may have been that earlier childhood experience, of co-parenting, that inspired her own choice of childrearing pattern. Clarissa re-created a communal home, first with her aunt, who she describes as a

> respectful aunt, not family aunt. She is someone I met when I first came over, one of my friends...because we're Trinidadians together, we all sort of cottoned on...so at the time when I got pregnant I stayed with her.[26]

And then with her daughter's child-minder, which was

> extremely convenient. I didn't have to go anywhere, to take [my daughter] anywhere, I just leave and go to work and come back. And that seemed to work out well enough...(She) *was, to be honest, like another mother.* She... really loved [my daughter]. [She] was the life and soul of her...she loved children.[27]

Such a pattern may be seen as a variant of child-shifting[28] although in the case of both Arianne and her mother, they remained present in the household. It may also be seen as an example of co-mothering, common in Latin America and now emerging as a recognized pattern in Latin American, and African-American communities in the United States.[29] Three generations had migrated, Arianne's mother from Venezuela, Arianne from the country to the city, and Clarissa from Trinidad to England and all adopted strategies that incorporated siblings—"blood" or "respectful"—in a co-parenting role. "I was" as Clarissa says "quite happy to bring (my daughter) up the way I was brought up."

Indira's Family

The final family is of Indian, rather than African origin and anticipates some of the discussion on Indo-Caribbean families and patterns of evolution developed in the next chapter. Indira was born in Trinidad in 1926. Her father was born on the boat that brought his parents from India to Trinidad at the turn of the century. As indentured laborers, the family lived in barracks until the indentures were expired and they moved out to farm their own land. Indira's grandfather, however, returned, suddenly and secretly, to India:

> I see my father crying...many times, when we were small, my father used to tell me. He used to cry and tell me, he say "My father gone back to India and leave me alone in Trinidad. And I have nobody, only three children I have."[30]

Her mother's parents were also East Indian, though born in Trinidad. Her parents' marriage, according to Hindu custom, was an arranged match. Her father indentured himself on a sugar estate and lived in plantation barracks until able to move out and build a house of their own.

Indira was one of three daughters, her mother the eldest of nine children. As adults, her mother's siblings and their families lived on, or close to, her parents' land in Monkey Town. Indira's mother and father worked as agricultural laborers. Her father, however, "did a little kind of hasty" (was quick tempered) and as a result was often out of work. On one of these occasions, he finally secured a job in Moruga, another part of Trinidad.

> My mother had she nice little house already...and my grandparents, everybody not too far, and all she brothers and everybody near...we know everybody. Well, when my father tell my mother he want to go there to live...my mother start to cry...she don't want to go...she own a little house and she don't want to go. My father say...she had to go...He sell the house...she don't want to come, so she crying...my father make mother pack up. They pack everything...my mother crying, crying...[31]

The family moved but after a while Indira's mother fell sick and, leaving her husband, returned with her children to Monkey Town to be close to her brothers and sisters. Her husband was forced eventually to follow her and it was there that Indira spent the rest of her childhood, recalling, as with Arianne and Beryl, the familiality of the village. In this case, the village had both East Indians and Africans.

> They used to live nice, the creole [African Caribbean] people in the village was nice people. We had good respects for them, because we used to call some of them 'grandmother', "grandfather," "grandpapa," "grandmama," the old people then, right?...so these aunts of we, and live like we're the same of it...if you go by them, they used to give you food to eat...they used to treat we good, the negro people where we lived nearby...we live well with them. And we still have some of ...those great-grandparents children still alive. We have of the boy living down the road here. He does call me 'Tanty' up to now. If he come up the road...if he come here, he does call me "Tanty," he said because he know his grandparents and my mother and them was friends, *so we live like family.*[32]

Indira lived close to her grandparents, sleeping there on many occasions, and close to her uncles in the village. When Indira was seventeen, her parents arranged her marriage. She was, however, married in a Christian Church, rather than according to Hindu rites. On marriage, following common patterns within this community, she and her husband went to live with his family, first with her mother-in-law, before they eventually built a house on land next to her and her husband's brother. Indira had six children. Although on marriage she moved away from her own family, she nevertheless remained very close to her two older sisters: "I respect my sister a lot, because they, my sister really love me the most....If I want anything, and I go and tell her, she give me. Any, any problem I have, I used to go to my sister...any little thing...I used to send and call she, and she always come."[33] One of this sister's children was sickly, and came to Indira,

> This child only sick, I know what to do. Well, you have so much children, four children, and your child, nothing do happen to them. "Take this child for me." So I say "Alright." So I pay she, and I take the child....Money, a little money now...she say 'Alright...this

child is your child from today." And he get better...I didn't bring him home. I say "Well, he is my child from today" but he stay with the mother, because she nurse him...she used to always tell him "I'm not your mother, your mother live in Lengua." Always, always used to say "Your mother live in Lengua." So he always say "Yes, who is my mother?"...And he come up big man, and he do still say "Who is my mother?" Yeh.[34]

Although Indira qualified the "buying" by saying that "me and she sister," she did in fact "buy" three more children, two of whom belonged to neighbors.[35] She explained it by arguing that if a child falls sick,

I say "This is my child from today" and I take it from you. And he get better...just for he get better is the reason why I do it. And they really get better. Look my neighbor, nobody would have a sick child, and I went and buy the child from the lady and the child get better...you have to consider the child. You does have to consider the child. This one over there is call me "Ma" up to now, does call me "Ma"...this one over here does call me "Ma," the little boy.[36]

The "one over there" was her nephew, Ajay, who migrated to England in 1972, joining two of his cousins who had arrived earlier. His birth mother, Indira's sister, worked first on the land and then in her own shop, employing relatives to look after her children while she did so. "Family. Cousins. Because some of my cousins had...very large families, nine, ten children. So I think it was a help for them, to send someone to stay with us."[37] The family was, according to Ajay, "very close," although the boundaries were clearly demarcated. His father was at times estranged from his younger brother for, as the eldest son,

you are the eldest son, you are the favourite and you are left in charge...my dad got, like me, got what was supposed to be the best. All the property and so...he (uncle) wasn't too please and there was always a bit of friction among them.[38]

Moreover, his father's "playboy" style resulted in two half sisters who Ajay did not meet until he became an adult, and whose existence was not condoned by his mother or her family. Nevertheless, Ajay, in England, tries to maintain the closeness with his mother's family "my two cousins will tell you, every Christmas I try to get them here, to try and re-enact what we used to have at home."

Although the neighborhood in many ways replicated an idea of the family, "Because we're so small a society... the neighbors, we forget some of them is not even our family and we grow up as family" it was not to neighbors, but to her sister that Ajay's mother turned in need, particularly when

He (Ajay's father) was violent. He used to beat her too. Many occasion he broke her arm...(then) she would go to her sisters, the first thing she'll do is go to her sister. I don't think she go to any neighbors or anything. She will go to her sister. When he hit her, she will leave home and go to her sisters. I remember, as children, about three occasions she pack her bags, and we trailing off to some aunt or somewhere. And then he will come back after a couple of weeks, and beg us to go back.[39]

The bond between Ajay and his aunt and her children is tight. Indira has come to England, staying with Ajay and his family, and Ajay remains in close contact with his cousins in England, and his siblings and other family in Trinidad, feeling strongly that his children must be made aware and proud of their heritage and parentage. He was, however, brought up as a privileged elder son, in a family in which the women were strongly protective of each other and of each other's children, where siblings played a vital role in providing support and sanctuary and where other collaterals offered closeness and companionship, a condition that Ajay attempts to replicate for his own children in England:

> I try to bring them up like home, to some extent. Not quite like home, but I make them aware of what I am from, and what I am, to know my culture, my background...the family closeness, I get my cousins, my nephews and nieces to come here, that they be together and close, more so than they do their parents...keep them close...to give them their cultural heritage.[40]

***

This chapter has described some of the features of the sibling relationship in West Indian family life. It has explored the role siblings have played in childhood, and the role uncles and aunts have played in childrearing. Smaller family size, and a generation not brought up in the close proximity of a "neighborhood family" may have an impact on the development and formation of those families in Britain, as the first case study suggests. On the other hand, although demographic change is clearly a powerful variable in family formation, family culture remains equally powerful in determining attitudes and behavior, as suggested by the final case study. Indeed, the continuities of family cultures, regardless of the material and social environment, suggest a remarkable resilience.

With the first generation of migrants to Britain, the role of kin and fictive kin was a powerful factor in determining migration and settlement, as suggested by the second case study, and fictive uncles and aunts were an important source of support in the early years of migration. They did not, however, emerge in a cultural vacuum but evolved as an organic extension of a common cultural experience.

Indeed, for many British-born Caribbeans, it was these fictive parental siblings who substituted for both "real" family and "neighborhood" family. One young woman recalled how, as a child, she pretended her close friends were cousins because she "liked the feeling that you had these people that were yours."[41] Fictive kin, particularly (but not exclusively) those who were involved in bringing up children, could forge very real bonds that could prove as enduring as those resulting from a consanguineal relationship. Thus loyalty and support, obligation and responsibility, override the logistics of living arrangements. These are values prided in and of themselves, and create a sense of solidarity; they also provide practical support, what may be described as a form of "cultural remittance": "if there is a support network that is needed, you can provide it with knowing who your family members are, so that not only you can provide help, but they can help you as well."[42]

Black led churches, regional solidarities, as organizations are vibrant features of West Indian communities,[43] and it may be that one explanation for their creation and survival, at least in the form in which they have emerged as offering particular fraternal support, may lie in the cultural roots in the Caribbean which saw the lateral family as a symbol and model for informal, fluid and non-exclusive social organization and support. It may be that the symbolic form of "family" is the feature that retains a resilience, transmits its influence, and shapes forms of social support across generations and cultures. Now, in later years, it could re-emerge as a source for care for the elderly, as Avis explained,

> Our people are not used to loneliness. Our people are very communal in mind, and communal in spirit...I'll tell you what I was working towards, but it hasn't come off yet. Hopefully it still will. I see myself as raising a large family and, to some degree, becoming a redundant mum...I felt that I'm not cooking for, say, six or eight anymore, so I feel that as our people get older, instead of sitting at home and eating on their own, if I'm more able bodied, let me cook for eight, and let them come and have the meal with me...I wouldn't be doing it for a profit...we would get together, sit and have a meal, talk about old times. Instead of feeling lonely, bored and depressed, the brain becomes more active...that's what I would love to see.[44]

Notes

1. Leonore Davidoff, Megan Doolittle, Janet Fink, Katherine Holden, *The Family Story. Blood, Contract and Intimacy 1830-1960*, (London/New York: Longman 1999), 79.
2. See, for instance, Linda Basch et al., *Nations Unbound*; Mary Chamberlain, *Caribbean Migration*. See also Ruth Glass *London's Newcomers* (Cambridge, Mass.: Harvard University Press, 1961).
3. This research on Caribbean families was one of the constituent research projects in this program.

4. Susan McRae, ed., *Changing Britain. Families and Households in the 1990s* (Oxford: Oxford University Press, 1999).
5. Davidoff et al. *The Family Story,* 70.
6. Leonore Davidoff, "Where the Stranger Begins: The Question of Siblings in Historical Analysis," in *World's Between: Historical Perspectives on Gender and Class* (Cambridge: Polity Press, 1995).
7. BF069/2/1/2/27.
8. BH118.
9. BI075.
10. Harry Goulbourne, *Ethnicity and Nationalism in Post-Imperial Britain* (Cambridge: Cambridge University Press, 1991).
11. BF069.
12. Susan Craig-James, "Intertwining roots" *Journal of Caribbean History,* 26:2, 216-228.
13. JI 028.
14. JI 028.
15. JI 028.
16. JI 028.
17. JI 063.
18. JI 063.
19. TM 098.
20. TM 098.
21. TM 098.
22. TM 055.
23. TM 055.
24. TM 055.
25. TM 055.
26. TM 055.
27. TM 055.
28. Gordon, "I go to 'Tanties.'"
29. Isa Maria Soto, "West Indian Child Fostering: Its Role in Migrant Exchanges" in *Caribbean Life in New York City;* Aminatta Forna, `The Girl with Three Mothers' *Independent on Sunday* 8 June, 1997.
30. TH 102.
31. TH 102.
32. TH 102.
33. TH 102.
34. TH 102.
35. The "buying" of children has been observed among the African and African-Caribbean community, and for the same reasons. It does not appear to have been common among the Indian-Caribbean community. As such, this may be seen as an example of creolization.
36. TH 102.
37. TH 051.
38. TH 051.
39. TH 051.
40. TH 051.
41. JL036/3/1/1/16.
42. (JF022).
43. See Harry Goulbourne "The Contribution of West Indian Groups to British Politics" in *Black Politics in Britain* ed. Harry Goulbourne (Aldershot: Avebury, 1990).
44. BF069/2/1/3/6.

Part 4

Comparison and Conclusion

9

Indo-Caribbean Families in Britain and the Caribbean

In Barbados and Jamaica, African-Caribbeans are in the overwhelming majority of the population. In Trinidad, on the other hand, the ethnic composition is markedly different. There, the largest ethnic group is the East Indians, who comprise 40.3 percent of the population, while the African-Caribbean population is 39.5 percent. (The mixed population stands at 18.4 percent, whites at 0.6 percent, Chinese and others 1.2 percent).[1] Although the focus of the book has been on African-Caribbean families, it is appropriate to sketch out some recent characteristics of Indo-Caribbean families, not least as a point of comparison. The central argument so far has been that explanation for the unique forms African-Caribbean families developed must be sought in the processes of cultural syncretism, as creative and innovative defenses against the inhuman and oppressive circumstances of slavery, rather than more contemporary reflections of economic circumstances and class positioning. The force of that culture of inventiveness and its continuing relevance in relation to family life can be seen not only in the retentions of living arrangements across the generations, within the Caribbean, but in the ways in which African-Caribbean families abroad continue to display characteristics most associated with those living arrangements in the Caribbean, and to draw from them a significant and active ingredient in their constructions of identity.

The ways in which Indian families have reconstituted themselves during, and since, Indian indentureship could be illuminating also. Like their African-Caribbean counterparts, Indo-Caribbeans endured poverty and low status. They were also subject to the inherently modernizing processes of the plantation regime, and to the social pressures that such discipline entailed by making redundant social forms that ceased to hold relevance, and demanding new ways of relating and socializing.² Likewise, they have migrated.³ To what extent did these social conditions influence family forms? To what extent, therefore, can we talk about "creolization" among the Indo-Caribbean community? (Bearing in mind, of course, that for many East Indians in the Caribbean, the term "Creole" refers historically and solely to African-Caribbeans).⁴ To what extent can we detect among Indo-Caribbean families evidence of Asian cultural retentions, albeit circumscribed by the particular exigencies in which they found themselves in the Caribbean and, later, abroad?⁵ Let us take Trinidad as an example.

***

Indians were brought to the Caribbean as indentured laborers to supplement what was perceived as a shortage of estate labor after the emancipation of the slaves and the ending of apprenticeship in 1838. The first Indians were introduced into British Guiana, but it was not until 1845 that they were brought into Trinidad and immigration to the island began on a systematic and consistent scale. Between then and 1917, 429,623 Indians came to the British Caribbean (many more went elsewhere in Asia and to the French and Dutch Caribbean), of which 143,939 arrived in Trinidad.⁶

For most of the nineteenth century, Indians were not considered by the colonial authorities to be anything other than transient, although the evidence suggested that throughout (and after) the period of importation, most Indians had chosen to settle in the Caribbean, rather than return to India, or re-migrate elsewhere.⁷ Yet, equally, throughout the period, the community was regularly replenished with new recruits from the Indian sub-continent, primarily, though not exclusively, from the North. Recruitment ceased relatively recently, in 1917. It is less than one hundred years since the last immigrants arrived in Trinidad, and for some of the older generation interviewed, India was an active memory. In addition, after the ending of indentureship, visitors and missionaries from India continued to travel to Trinidad, continuing the material and spiritual contact with the subcontinent. The Nationalist movement in India, and Indian Independence, increased the sense of cultural and political pride, a sense that has been given regular fillips since, through periods of conscious revivals of Indian culture.⁸ Ironically, identification with "Mother India," particularly in the 1930s and 1940s, represented a degree of disengagement with the growing movement toward nationalist identification in Trinidad, which was associated primarily with creole, that is, African-Caribbean politics.[9]

Living in Trinidad, but estranged from its national and political ambitions, East Indians existed in a liminal state of identifications and belongings, neither fully part of India, nor accepted (or wishing to be, in many cases) as part of Trinidad. Yet they were not immune from the circumstances in which they lived and worked. Those cultural values and processes they had brought with them from India were adapted, merged, eliminated, reclaimed or re-invented over time, as settlements metamorphosed into stable communities within a tight geographic area, and as they interacted with other cultural forces, values and practices. At the same time, as Kusha Haraksingh points out, the Indian community in Trinidad has been characterized, throughout its history by "periods of heightened concern...about traditions and culture." In all periods—and he points to several in the twentieth century, including the most recent in the 1980s—there have been present,

> the twin forces of replication and substitution, of seeking sustenance from the past while responding to the challenges of the present. Repeated exposure to these forces has produced a degree of versatility within the Indian community, traceable to the very origins of the Indian presence here when, for example, the enduring ties of *jahaji bhai* or brotherhood of the boat, transcending as it did ordinary divisions of caste and religion, indicated how prepared the community was to devise new approaches to suit new circumstances. These examples can be multiplied, like the *betis* dancing calypso music; the problem is to identify them as a strength, not a weakness, of the culture.[10]

As Thomas Erikson has argued, "Indians in a poly-ethnic society outside of India cannot adequately be viewed simply as Indians. They are Indians embedded in a particular historical and socio-cultural context."[11]

What was the impact of this on families? Despite the imposition of quotas determining the ratio of male and female immigrants, the demographic composition of the community was heavily imbalanced in favor of men. It was not until 1917 that families were encouraged to migrate to the West Indies, and not until 1946 that a normal sex distribution was secured.[12] The distorted sex ratio was, therefore, one of the first elements to factor into the development of Indian family forms (as it was with the slaves earlier). As a scarce resource, women should have been able to exploit their position and their status as wage earners to secure for themselves the most beneficial personal and domestic circumstances. Yet many women found themselves in a situation where they were exploited sexually, domestically and in their pay and working conditions.[13] The character of those who migrated, particularly the women, was, however, significant. As Rhodha Reddock [14] argues, the majority of women who came as indentured laborers in the nineteenth century came as independent women, not as the wives or daughters of male migrants. Once in the Caribbean, many remained as wage laborers, representing a continuing challenge to Indian gender hierarchies in the period. A shortage of Indian women in the Caribbean resulted in a substantial increase in the bride price and in some cases replacement of the dowry system. The antagonism between the former slaves —creoles—and the East Indian laborers, triggered largely by economic rivalry over scarce jobs, and by a mutual resistance, disapproval of religious rites and living patterns, and distrust, meant that very few interracial relationships, let alone marriages and families, developed. Reconstituting the Indian family could never, therefore, be straightforward, assuming that this family was itself a monolithic, unchanging and uncontested entity. Nevertheless, attempts were made to reconstruct domestic structures and hierarchies, in which men became the dominant partner, women the submissive wives, and the children dutiful, below him, and to reconstitute extended families in which the sons and their wives continued to live within the patriarchal household, and where the older woman was able to wield considerable power over her daughters-in-law. Undoubtedly many women colluded in this, for family life is a central human need, and many women, and men, may have sought comfort in familiar cultural and social domestic forms.[15] But that many clearly resisted is attested to by the levels of domestic violence (including murder) in the late nineteenth century[16] exacted on recalcitrant or unwilling wives on the one hand, and the reports from missionary and other authorities on the flagrant disregard of many women of their marriage vows, on the other. "The loose notions and prevailing practices in respect of marriage here are quite shocking to the newcomer," wrote Sarah Morton, the Canadian Presbyterian missionary, and the first (with her husband) to proselytize among the East Indian community, continuing,

> I said to an East Indian woman whom I knew to be a widow of a Brahman "You have no relations in Trinidad, I believe." "No Madame," she replied, only myself and two children; when the last (Immigrant) ship came in I took a papa. I will keep him so long

as he treats me well. If he does not treat me well, I shall send him off at once; that's the right way, is it not? This will be to some a new view on woman's rights.'[17]

Clearly such behavior offended Christian sensibilities as much as Indian, both Hindu and Moslem. In that sense, both groups shared an interest in establishing a patriarchal family in which the man was the breadwinner with his wife and children as dependants. Conditions on the ground, however, militated against this. Many women needed to work to supplement the family income, a condition that continued in the twentieth century (and still continues). Patterns of plantation housing in the nineteenth and early years of the twentieth century also militated against "traditional" extended families, while out migration, particularly of men, necessarily introduced high levels of female, and male, independence. In other words, many of the structural conditions present for African-Caribbeans were also present for Indo-Caribbeans.[18] Notwithstanding that, the move by East Indians away from plantation labor and into small-scale agriculture, a common transition for many laborers whose indentures had expired, resulted in the formation of villages where it was possible to reconstruct domestic arrangements following seemingly traditional Indian models.

The majority of indentured laborers were Hindu, although a sizeable minority were Moslem. Marriage under Moslem rites was not recognized in Trinidad until 1936, and 1946 for Hindu. By then, substantial numbers had also converted to Christianity largely as a result of the activities of the Canadian Presbyterian Church, which began its missionary work in Trinidad in 1862. None of these religious groupings can be assumed monolithic, incorporating devout and lapsed followers, as well as absorbing new movements, such as the Arya Samaj from India in the 1930s. While both Hindu and Moslem shared many social values, particularly relating to gender and the role and status of women, this may have been undermined by Christianity, which was perceived to accord women a measure of status and esteem (albeit heavily circumscribed by domestic and family duties), and actively sought to educate and convert them. Similarly, caste, which had been a vivid social marker in India, had to be realigned under the prevailing social, economic and demographic conditions in Trinidad, becoming in practical matters redundant. Despite retaining some symbolic significance, caste endogamy could not, on the whole, continue to be practiced, although status remained relevant in marriage alignments, as did ethnicity.[19] Indeed, to an extent caste endogamy has been replaced by religious and ethnic endogamy, with relatively few marriages taking place historically or contemporarily between the Hindu and Moslem East Indian community,[20] and between that community and other ethnic groups.

Nevertheless, Morton Klass's classic study *East Indians in Trinidad: A Study of Cultural Persistance*,[21] revealed that, forty-four years after the last indentured laborer arrived from India, there was still strong evidence of the persistence of many aspects of Indian culture and social organization. Extended families were the norm and kinship remained a vibrant force; marriages were arranged, although young couples were introduced before the ceremony. Education for girls was not considered necessary or desirable, and they were considered marriageable at fifteen years of age. On marriage, girls would be required to take up residence with their husbands' families under whose jurisdiction and authority they would remain.

As Patricia Mohammed has argued, however, Klass's work obscured some changes that had been taking place over time in both rural and, in particular, urban areas. Moreover, the introduction of widespread secondary education after independence in 1962, and the growth of a cash economy in the 1960s and 1970s, resulted in observable changes in East Indian families.[22] The rapidity of these changes was confirmed by Joseph Nevadomsky who, returning to "Amity," the village studied by Morton Klass in 1980, revealed that within twenty years nuclear, rather than extended, families were the norm. Girls, moreover, were widely educated and education improved their value as wives; young people chose their marriage partners themselves and if they moved to the husbands' family home, such a move was considered temporary.[23] On the face of it, it would appear that the changes in family life and formation had been the result of rapid modernization as rural families (and the majority of East Indians, even in the 1980s, were rural) were catapulted, by education, increased wealth and the rapid development of consumerism, into the twentieth century. How do these elements play out in practice? This chapter, like the earlier ones, uses case studies to illustrate the diversity of family forms, and the shifting practices around marriage and family formations. Like other case studies, the families here have been molded by migration to Britain. In many cases, the migration experience has brought into sharp profile issues of ethnic and cultural identity.

Vivien's Family

The first family may be seen as a microcosm of the evolution of an Indian-Caribbean family. Vivien was born in Trinidad in 1935, one of three children. Her parents, both born in Trinidad, were Moslem. Her paternal grandparents were born in Trinidad but her maternal grandfather was born in India, immigrating, it was thought, as a child. He returned to India twice to re-establish contact with his family but, as Vivien recalled, he "had no contact, because he had no roots, [no]where to go...so he couldn't get anywhere."[24] Her parent's marriage, in 1929, had been arranged by these grandparents.[25] Her mother was twenty-years-old and "said that she only saw him [husband] once before, that is for the engagement."[26] On marriage, she went to live with her in-laws,

> and then, after a time, they go and start having kids, then they get their own place...they go and live their own lives then...in those days the daughters-in-law are stay at home, and sort of cook and wash and do all the housework and so on, you know...until they are ready to leave.[27]

Her paternal grandmother had, however, married twice. Her first husband had died, and she remarried, to a widower, adopting his children as her own. Despite the proximity to this grandmother in the early years of marriage, it was her maternal grandparents and family with whom Vivien was closest. Her maternal grandfather owned a coffee and cocoa plantation, a shop, and land, giving each son a plot on which to build a house after marriage, and distributing the rest to his children in his will. Her maternal grandmother had ten children,

> In those days...they never used to have help in the house....They had all the daughters-in-law and what not, used to help them cook, because the daughters-in-law... when the sons get married, they used to stay home for a while, until they start picking up themselves...all round here had all my uncles.[28]

Vivien and her parents lived nearby, moving to be close to her grandparents in order to care for them. Although Vivien was not brought up in an extended household (and more particularly her parents moved back to be close to her maternal grandparents), she was brought up close to her uncles and their families, all of whom lived on land provided by, and close to, her grandfather.

The family considered themselves well off. Although they did not have electricity, there was running water in the house, a wireless (run off batteries), the children all had bicycles, and her grandfather had a car. Her mother, a "staunch" Muslim, made sure that the children were brought up in the faith, and Vivien's particular chore was to clean the local mosque every Friday before she went to school. In addition to this, Vivien and her sister were required to help their mother in the house. Their brother "never used to do anything, being, in those days, boys were...what I should say, God-gifted child. They don't hardly do anything."[29] When he was quite young, he went to live with his maternal grandparents whose other children, with the exception of the youngest son, had all left home. From there he went to school, and to college, working in the family store at weekends. At the same time, Vivien left secondary school—which she had just started—to care for her grandmother, although unlike her brother, she continued to sleep in her parents' home. She was twelve years old. In time, she began to work in the family store.

> I don't think they even ask me! Because I think it's automatically, I went in the store and started working. And I started working there until I decided, well, I had enough of store work. I just want to go away....So I worked there, started selling in the store, going buying shopping and so on...going San Fernando, buying jewellery and all this kind of thing for the store, you know....Remain there for a good few years until I left.[30]

In the meantime, she took a number of courses in commerce, typing, and sewing until, aged twenty, she decided to go to England, to join her brothers who had already gone there to study. She

> went with intention. I had liked nursing, right, because I had joined the Red Cross [in Trinidad]...and I decided...I'll see what it is like and go and do nursing....[my parents] were upset, really, because my brother had just left, and then I was going...and I said "Well, look, I'm just going to see what it is like, and we'll see how it goes." But then, eventually, it turned out to be 39 years![31]

In contrast to her mother, who had never worked before or after marriage, Vivien was intending to pursue a career. Her father, acknowledged as the strictest of her parents, nevertheless recognized that "time was changing...so he didn't sort of stop me, or anything like that."[32] On arrival, Vivien applied for admission to do nursing, and was accepted by a hospital in London's East End. Prior to that, however, and shortly after arriving in Britain, she had met her future husband, "Mr. Right!" He was the uncle of a friend of hers from Trinidad, one of a host of names she was given to contact on arrival. Once it was clear that they intended to marry,

> he told his parents and his parents came to see my parents, although we were in England, they came to see each other...his father came and said "Well, look, you have a daughter in England and my son is there, and I think they're going to get married..."

And so they met each other...they went to test each other out! ...But they're from a very good background too, he's their kind...and...they're well known to my grandfather.[33]

With their parents approval, Vivien and her husband were allowed to marry, a choice that marked a further shift from the practice of their parents. Furthermore, after her marriage, she continued to train as a nurse, living in the nurses' home when she was on duty, and commuting to her husband's flat at weekends. Clearly, as a young couple alone in England, there could be no question of sharing the household with her in-laws, as had been the experience of her mother and her aunts. Accommodation in London was, however, difficult to secure particularly after the birth of their first child. Their landlord would only let them have their child at home at weekends. They found a nanny to look after the baby during the week, but

> it was hard...and in those days...there wasn't register [of childminders]...when I had my days off I used to go and bring her home...it was hard, because I was studying and then you had to come and look after a baby....Eventually, I tell my husband.... "Look, we must go and get...a place...because it's not nice leaving your daughter away, your child."[34]

As a result, Vivien and her husband bought a small house, enlarging it as their family expanded. With the exception of a short break after the birth of their third daughter, Vivien worked as a nurse until she retired, when she and her husband (who worked as a postman) returned to Trinidad, to a house they built on land bought from an uncle in the United States, which he had inherited from her maternal grandfather. She now lives in the same street in which she was brought up, opposite the mosque she cleaned as a child, which she now attends. They live with, and take care of, her elderly father. In many ways, her life has come full circle and, according to her daughter Karole,

> she's becoming more Moslem. I mean, she's got involved with a Moslem group, she was trying to raise money for a new Mosque...she follows all the...religious holidays again...I think in the last ten years it came back to her. I think she has found her way.[35]

Vivien found it difficult to practice her faith when she first came to Britain. At the time, there was no mosque near to her in London, so she "used to go to any other church because, to me, I think it's one God, so I used to go to the other [Christian] church."[36] As a result, she chose to bring up her own children as Christian. Her husband, though brought up Muslim, had long ceased to practice ("he was as Moslem as a brick!"[37] was how his daughter described him).

Clearly, her experience of motherhood was very different from that of her mother. Not only did Vivien work outside the home throughout her married life, but she and her husband brought up their children in a small, nuclear family, unable to draw on help from their extended kinship networks in Trinidad. Compared with her own childhood, that of her three daughters was isolated, to the extent that her daughter, Karole, despite visits to Trinidad,

> always felt...because we lived here, they [maternal grandparents] didn't actually think of us as grandchildren. I mean, the rest of all their other grandchildren...live in the vicinity of them and everyone is around them...I always felt that...they thought that because we lived in England, we weren't actually part of that family, you know...I felt I was an outsider, I never felt like a real grandchild, you know.[38]

Her paternal grandparents she knew even less well. Her paternal grandfather died before she was born, her grandmother she met only once, as a five-year-old, and her memories of her are limited. Similarly, she does not know well any of her parents' siblings, with the exception of one aunt who lives in England, and who lived for a while with her family. This aunt they were close to,

> because my mum was quite narrow minded then...my aunt was that bit younger...she was very modern in her thoughts...and if you wanted to get anything, you used to ask her.[39]

Although her father's family were Moslem, and her uncles continued to live in the family home, her father she describes as "very Westernised...he used to sort of let us have a free life. He's very quiet. He never ever lost his temper with you. Very generous...I don't think anyone ever said a bad word about him."[40] Karole feels a similar warmth toward her mother and

> over the last ten years we have grown very close. Yes, very close. Far more close than I ever would have expected in my whole entire life, you know. So that now that she's gone, it's like losing my right arm, you know?...I said to someone the other day 'You really can have a broken heart. I've just got one now.' I miss her a lot.[41]

Karole is the middle of three sisters, with whom she was and is close. Her parents she described as "easy-going...they didn't make us do anything [around the house]. Washing up, we never did it."[42] In this, her father shared many of the domestic chores with her mother, particularly cooking. Although the neighborhood and the school in London was predominantly white, Karole did not experience racism. However,

> when we were... teenagers...you start going out with boys and things like that, my mum suddenly became an avid racist, but against blacks...you know, this was a no-no, it really was a no-no.[43]

Karole left school at seventeen, and worked in a shop,

> and I suppose you think, "Oh, great! I'm getting this money!" And that's all I was interested in, money, you know...and then...I moved out...a friend at work...she had a flat and we used to go out all the time, drinking and partying...staying out all night...My mother wasn't having it...One day she said to me "Why don't you just move out?" I thought, this is the life! So I moved out of home...in with my friend.[44]

She did not stay long in this flat, for she met a young man, gave up her job, and went to live with him in

> a non-existent life I would say now...we didn't have anywhere to live, right, so we were living...with his friends [who] were basically the same as him, so the houses weren't nice. I'd literally gone from one extreme of my life to the other. Really low...I mean, probably there is lower, being out on the streets...or being in a hostel. These were people's homes, but they weren't what I'd call a home...our life was spent sitting down watching TV, didn't have any money, so we couldn't really go out...doing nothing. And that was day in, day out, seven days a week.[45]

Her boyfriend was mixed race, his mother German, his father African-Jamaican. Her parents, and her mother in particular, was "extremely upset," Her parents tried to remove her from the situation, but "it didn't work. I was at a very rebellious stage. Then I got pregnant. So there was no going home."[46] After her son, Dillon, was born, they secured a council flat but after a year Karole decided she wanted to go to college.

> So, this is where Mum and Dad come in...they paid for me! Well, they paid for the first year, which was like a birthday present, which I thought was lovely. So they got me back into...humanity...and mum and dad looked after my son all week, they used to have him all week, and I had him at weekends. So we did that for two years.[47]

She continued to live with Dillon's father, and although her parents grew to accept the situation,

> they didn't really like him, because they knew what he was like, you know...it wasn't his colour...they just didn't like him...they knew he wasn't right for me. So when...I finally got rid of him, they were quite happy...they were always there for Dillon, and they've always been there for their children.[48]

As Karole argues, her mother has "mellowed," and Vivien admits that "eventually I change," and insists now that she and her husband are quite "broad minded" about it all. Karole subsequently met a South African Asian, a Hindu, by whom she has another son, and whom she is hoping to marry in a Hindu ceremony when his divorce is finalized. Being a single parent has not posed any problems for her "because it is acceptable now. I mean, single parents in England are one a penny, aren't they?"[49] Her new partner is both acceptable to her parents ("[Mum] is a very happy woman now!"[50]) and to Dillon, who remains close to Karole's parents, particularly her father. Although Karole's life is the most divergent of Vivien's children, the other daughters have also followed a unique trajectory. Vivien's eldest daughter, presently working in the Far East, has lived with a young Englishman for the last eight years. His parents are "anxious for them just to put the ring on her finger, but she says 'Wait!'"[51] Her youngest daughter is, perhaps, the most conventional. She married her partner of choice in the Church of England and is now expecting her first baby.

How are we to make sense of the substantial changes that this family has shown in three generations? For Vivien, the kin and social structures she experienced as a child in Trinidad were missing in Britain, and it was impossible to draw on family resources the way her parents clearly had. Necessarily, she brought her children up in a small, nuclear context, to the extent that they felt isolated and excluded from the wider family setting which, for Karole, was enabled by, and identified with, location. But in many ways, some of the changes in the Indian family patterns were in evidence before then. Vivien's parents had moved out from her paternal grandparent's house, to occupy a house on land owned by her maternal grandparents. Equally, her maternal grandfather chose to give his sons a houseplot, albeit on his land, to enable them to establish independent homes. Vivien's father had permitted her to travel to England, and raised no objections to her marrying the man of her choice. There were, therefore, already significant evidence of adaptation to changing circumstances. Yet while the practices and the structure of family life may have changed—and in this family perhaps beyond recognition—this does not mean that the values that the family endorsed have shifted. Although Vivien disapproved of Karole's behavior, they supported her and Dillon, taking an active part in Dillon's upbringing and taking joy in their grandchildren. Vivien and her husband have now returned to Trinidad, back to the village and kinfolk they left behind. Both Karole and Dillon consider themselves to be Trinidadian and the links with Trinidad will be rejuvenated. For Karole, however, the close links with the extended family are absent:

> As for my cousins...when I'm away from there I don't have any contact with them and they don't have any contact with me. So we're forgotten...I don't think they feel like they think of us as part of the family...because we live here...we never get thought of...we never

had forged a bond. There is a real bond between all of us [immediate family]…because we're so far from them…we've never felt part of them…or any part of the family…My mum used to say to my grandmother, "Is it because they're living here, that you forget them?" …It's sad. It shouldn't happen, but it does happen.[52]

And, in a similar vein, she believes that although Dillon knows the names of his uncles, aunts and cousins in Trinidad, his kin trajectory is "two aunts…their partners. And a brother. You know. And that is his family. Grandmother and grandfather."[53] It is a loss that they all feel.

George's Family

The second family represents a very different trajectory and social environment. George was born in Trinidad in 1941, the first of his mother's three children by his father. His paternal great-grandparents had migrated from India in the nineteenth century. This great-grandfather returned to India a wealthy man, after his indentureship had expired, but found that "life in Trinidad was better than India'"[54] and came back, but,

> when he returned to Trinidad, my great-grandmother was on her way back to India for a visit. Even in those days, they had a lot of money in gold, and I was told that she had so much jewellery on her arm, and around her waist, and on her body, that she suffocated with all the jewellery! She had so much, because in those days, Indian people wore bracelets all over, around her neck, and waist, and ankles and what not…No one knew what became of the jewellery…I suppose they threw her overboard.[55]

Their son, George's grandfather, had a dry goods shop but the business, and the marriage, failed. Shortly after, this grandfather suffered a stroke and George's father had to leave school early to care for him.

His maternal grandparents had migrated—but as an already married couple—from India in the twentieth century. Both sets of grandparents were Hindu. His paternal grandparents had, however, sent George's father to school, run by the Canadian Presybterian Missionaries. As a result,

> he grew up in the Presbyterian Church. Most, not all, but most people of Indian extraction were [persuaded] by the Presbyterian Canadian Mission to join the Christian faith, for various reasons, because of better jobs, better prospects etc. And when the Canadian Mission came to Trinidad…they purposely set up schools for Indians…calling them CMI schools, which is Canadian Mission Indian Schools, meaning you had to be an Indian to attend one of their schools, thus becoming a Presbyterian…the Canadian Mission saw a gap and came in and set up schools, educating people of Indian extraction, and thus converting them to Christianity.[56]

Although George's father had to leave after fourth standard, he maintained contact with the headmaster of his school, who remained an influential presence in his life. It was this man who

> actually got him married to my Mum, and they took the responsibility in godparent me. And they guided my dad, and they told him how to save, and how to look after his family because, being a Headmaster, in those days, was very significant in the community, and everyone looked up to a Headmaster...my dad had very, very close links with them, and thus I had close links with them.[57]

George's mother was, however, pregnant at the time of her marriage and George was born, in the headmaster's house, on the day of his parents' wedding. Two more children were born before his mother was accused of adultery, and his father given a divorce. George, then aged three, stayed with his father, and his two younger siblings stayed with their mother, who subsequently set up house with her lover, by whom she had five more children. Despite what must have been a charged emotional, domestic and, indeed, social situation, the two men conducted amicable relations, and although George never became close to his mother or his younger brother and sister, and did not know his half-siblings, he described his stepfather as a kind and caring man, and a gentleman. His mother had had no education, and even if she had converted to Christianity, she was not a practicing Christian, nor Hindu.

After the divorce, his father worked first on the cane fields, living in barrack accommodation, "you had your own kitchenette and one bedroom, which was your bedroom, sitting room living room, the lot...I remember that."[58] Tate and Lyle, who owned the plantation, subsequently demolished the barracks and provided the tenants with a house-spot on which to build a house. He then found better work as an engineer in the sugar factory. He never remarried, and brought George up alone, albeit in a community where

> the neighbors, the friends ...treated [you] as one of their children in the village...we used to exchange dishes...with the neighbors...we will give half of what we have, and they will give half of what they have...and looking after children, like myself, from a single parent, they were well-cared for by the community, and no abuse, as far as I know. Discipline was there, but there was no abuse. And that, I have a lot of regard for.[59]

The headmaster, who had played such an influential role in his father's life, also took George under his wing. He guided his education and George boarded with him during school terms. George, therefore, continued to be brought up and educated by the Presbyterians. At eighteen, however, he decided to migrate to England, enrolling—as intended—to complete his City and Guilds certificate but leaving the course when he failed to find work experience, largely as a result of the "closed shop" union policy. Although he was never able to secure work in this field, he continued to educate himself, and before he took early retirement, held a senior position in local government.

England proved a shock. Accommodation was inadequate and hard to secure; washing and cooking facilities were minimal; England, he thought, was unprepared for foreigners and, moreover,

> having come from the West Indies where discipline and morals are very high, to see people kissing each other at the train station, and on the train and on the platform, and hanging out the carriages and kissing...to see the same thing in the park and on the streets and so on, it was quite an experience.[60]

Although his inclination was to leave, he was persuaded to stay. After a few months, his father joined him "he wrote me a distinctly pathetic letter that he was on his own, he was lonely and whatnot..."[61] His father recently died in England, and neither George nor his wife harbor any desire to return to Trinidad.

He first met his wife, a nurse, in Trinidad. They married in England, in the Canadian Church in London, and although they brought up their two daughters as Christian, George now considers himself an atheist.

> You have what I call "The Guinness Syndrome," that you have a few whites, and they're always at the top...no matter how you turn the glass of Guinness, you always find the white at the top...the black is always at the bottom...that's why I said "What sort of a God is there? If there is a God, He must be a white man." White people are doing more wrong than black people...and they seem to be prospering. What is wrong with us Black people? We believe in the same God. And then when the South Africa thing was on ...you go into the same church, a white man preaching to you, but you're in two separate sections, black on one side, white on one side. How could you be worshipping the same God? So where is this God, you know? What sort of a God is He? Well, how can you tell me that you must believe in God, and become a Christian...and in the same church you tell me I can't sit with you?[62]

His wife stayed at home to care for the children when they were small, returning to work when the youngest was seven. His father also helped share the childcare. George admits that, until they were eighteen, he did not give them much freedom, emphasizing their education as a priority above boyfriends. Even now, he still tries to guide them. His youngest daughter lives with a musician, his eldest daughter, an engineer, now lives with them at home. As children, he made sure that they had contact with their family in Trinidad, that they visited for holidays, that they know about the Caribbean, and that they know about their Indian origin. As a result,

> they know who they are and what they are...the younger one...has even told Indian people from India, and Kenya, and so on, who try to say that she's Asian or Indian, she says, "Yes, I'm of Indian origin, but I'm from the West Indies. My parents are from the West Indies," she made that quite plain, not from India, or anywhere else, but from the West Indies."[63]

Indeed, for George, although he has no plans to return to Trinidad, he still argues that,

> in this [British] society, first and foremost, I'm a Trinidadian. Secondly, a West Indian and black West Indian. *Thirdly, I'm Indian*.[64] (emphasis added)

His eldest daughter, Cilla, takes, however a very different perspective. Her narrative is haunted by India, and her childhood recounted through an Asian filter. Her father, whom she "idolises" was, nevertheless,

> strict, in the traditional sense of the word, or probably in a very, very Asian sense of the word that, you know, girls don't go out late, and are encouraged to study, and not think about boyfriends, and not go out and get yourself pregnant...we know what to do, and what not to do, or what will get approval and what wouldn't. And what doesn't get approval and we want to do it, we'll do it, but we tend to try and do it discreetly![65]

Her mother, she argues, is less strict but "can turn on the emotional blackmail...which I think Asian parents are willing to do."[66] But both parents—and their families are, she insists, "very, very Asian. They still listen to the music, hold the traditions, and you're expected to fit in...it hasn't been lost, coming to England. If anything, it's probably reinforced, more so."[67]

In contrast to her father, who insists that he is a Trinidadian first, Cilla finds little to endorse in Trinidad or the Caribbean. "I can't identify with the life there, I just don't see it as being progressive" she argues,

> I probably sound very...bigoted, but I see Trinidad, basically, as a stopover place, where the Africans came, because they were slaves, and the Asians came, because they were indented [sic] labor, and were basically stuck there...I don't see Trinidad like how a lot of people see it here, as being a race. I see it, maybe, as a nationality, or a place, but I really think we should look further back into their own roots, and learn more about it, and be proud about it...Asian culture has so much history and value, and so many things to be proud of...I think a lot of the Asian West Indian kids that I know feel actually ashamed of their identity and they try and emulate being black.[68]

She places her sister in this category, "she's going through the phase where she finds it very difficult to identify, or admit, that she's

Asian, or Indian or Persian origin. That she's very un-West Indian, and she'll put on this silly Jamaican accent, you know."[69] She is similarly scathing toward a cousin who has become "a pseudo-black person. A typical Asian child that thinks he's black."[70] This cousin

> doesn't like...if somebody calls him "Paki" or Indian, he gets really up-tight about it. He says, "Oh no I'm not. I'm from Trinidad," you know? *So there's still that kind of not accepting where your real racial identity comes from.*[71] (emphasis added)

Cilla is convinced that her own Indian origins are not straightforward. Her mother, she believes ("although she'll disagree with me" can find her origins

> as Parsee, or Persian, because...looking at her features, and looking at the other East Indian people from Trinidad, her features are very different...I always see Mum as being Persian...On my Dad's side, Northern Indians, and that's quite easy, probably, to trace back and to know about the culture and the clothes and the food. On Mum's side, it's not so straight cut because herself, and her side, they don't fully know.[72]

But Cilla is also proud of her grandmothers. Her maternal grandmother, a Hindu, "was probably more modern than ...my own mother,"[73] in that she defied her parents and eloped to marry Cilla's grandfather, a divorced man with three children. Widowed young, and illiterate, she supported her family selling dry goods and eventually running a rum shop. Her paternal grandmother she also considered "strong" since she, too, had to support her children after being widowed, and she, too, chose her partner, risking ostracism in the process.

Although Cilla did not know her maternal grandfather, he was a "typical Asian...strict male...I knew his father actually came from North India, or Persia, came to Trinidad...I know he was tall, he was fair haired and dark eyed, and just very, very strict."[74] Cilla had a very special bond, however, with her paternal grandfather, who lived close to them in England. As a child, Cilla visited Trinidad regularly, getting to know the wider family of uncles, aunts and cousins on both sides. Unlike Karole, she feels fully integrated with her family in Trinidad, and makes a point of maintaining contact, "I suppose, in a sense, retaining the ties."[75] Not surprisingly, given her father's estrangement from his siblings, she is closer to her mother's family than her father's. But family gatherings, in Trinidad and Britain, are common and "what seems to happen, quite naturally, is the men will end up staying in here, and the women will end up being in the kitchen."[76] Although under other circumstances this division is not something Cilla endorses, in this context she suggests that she has "accepted the duties that go with being an eldest daughter and being part of Asian culture."[77]

George did not mention it, but Cilla converted to Islam in her late teens. She met and married, against her parents' wishes, a Palestinian. She insists that he was not influential in her decision to convert to Islam "although my parents think so." The marriage did not last, but Islam, is "something I've retained...if it was done purely for him, I would have given it up a long time ago."[78] Cilla is now considering marrying for a second time, to another Palestinian, a "big decision,"

> The language isn't a problem. I speak Arabic fluently enough to be understood...[and] I actually find myself identifying with the Arab culture, or I'd say in inverted commas the "Asian culture," taking Arabia as part of the Asian continent, a lot more than the culture from the Caribbean or here.[79]

She argues that she can "relate to somebody who's probably from India...probably more clearer to some of the West Indian[s],"[80] and she guesses that she would

> probably feel more comfortable living in a Middle-Eastern country or an Asian country...I haven't live there, but it's more the way you feel at home, where you feel that you belong, or where you feel that life will be easier for you. Certainly you don't feel that here. I have never done really. It's always been searching for something...Trinidad doesn't come into my life at all. I mean, okay, my aunts and uncles are there and...if I had children, [they] would know about that, but...it's not somewhere that I identify with, or that I particularly miss.[81]

As further endorsement, Cilla can see her father "going back to India," for she feels "that he identifies with India much more than Trinidad, and I feel that he would be happier and that he would actually integrate."[82]

Despite Cilla's conversion to Islam, her wearing of the *hejab*, her experience of prejudice against Moslems, and her espousal of an Indian, or Asian, identity, there is little in this family that particularly marks it out as anything other than Caribbean. Neither of her grandmothers, whom one would have thought of as the most rooted in Indian practices, behaved according to expected norms. One eloped, the other was pregnant prior to marriage, and then committed adultery. Cilla's mother, and Cilla herself, are highly qualified professional women. The female line reveals levels of independence attuned as much to creole as to contemporary Asian behavior. Despite Cilla's denigration of Trinidad, she retains links with the wider family there, as does George. Indeed, he now helps support his mother by sending over remittances. More particularly, Cilla's insistence on not only the Asian heritage of her family, but its culture, and her own quest toward an Asian identity and lifestyle, accord with comparable political and cultural moves to reclaim India in the contemporary Caribbean, and to re-establish the importance of those roots, of which Hindu fundamentalism, and the politics of gender and ethnic identity, may be considered to be recent manifestations.[83]

Rani's Family

Rani was born in Trinidad in 1915, one of three children of an Indian-born indentured servant, and a Scottish estate manager. Her mother, as Tracey, the granddaughter explained, "was a concubine of the Scottish plantation master....There was no formal marriage there."[84] This man, according to family lore, drunk his inheritance, "maintained a very selfish existence," and made Rani's mother "the donkey in the relationship."[85] Sexual exploitation of female indentured servants was common and—like slave women before them—they had little redress, even though sexual abuse was one of the concerns of the Protector for Immigrants. Although her mother was Hindu, her father sent the three children to the Presbyterian Mission School, and it was there that Rani was educated, converted and taught the Lord's Prayer in Hindi—a memory that structured and bounded her recollections. She married a young Trinidadian-born Indian who had also been converted to Christianity, and educated by the Presbyterian missionaries. The marriage was not arranged according to Hindu custom, but, as her son explained, "we were in a transition stage from an Asian culture to a Western culture."[86] As a result, although the choice to marry was made by the couple, "the Asian culture didn't permit that sort of courtship society at the time."[87] According to her granddaughter, Tracey,

> my great grandmother was pleased to get her married off because they were always sort of illegitimate children, really...and here was this very upstanding religious person in the community, my grandfather, so she was obviously quite pleased to get her married to him.[88]

Her husband worked for the government, but also farmed a little in his spare time, sufficient to provide most of the food his family needed. Although he was strict with his children, Rani was stricter "she would consider stepping out of line in the slightest as a great transgression...but...Dad would say 'They're kids, what do you expect?'...and if you did step out of line more than was acceptable, then he may have a talking to you. But in those days, just a type of glance was a form of discipline."[89] Indeed, as Tracey observed, while Rani would give you the impression that whatever the man says, goes, in terms of the grandfather she was, in practice, a "very strong, sort of matriarchal figure...she had quite a stronghold."[90] Her son, Brin was, however, more measured in his assessment of his mother and her influence. She was, according to him, "very dutiful...she made sure that, within the resources, everything was in place for a meal, and clothes were sorted out...she always deferred to my Dad's decision [but] if she didn't agree with a particular thing, they would argue."[91]

Rani and her husband had six children and, as her son Brin points out, educating the children was their first priority. Money for this was, however, scarce but was democratically apportioned.

> When my brother was at college and I was at college, my sister, being the only daughter...was enlisted at a convent school...after I'd been to college for about a year, the fees went up...and we had a family discussion. Somebody had to discontinue, because there wasn't enough funds to pay. And I said, "well, my older brother should discontinue, because he's had two years benefit," because my dad said that my sister discontinuing was not negotiable, so she was out of the fray...but then the discussion turned on the fact that so much had been invested in him already, as the investment angle.[92]

In the event the older brother was allowed to stay on at college, and Brin was apprenticed to a tailor. After two years, his brother won a scholarship to study in Canada and Brin was able to return to his studies. In time, his sister migrated to Britain to study as a nutrionist. Another brother followed her to Britain shortly after to study engineering, another remained in Trinidad to study agriculture, and the youngest brother similarly remained in Trinidad and he and his family continue to live with his parents in the family home. Although the family are dispersed, they share the cost of caring for their now elderly parents. The wider family of uncles, aunts and cousins is similarly dispersed around North America and the Caribbean, where they are all "doing well," but even as children many did not live close by in the neighborhood but what Brin described as "an independent existence, scattered around."[93] As a result, although family news is passed around, the family lacks a closeness.

Brin left school with a higher school certificate, which qualified him to teach. As a Presbyterian and a graduate of their own education system, he had no difficulty securing a job. He wanted to study law, and had a place at Dalhousie University. But as the second son, the family could not afford it, and when the Bahamian authorities were recruiting police, on what appeared to be substantial salaries, Brin applied for a place, and was accepted. He arrived there and "if there was a Heaven and a Paradise, at the same time, the Bahamas was the stop before Heaven."[94] The police force was not, however, to his liking. He worked out his three-year contract and decided to leave. By then, however, he had married and was starting a family. "My...desire to do law was drifting further and further away from me."[95] They decided to stay in the Bahamas, and Brin found work first in the nascent tourist industry, and then with an American company, before deciding in 1970 to leave the Bahamas and come to England. His children were still quite young but

> we were conditioned to thinking that when you're talking about education, Britain offers the best...as far as we were concerned, there were only two universities in England, Oxford and Cambridge.[96]

Brin found work with the civil service, and bought a house so that, three years after his arrival in Britain, he was able to bring his wife and children over when the latter were aged eleven and thirteen. Once reunited with them, he gave up work to study full time for a law degree, and after graduation secured work as a senior race relations officer. Brin plans to retire within the year but has no intention of returning to Trinidad or the Caribbean, although he identifies himself "as a Caribbean person, plain and simple."

Brin's son and daughter attended secondary school in Britain. Both went on to university, graduating with Masters degrees. His daughter, Tracey, is a civil servant. She describes her father as "the life and soul of the party," committed to family life but in a "traditional male role of parenting...making sure there was food on the table...a great provider. But in terms of reading bedtime stories and...changing nappies, that wasn't his scene."[97] Her mother, by contrast, was the nurturing parent. Tracey's maternal grandparents were Hindu, although Tracey's mother became a Roman Catholic, before re-converting to Presbyterianism when she married Tracey's father. As Tracey points out, both her parents were brought up strictly "the Indian way." Their marriage was not arranged, but both families became involved once it was clear that the courtship was serious, and marriage would result. In other ways, Tracey feels, her parents were traditional. "We had no touch at all in our family...I suppose that was part of the tradition....There are boundaries and that was very clearly adhered to."[98]

And yet, in other ways, she feels her parents were both progressive and supportive, encouraging education and a career. Her mother always worked as an administrator, paying for childcare for Tracey until she went to school, sending her brother to Trinidad to his grandparents until he was five years old. Both in the Bahamas and in Britain, the family was "nuclear—mum, dad, brother and sister." Neither family, as we have seen, was close and both were dispersed around the globe. Visits home, for Tracey as a child, were few, and unlike her brother who spent his early years in Trinidad, she felt alienated and isolated there. Her maternal grandmother, for instance,

> was a strict disciplinarian, and she used to beat us a lot, because we wouldn't eat the food and dhal and rice and so forth...so I never have sort of pleasant memories...because I was brought up in the Bahamas I don't feel a kindred spirit to her, and to Trinidad...we never had any bonding as such...and there were other things...her home...was more rural, and they had outside toilets, the latrines, and I couldn't cope with that. And I couldn't cope with the chickens and all the rest...what I now come to respect in the ways and traditions brought over from India.[99]

Her paternal grandmother, Tracey recalls, was strict not only in her religious beliefs, but despite—or perhaps because of—her mixed race parentage was "very strict about Indians should remain as Indians, didn't like the thought of mixing, even with friends of different races."[100] Her paternal grandfather, she recalled, was "quietly strong, quietly assertive," a respected member of the local community. It is to her father's family that she feels most connected, although her uncles and cousins are dispersed in Canada, the United States and Trinidad. Her relationship with her own brother was strained in the early years through separation in Trinidad, and although the subsequent years have improved it, they are still quite distant. This distance has now been aggravated by his disapproval of her lifestyle. She is not married, but lives with her partner and "maybe in terms of culture, I don't know how he feels about the person not being of Asian origin."[101]

Her choice of partner, of African-Caribbean heritage, has also caused problems with her parents. Despite her father's professional position as a race relations adviser, and his insistence that race would make no difference in their choice of partner, Tracey insists that

> they're not at all happy about it. And they will tell you something different...but it's absolutely not true. They are entirely unhappy with it. They do not believe in the mixing of the races, or a particular race. They have no problems if the person was white...I believe that Caribbean Asians, the Indo-Caribbean people, have an even more racist view, for want of a better word, of black people, than probably Asians.[102]

As a result, Tracey has become close to her aunt, her father's sister, who lives in the United States, but who was ostracized by the family when she married an African American.

Despite her criticisms of what she considers her parents' racism and, by extension, that of the Indo-Caribbean community, she is proud of her heritage. "I see myself as a Caribbean Asian person ...I have a British passport, and have a British accent and ...I live here and I don't see myself living anywhere else....But...if someone said to me 'Are you British?' I would say, 'No, I'm Caribbean. Caribbean Asian."[103] It is a heritage in which the Caribbean is as important as the Indian.

> My father uses a phrase, which seems quite derogatory to some extent, but there are elements that I agree with, which is he "blesses the day that our forefathers left the shores of India"...lthough they were indentured labor...we've come to a different part of the world, where there's lots of sort of multi-cultural, lots of different influences, and we may not have had that if we were still in India...we've had more opportunities available to us...as Indo-Caribbeans...we fit into all sorts of pockets...we still have some of the Asian traditions...equally...Caribbean ...and all the traditions there. We understand some of the British way of thinking because...we've been colonised...we have a mixture of a lot of things that can enhance us...that's an advantage.[104]

***

The three families represented here all display evidence of adaptation, both to life within Trinidad and the Caribbean, and beyond. They also represent the uneven origins of family formation, with the transgressive behavior of one grandmother, and the sexual exploitation of another. Unlike many African-Caribbean families, the kinship networks do not appear as multilateral, nor are the families so characterized by the rhetoric of closeness, or so shaped by histories of emigration from Trinidad. In all three families, the religion of origin has been abandoned and faith has ceased to be one of the family bonds.[105] Yet all three retain links with the Caribbean, and, with the exception of Cilla, espouse a strong Indo-Caribbean identity in which the Asian heritage is asserted as an equal partner.

Despite the adaptations, there are clearly some elements of this heritage that are reflected in family patterns. For instance, as Godfrey St. Bernard[106] shows, East Indians show a stronger propensity than their African-Caribbean counterparts for marriage as a first union, (although numbers of common law unions are increasing) and lower proportions of female headed households. In Trinidad and Tobago, for instance, the 1991 census showed that 28.1 percent of households were female-headed. (By contrast, in Barbados, with a majority African-Caribbean population, 48.3 percent of households were female-headed.) At the same time, as our case studies show, many of the traditional forms of family formation and living—arranged marriages, extended households—were no longer accepted or relevant to the young generation, and certainly not in the Caribbean-Asian community in Britain. To this extent, Indo-Caribbean families have changed significantly within a relatively short space of time, from what may be identified as "traditional" forms into forms approaching modern, European models. Distinguishing to what extent this is the result of modernization, or creolization, as Patricia Mohammed argues,[107] is almost impossible, for the modernising impulses that have transformed Trinidad in the years since Independence have contributed to the continuing movements of creolization, as new values and behaviors are formed, articulated and shared, including a shared commitment to Trinidad as a nation state, and a shared participation in its political governance. And, as Mohammed, Erikson and others point out, there is nothing in creolization that precludes affirmation of ethnic and cultural identities. "Being creolised does not… imply losing one's Indianness; to think so would be an essentialist error."[108] While family forms have metamorphosed, in some cases beyond recognition from their Indian progenitors, and as other elements of Indian culture appear to be disappearing or fast transforming, this does not imply, as Erikson argues, "that Indianness disappears as a form of social identity…but that its content changes." Indo-Caribbeans are as committed to families as those of their African-Caribbean counterparts. As with African-Caribbeans, versatility and adaptation appears to be the name of the game: retaining those elements of family forms that maintain a cultural and practical relevance while employing a flexibility best adapted to the exigencies of historic, and contemporary, Caribbean life, and using those to retain and affirm a sense of belonging and self.

Notes

1. In Guyana, East Indians comprise 51 percent of the population, African-Caribbeans 29-36 percent. (The mixed population is between 7-13 percent, Amerindian 4.7 percent, Chinese 1 percent) www.library.uu.nl/wesp/populstat/Americas/guyanag.htm (accessed 9 July 2004).
2. For a discussion of the modernizing pressures of plantation societies see Sidney Mintz, "Enduring Substances, Trying Theories: the Caribbean Region as Oikoumenê," *Journal of the Royal Anthropological Institute* 2:2 (June 1996), 295, as cited in David Scott, "Modernity that Predated the Modern: Sidney Mintz's Caribbean, "*History Workshop* 58 (Autumn 2004), 196-215.
3. Verene Shepherd, "Indians, Jamaica and the Emergence of a Modern Migration

Culture" in Chamberlain ed. *Caribbean Migration.* See also Look Lai, *Indentured Labor;* Laurence, *A Question of Labor.* Watton Look Lai, *Indentured Labor, Caribbean Sugar, Chinese and Indian Migrants to the British West Indies 1838-1918* (Baltimore : Johns Hopkins University Press, 1993); K. O. Laurence, *A Question of Labour: Indentured Immigration into Trinidad and British Guiana 1875-1917* (Kingston: Ian Randle Publishers, 1994).

4. Patricia Mohammed "The 'Creolization' of Indian Women In Trinidad" in *Questioning Creole. Creolization Discourses in Caribbean Culture,* eds. Verene Shepherd and Glen L. Richards (Kingston: Ian Randle, 2002). See also notions of "Douglarisation" (a Douglar is a person of mixed African and Indian descent) in Thomas Hylland Erikson "Indians in New Worlds: Mauritius and Trinidad," *Social and Economic Studies* 1 (1992), www.caribvoice.org/Caribbean Documents/Indians. html (16 July 2004); Percy Hintzen, "Race and Creole Identity in the Caribbean'"in Shepherd and Richards *Questioning Creole,* 92-110, esp. 101.

5. Christine Barrow, *Family in the Caribbean.*

6. Walton Look Lai, *Indentured Labor;* Keith Laurence, *A Question of Labor.*

7. Walton Look Lai, *Indentured Labor;* K.O. Laurence, *A Question of labor.* Verene Shepherd *Transients to Settlers. The Experience of Indians in Jamaica 1845-1950* (Leeds: Peepal Tree Books/Coventry, Centre for Research in Asian Migration, University of Warwick, 1994).

8. Steven Vertovec, "Religion and Ethnic Ideology: The Hindu Youth Movement in Trinidad," *Ethnic and Racial Studies,* 13:2 (1990), 225-249; Patricia Mohammed "Ram and Sita: The Reconstitution of Gender Identities among Indians in Trinidad through Mythology" in *Caribbean Portraits.* Christine Barrow ed. *Caribbean Portraits: Essays on Gender Ideologies and Identities* (Kingston: Ian Randle Publishers 1998).

9. Selwyn Ryan, *Race and Nationalism in Trinidad and Tobago* (Kingston: University of the West Indies, Institute of Social and Economic Research, 1974).

10. Kusha R. Haraksingh, "Structure, Process and Indian Culture in Trinidad" in H. Johnson, *After the Crossing, Immigrants and Minorities in Caribbean Creole Society* (London: Frank Cass, 1988),12,; See also Arthur Niehoff, "The Survival of Hindu Institutions in an Alien Environment" *The Eastern Anthropologist,* 12:3 (1959): 171-187.

11. Erikson, "Indians in New Worlds."

12. Patricia Mohammed "Writing Gender into History. The Negotiation of Gender Relations among Indian Men and Women on Post-indenture Trinidad Society 1917-1947" in *Engendering History. Caribbean Women in Historical Perspective'* eds. Verene Shepherd, Bridget Brereton, Barbara Bailey (Kingston: Ian Randle Publishers, 1995).

13. Verene Shepherd, *Maharani's Misery. Narratives of a Passage from India to the Caribbean* (Kingston: University of the West Indies Press, 2002).

14. Rodha Reddock "Indian Women and Indentureship in Trinidad and Tobago 1845-1917" in *Caribbean Freedom. Economy and Society from Emancipation to the Present,* eds. Hilary Beckles and Verene Shepherd (Kingston: Ian Randle Publishers, 1993).

15. Patricia Mohammed, "The 'Creolization' of Indian Women."

16. David Trotman, "Women and Crime in Late Nineteenth Century Trinidad," *Caribbean Quarterly,* 30:3 & 4 (1984):60-72; Bridget Brereton, *Race Relations in Colonial Trinidad, 1870-1990* (Cambridge: Cambridge University Press, 1979).

17. Sarah E. Morton *John Morton of Trinidad,* (Toronto: Westminster Ca, 1916) 342, quoted in Reddock, "Indian Women and Indentureship," 237.

18. Chandra Jayawardena "Family Organisation in Plantations in British Guiana"

International Journal of Comparative Sociology 3 (1962), 43-64; M. Agrosino, "Sexual Politics in the East Indian Family in Trinidad," *Caribbean Studies*, 16:1 (1976): 44-46.
19. Niehoff, "The Survival of Hindu Institutions;" J. Nevadomsky, "Changes in Hindu Institutions in an Alien Environment," *The Eastern Anthropologist*, 3:1 (1980), 39-53.
20. Although more marriages do take place between Hindus and Christians
21. Morton Klass, *East Indians in Trinidad: A Study of Cultural Persistence* (New York: Columbia University Press, 1961).
22. Patricia Mohammed "'The 'Creolization' of East Indian Women.'"
23. Joseph Nevadomsky "Abandoning the Retentionist Model: Family and Marriage Change Among the East Indians in Rural Trinidad"*International Journal of Sociology of the Family* 10 (1980), 181-198.
24. TR097/1/2/7.
25. Arranged marriages were common practice in both Hindu and Moslem families and, indeed, in some Christian families. The ways in which some cultural practices superseded religious differences is discussed in Mohammed, Patricia, "From Myth to Symbolism: The Definitions of Indian Femininity and Masculinity in Post-Indentureship Trinidad" in *Matikor. The Politics of Identity for Indo-Caribbean Women,* ed. Rosanne Kanhai (St. Augustine: University of the West Indies, School of Continuing Education, 1999).
26. TR097/1/1/1/3.
27. TR097/1/1/1/7.
28. TR097/1/1/1/5.
29. TR097/1/1/1/11.
30. TR097/1/1/1/12.
31. TR097/1/1/1/15.
32. TR097/1/1/1/15.
33. TR097/1/1/2/19-20.
34. TR097/1/1/2/22.
35. TR038/2/1/1/3.
36. TR097/1/1/2/25.
37. TR038/2/1/1/1.
38. TR038/2/1/1/6.
39. TR038/2/1/1/12.
40. TR038/2/1/1/1.
41. TR038/2/1/1/3.
42. TR038/2/1/1/14.
43. TR038/2/1/2/17.
44. TR038/2/1/2/19.
45. TR038/2/1/2/20.
46. TR038/2/1/2/21.
47. TR038/2/1/2/22.
48. TR038/2/1/2/22.
49. TR038/2/2/1/34.
50. TR038/2/1/1/17.
51. TR097/1/1/2/27.
52. TR038/2/2/2/42.
53. TR038/2/2/2/42.
54. TE044/2/1/1/11.
55. TE044/2/1/1/11.
56. TE044/2/1/1/1-2. Other Christian denominations focused their missionary activities

ties among the former slaves of African origin. See Carl Campbell, "The East Indian Revolt Against Missionary Education 1929-1939" in *Calcutta to Caroni. The East Indians of Trinidad,* ed. John La Guerre (St. Augustine, The University of the West Indies Extra Mural Studies Unit, 1985).

57. TE044/2/1/1/17. The Missionaries considered it their duty to instruct their converts not only in Christian theology but in its sexual and economic values. At the same time, they also arranged marriages to ensure that Christians married each other. Indeed, part of the impetus to educate girls to was to provide a pool of suitable wives for their educated young men. In this case, however, the marriage was arranged to avoid the stigma of illegitimacy.
58. TE044/2/1/1/19 . This accommodation was originally provided by the plantation owners to house their indentured laborers.
59. TE044/2/1/1/7.
60. TE044/2/1/2/28.
61. TE044/2/1/2/29.
62. TE044/2/2/2/38.
63. TE044/2/2/2/47.
64. TE044/2/2/2/47.
65. TE043/3/1/1/2.
66. TE043/3/1/1/3.
67. TE043/3/1/1/4.
68. TE043/3/1/1/4.
69. TE043/3/1/1/14.
70. TE043/3/1/1/16.
71. TE043/3/1/1/16.
72. TE043/3/1/1/5.
73. TE043/3/1/1/9.
74. TE043/3/1/1/10.
75. TE043/3/1/1/13.
76. TE043/3/1/2/19.
77. TE043/3/1/2/19.
78. TE043/3/2/2/36.
79. TE043/3/1/1/3.
80. TE043/3/1/2/32.
81. TE043/3/2/1/37.
82. TE043/3/2/1/38.
83. There have been periods of revivalism throughout the twentieth century, increasingly linked with politics and political representation.
84. TD053/2/1A/12.
85. TD039/2/1/1/8.
86. TD039/2/1/1/2.
87. TD039/2/1/1/2.
88. TD053/3/1/1/11.
89. TD039/2/1/1/3.
90. TD053/3/1/1/11.
91. TD039/2/1/1/4.
92. TD039/2/1/2/13.
93. TD039/2/1/2/17.
94. TD039/2/1/2/21.
95. TD039/2/1/2/22.
96. TD039/2/1/2/24.
97. TD053/2/1A/1.

98. TD053/2/1A/4.
99. TD053/2/1A/9.
100. TD053/2/1A/11.
101. TD053/2/1A/15.
102. TD053/2/1A/15.
103. TD053/2/2A/37.
104. TD053/2/2/30.
105. I am grateful to Kate Hodgkin who pointed this out to me.
106. St. Bernard, "Demographic Characteristics."
107. Patricia Mohammed, 'The "Creolization" of East Indian Women.'
108. Erikson, "Indians in New Worlds," 8.

10

Conclusion

The family stories presented here span most of the twentieth century, offering an insight into the social history of the British Caribbean during periods of emigration, social unrest, and political change. What appeared to provide continuity in this period was—despite views to the contrary—the strength of family connections and support. These strengths clearly derived from the constancy of African- Caribbean families despite, again, views to the contrary. One of the prevailing themes in the Caribbean was the assumption that, because families failed to meet the prescribed norms of European behavior, they represented inchoate and anarchic social structures that provided inadequate models upon which to build cohesion and stability in the wider society. Indeed, it was assumed that Caribbean families militated against social stability and the building of citizenship.

One of the pulses driving social organization was the extensiveness and inclusiveness of African-Caribbean families, in which children were second only to mothers as carriers of lineage, but first in terms of symbolic wealth, where the neighborhood saw it as a collective responsibility to socialize children and could use the concept of family with its hierarchies and equalities as a metaphor and model of social behavior at home and abroad. Thus the strength and linkages of family networks provided powerful, alternative, examples of social organization. Neighborhood networks became the networks of migration, while the patterns of support (and censure for miscreants) emerged as vital memories for those brought up in the Caribbean, and powerful directives for survival in the new and often hostile environment of the United Kingdom. The role women performed as family providers, in nurturing and supporting children and other kin, equally provided models for communal behavior. They also provided flexibility that enabled resources—symbolic and actual—to be redirected to where they were most required, including enabling parents to migrate for the improvement of their kin. Families reveal complex structures based on a communitarian philosophy of social organization and of the "self."

The failure by colonial and other authorities to recognize the strength of families and the powerful ideologies they represented, to acknowledge creole cultural forms and social practices—black Caribbean society—offered, paradoxically, a protection against vilification by the colonial authorities, while the failure to "reform" family structure represented a continuing point of independence, if not defiance. It provided Caribbeans with the freedom to develop and indulge an alternative set of values which were held as the basis of communal living. Such values were articulated in metaphors and narratives, codes in which were inscribed prescriptions for appropriate behavior, and which represented resistance to the hegemony of the white elites. Family values metamorphosed into pride in family structures, loyalty for the land of birth and the land of burial of the old "ancestant," and a pride in national belonging. Accompanying this was a powerful ideology of family closeness and loyalty which tied the families together, an ideology which similarly linked together the African-Caribbean community, at home and abroad, and which has bound African-Caribbeans into a shared understanding of nationhood and nation. Creolization has, to a large degree, had its contemporary parallel in nation making.

***

The strength of African-Caribbean families is undoubtedly the result of the complex processes involved in creolization, processes that changed over time as new influences and circumstances emerged and interacted. Indo-Caribbean families have taken a markedly different course, but have no less emerged into forms that are equally unique to the Caribbean. Their cultural influences, however, were circumscribed by very different political and historical contexts from those which surrounded the African-Caribbeans. Unlike the slaves, the Indian indentured servants were not forcibly removed (at least, not in theory), nor was their country of origin obliterated or denied. Treated as transient, for the most part colonial authorities were indifferent to the language, rituals, cuisine and other customs (except when they breached the law, or interfered with labor requirements or productivity). There was no deliberate attempt to eradicate origins; contact was maintained between India and the Caribbean, at both personal and governmental levels, while a degree of vigilance was exerted over the fortunes of the indentured laborers by the Indian, British and colonial governments. While Indo-Trinidadians rarely participated in pre-Independence politics, post-Independence has seen a transformation in the political fortunes of Indians and with it a more conscious affirmation of ethnic and religious identities. This affirmation is, ironically, because of, not despite, creolization, and abroad Indo-Trinidadians express the same identifications with Trinidad as their families at home. Indeed, as with African-Caribbeans, the link between families and national belongings may be equally strong, for the points at which the Indo-Caribbean community began to engage in the national political imaginary were also the points at which Indo-Caribbean families emerged as creolized Caribbean entities.

***

The question posed by nineteenth and twentieth century observers and commentators on Caribbean families related to their success in performing the duties required of parenthood: How to achieve the successful socialization of children into responsible workers and dutiful citizens. As we have seen, for many of those commentators, the poverty and political instability prevalent in the region, was linked to the lack of partner permanence in family life, a lack which led, it was argued, to poor emotional and psychological adjustments on the part of children, and a lacuna in village and community life. "Such problems as the unsatisfactory upbringing of children, the low social status of women, and the neglect of the aged, can only de dealt with satisfactorily," as Sir Frank Stockdale suggested, "if the family takes its place in the hierarchy of social institutions."[1]

Contemporary thinking confirms the importance of families in generating the necessary emotional and cultural "capital" in order for children to succeed in education, employment and in life more generally, with much of the debate focusing on the potential difficulties of single-parent mother-headed households in providing the necessary material resources and emotional stability for successful child development. While this thinking relates to all families, regardless of race or ethnicity, the predominance of such family forms in the Caribbean and among the African-Caribbean population in Britain, and the persistent poverty in the region, coupled with relatively low levels of economic achievement by this community in Britain (and the U.S.A.), has meant that, for the African-Caribbean community, the correlation between family and social disadvantage has remained live. Commentators point also to the long-term effects of the alienation of black men from both the labor force and the family, blamed variously on the legacy of slavery,[2] on women,[3] and on the corrupting impact of unemployment itself in robbing men of their masculinity by depriving them of their role as breadwinner.[4] As a result, the absence of appropriate black male role models and mentors for young people has led to some young, alienated, black men becoming attracted by a "gangsta" street culture with its allure of masculinity, status and, of course, drugs.[5] In such contexts, sexuality and in particular fathering a child may emerge as an affirmation of self and identity, particularly for younger (and often teenage) men—thus replicating this pattern of family life.[6]

But while lone parenting is linked with poverty and other forms of disadvantage, it is not necessarily the cause of them. In Britain, for instance, the poorest ethnic minorities are the Bangladeshi and Pakistani communities,[7] that also have the *lowest* rates of lone parents. Similarly, lone parenting cannot be castigated for low attainment. In the Caribbean, although there is concern about boys' low educational achievements, and about male unemployment (notably in urban areas such as Kingston or Port of Spain), single-mother parenting is not so easily implicated, for such parenting was equally present with the general *rise* in the standard of living and in education which has taken place across the former British West Indies since Independence. One single-parent, mother-headed household may produce successful and well-adjusted children, and another result in less fortunate outcomes. In these cases, variables other than single parenthood need to be examined.

A further concern linked with material deprivation is the perceived vulnerability of women and children to domestic violence and child abuse. Domestic violence and child abuse, however, occurs across all family types, classes and ethnicities[8] There are no data that suggest that African-Caribbean families are more prone to violence and abuse than people in other forms of family life, although as we have seen, there was a wide acceptance of corporal punishment as an appropriate method of disciplining children. At the same time, however, there is an increasing awareness of domestic violence as an issue that has resulted in a rise in reporting and prosecuting rates. In the case of sexual abuse of children, this is more likely to occur in two-parent households than in one.[9]

Yet, as Constance Sutton observed in the introduction, the Caribbean community is the only community where family life has been consistently blamed for every form of economic, social and psychological dysfunction, even though there is no evidence to suggest the link.[10] And many of the trends associated with African-Caribbeans can also be discerned in the community at large. Domestic violence and child abuse, for instance, are generally high and rising, in Britain, the Caribbean and North America, and the consistent underachievement in education of *all* boys is equally a matter of concern. In the case of African-Caribbeans, there are other, equally plausible explanations to account for low levels of economic and educational attainment.

Contemporary Caribbean economies, for the most part based on monoculture or tourism, are particularly vulnerable to the vagaries of the global market, and to disadvantageous World Trade Organization rulings, and for a variety of reasons have found it difficult to diversify or expand.[11] In some parts of the region the failure of experimental economic policies (such as in Guyana under Forbes Burnham, or Jamaica under Michael Manley), compounded the problem. At the same time, the economies are dominated by their historical legacy of ownership, and much remains in the hands of individuals or institutions, including multi-national companies, so that wealth generation is not always evenly or fairly distributed. Many families survive precisely because the migration of family members guarantees an income, however small. In turn, those migrations were permitted by the fluidity and flexibility of families that could step in to provide childcare for parents migrating abroad.

As a result, in many parts of the Caribbean low wages and under- and unemployment remain as persistent a problem as they were in the decades prior to independence, compounded by a fall in social service provision and in many areas, particularly inner-city areas, by rising levels of crime and a resulting reluctance to participate in neighborhood life. All this has led to a breakdown of local community mores, a heightened sensitivity around male personhood, and an increase in street and other types of violence.[12] Problems of social exclusion, however, are more appropriately apportioned to the structure of the economy and its consequences than to the structure of the family.

For many African-Caribbean communities abroad, unemployment or low economic achievement is a depressing characteristic. In the United States, as Mary Waters has shown, while first-generation West Indians initially move toward successful social and economic integration, their children emerge as socially disadvantaged as their African-American counterparts, subjected to comparable levels of discrimination, poor housing, education and employment prospects.[13] In Canada, similarly, first-and, particularly, second-generation West Indian immigrants have been confronted by levels of discrimination that militate against economic success and upward mobility.[14] In Britain, the West Indian community has relatively low rates of achievement, as measured by home and car ownership,[15] and, as with the United States and Canada, it is the second generation that has the lowest employment levels and its concomitant state housing, often located in deprived inner-city communities with poor schools. As we have seen, second generation African-Caribbeans are more likely to suffer from mental illness; black and mixed-race children are more like to be taken into local authority care, and for longer periods than their white counterparts, and black British nationals accounted for eleven percent of the sentenced population in prison (by far the largest ethnic minority), and thirteen percent of the remand population.[16]

In terms of education, the picture is equally unsatisfactory. A recent report from the London Development Agency showed:

> The English schooling system has produced dismal academic results for a high percentage of Black pupils for the best part of 50 years. Even after the considerable educational reforms of recent times, after up to 10 years of schooling, for 2002 and 2003 approximately 70 percent of African-Caribbean pupils left school with less than five higher grade GCSEs or equivalent GNVQs. This represents the lowest levels of achievement for all ethnic groups at Key Stage 4. The biggest casualty of the educational system is African-Caribbean boys. In London, for three consecutive years –2000, 2001 and 2002– they have been the lowest achieving group at Key Stage 3 in English. Results for this group for all key stages and subjects are alarming.[17]

While the reasons for this are complex, the report found that "low teacher expectations played a major part in the underachievement of African-Caribbean pupils...[and] inadequate levels of positive teacher attention, unfair behavior management practices, disproportionately high levels of exclusion and an inappropriate curriculum took their toll on levels of attainment."[18] Such findings paralleled those of the 1999 Macpherson Report, which detailed the failures of the Metropolitan Police in their investigation into the murder of the young Jamaican-heritage student, Stephen Lawrence. This report identified what it termed 'institutional racism' which, it claimed, permeated London's Metropolitan Police Service and inhibited the delivery of a fair and equitable service. It defined institutional racism as

> the collective failure of an organization to provide an appropriate and professional service to people because of their colour, culture or ethnic origin. It can be seen or detected in processes, attitudes and behavior which amount to discrimination through unwitting prejudice, ignorance, thoughtlessness, and racist stereotyping which disadvantaged minority ethnic people.[19]

Certainly, discrimination and racism were one of the central causes of schizophrenia identified by Dinesh Bhugra,[20] and remain as a major factor in social exclusion, whether from education, health provision or employment. Yet, as Ceri Peach has shown, despite the barriers to mobility posed by unemployment and other structural factors for African-Caribbeans in Britain, the levels of spatial segregation in urban areas, compared with cities in the United States, are not only moderate but decreasing.[21] Furthermore, successful African-Caribbean families have tended to return to the Caribbean or re-migrate (primarily to North America). As a result, the accumulation of capital and assets in Britain may appear low, but the levels of investment in the Caribbean region in terms of home ownership, pensions and remittances, are relatively high.[22] Equally, African Caribbeans have the largest number of exogamous partnerships of all ethnic minorities. Of those born in Britain, half of Caribbean men and a third of Caribbean women have a white partner, and almost half of Caribbean children have one white parent,[23] which suggests (as George Beckford indicated, though for the Caribbean region, not Britain) one measure of integration.[24]

Yet if no direct link can be made as yet—for the jury is still out—which posits African-Caribbean families as the primary or sole cause of social dysfunctionality and economic exclusion, this is not to say that there are no issues of relevance to policy makers. Although, as we have seen, lone mothers are not necessarily "alone" and can rely on the support of kin, and in many cases the fathers of their children,[25] much as happens in the Caribbean, demographic and social change may challenge this support. Grandmothers, for instance, in the United Kingdom are now often in paid employment (and need to be) and may not have the flexibility or freedom to assume care and control of grandchildren. The difficulty of securing appropriate housing in city areas, particularly in London, means that many families may no longer be able to live close to each other, thus complicating the ability for easy childcare. Alternatively, many Caribbean elders have retired or plan to retire to the Caribbean, leaving their children and grandchildren in the U.K. Returning nationals, too, face problems at governmental, societal and domestic levels.[26] Smaller family sizes mean that the kinship networks will also diminish over time, which could further threaten these informal systems. Even if this were not the case, lone parenting is tough and women carry a disproportionate amount of the economic and emotional responsibility for childrearing. Many lone mothers are concentrated in the poorer areas of inner cities where there are inferior educational facilities and limited employment prospects, with little opportunity to move or to improve the environment for their children. In some cases, an easy and seemingly attractive street culture (of violence and drugs) seduces some, particularly young, black males. As the African-Caribbean population in Britain ages, additional problems are emerging in terms of health, institutional and pension provision. Many of these elders are single men, bereft of family of both origin or creation.[27] Institutional care, whether in residential homes or day care centers, does not always accommodate the dietary preferences of African-Caribbeans, nor, particularly in cases where African-Caribbeans are in a minority, can it always offer the therapy of reminiscence so important to the well-being of the elderly. There are also health problems, such as diabetes, or sickle cell anemia, which are experienced to a greater degree by members of the African-Caribbean population, and which have implications in terms of health provision and policy.

If issues of social exclusion are to be addressed in a meaningful way, then the societal and structural factors that impede inclusion need to be identified and appropriate action undertaken. It is insufficient, and unfair, to blame African-Caribbean families, particularly the poorer families, who often struggle against almost insurmountable odds, while excluding mention of the many African-Caribbean organizations, such as the black-led churches, the Saturday schools and the bookshops and presses, that provide coherence and support to so many people of African-Caribbean descent, and promote a celebration and pride in African-Caribbean intellectual, political and social achievements.

***

For all the problems that some African-Caribbean families face, particularly in Britain, for now and the future it is hoped that the descriptions of the families here, and their location within a variety of contexts and roles, in the Caribbean and elsewhere, will contribute to an understanding of African-Caribbean families in the Caribbean region and in Britain. It is also hoped that the "family pictures" in this book will produce the recognition that, for all their historical and contemporary hybridity, African-Caribbean families are for the most part, loving, functioning and vibrant units that have developed and survived against remarkable odds, and which continue to do so. Their differences with European and Western-model families may point also to their strengths. The Caribbean emerged as an essential modern society, long before modernity had impacted so powerfully on European and North American societies. A central part of the adjustments to modernity was the creation of new family forms from what could be salvaged and from what proved durable and practical. It may be that those same families—African-Caribbean families—indicate the directions in which contemporary European and Western families are now heading. Far from vilifying such families as a threat to "family" or "traditional values", we should perhaps learn from them and laud the ways they have developed to maintain contact, closeness and the powerful bonds of love across the seas, the years and the generations.

Notes

1. Sir Frank Stockdale, *Development and Welfare in the West Indies 1940-42*, Report. London: HMSO, 1943, p.52. Stockdale appointed as his adviser Professor Thomas Simey, Charles Booth Professor of Social Policy at the University of Liverpool. See also Thomas Simey *Welfare and Planning in the West Indies*, (Oxford: Clarendon, 1946), for further discussion of family weaknesses and its consequences for village and social welfare.
2. Franklin Frazier, *The Negro Family in the United States* (Chicago:University of Chicago Press, 1996 [1939]).
3. Daniel Moynihan, *The Moynihan Report: The Negro family, the case for national action* (Washington DC: Government and Printing Office, 1965).
4. William Julius Wilson, *The Truly Disadvantaged: The Inner City, The Underclass, and Public Policy* (Chicago: Chicago University Press, 1987); William Julius Wilson, *When Work Disappears: The Work of the New Urban Poor* (New York: Random House, 1996).
5. Clement Branche "Boys in Conflict: Community, Gender, Identity and Sex," paper presented at Workshop on Family and the Quality of Gender Relations, University of the West Indies, Mona, 1997.
6. Graham Dann, *The Barbadian Male. Sexual Attitudes and Practice* (London: Macmillan Caribbean, 1987). See also, for the UK (all groups) Kaye Wellings and Jane Wadsworth , "Family influences on teenage fertility" in *Changing Britain. Families and Households in the 1990s,* ed. Susan McRae (Oxford: Oxford University Press, 1999).

7. Tariq Modood et al., *Ethnic Minorities in Britain: Diversity and Disadvantage* (London: PSI, 1997).
8. Roanna Gopaul and Paula Morgan "Spousal Violence. Spiralling patterns in Trinidad and Tobago," proceedings of a Workshop (Kingston: Institute of Social and Economic Research, 1997).
9. Elsie Le Franc et al "Family Structures and Domestic Conflict in Jamaica," in *Caribbean Families in Britain and the Trans-Atlantic World.* (London: MacMillan, 2001).
10. There is a research program currently underway at the University of the West Indies on "Migration, Family Structures and Morbidity from External Causes: A Comparative Study on Jamaica, Barbados and Trinidad and Tobago," under the directorship of Elsie Le Franc, which is attempting to establish whether any links can be made between family form and interpersonal violence, including domestic violence. To date, the extant literature is inconclusive.
11. Soil erosion, lack of investment, high production costs and competitive markets are some of the explanations put forward to explain this difficulty.
12. Clement Branche "Boys in Conflict: Community, Gender, Identity and Sex," paper presented at Workshop on Family and the Quality of Gender Relations, University of the West Indies, Mona, 1997. See also Wilma Bailey "Conflict and Accommodation: Female Gendered Existence in the Inner City of Kingston," paper presented at Workshop on Family and the Quality of Gender Relations, University of the West Indies, Mona, 1997.
13. Mary Waters, *Black Identities: West Indian Immigrant Dreams and American Realities* (Cambridge, Mass.: Harvard University Press, 2001).
14. Dwaine Plaza "Migration and Adjustment to Canada: Pursuing the Mobility Dream 1990-1998, *Society for Caribbean Studies Annual Conference Papers*, ed. Sandra Courtman, Vol. 3, 2002; "Strategies and Strategizing: The Struggle for Upward Mobility Among University Educated Black Caribbean-born Men in Canada" in *Caribbean Migration. Globalised Identities*, ed. Mary Chamberlain.
15. David Owen, "A Profile of Caribbean Households and Families in Britain" in *Caribbean Families in Britain and the Trans-Atlantic World,'* ed. Harry Goulbourne and Mary Chamberlain.
16. White males made up 84 percent of the prison population in 2002. *National Statistics. Census 2001* www.statistics.gov.uk.
17. *Educational Experiences and Achievements of Black Boys in London Schools 2000-2003*, London Development Agency, 2004. (Conclusion).
18. *Educational Experiences and Achievements of Black Boys in London Schools 2000-2003*, London Development Agency, 2004. (Key findings).
19. *The Stephen Lawrence Inquiry. Report of an Inquiry by Sir William MacPherson of Cluny* (London: The Stationery Office, 1999).
20. Dinesh Bhugra "Migration and Schizophrenia" *Acta Psychiatrica Scandanavia* 102 (suppl. 407) 2000, 68-73.
21. Ceri Peach, "Trends in levels of Caribbean segregation 1961-1991" in Chamberlain, ed., *Caribbean Migration. Globalised Identities.*
22. Harry Goulbourne and Mary Chamberlain *Living Arrangements, Family Structure and Social Change of Caribbeans in Britain*, Final Report, ESRC 1998.
23. Tariq Modood et al *Ethnic Minorities in Britain*. See also David Owen 'A profile of Caribbean households and families in Great Britain' in *Caribbean Families in Britain and the Trans-Atlantic World.* Goulbourne and Chamberlain, ed.
24. "We in the Caribbean are already integrated. It is only the governments who don't know it." The comment referred to transnational families in the region, and their

relation to Caribbean regional federation. Cited by George Lamming, "Coming, Coming, Coming Home" in George Lamming, *Coming, Coming Home. Conversations II* (St. Martin, Caribbean: House of Nehesi Publishers, 2000), 33.

25. Tracey Reynolds "Caribbean Fathers in Family Lives in Britain' in *Caribbean Families in Britain and the Trans-Atlantic World* Goulbourne and Chamberlain, ed.

26. For a case study, see Frank Abernaty, "The Dynamics of Return Migration to St. Lucia" in *Caribbean Families in Britain and the Trans-Atlantic World,* Goulbourne and Chamberlain ed.

27. Dwaine Plaza, "Aging in Babylon: Elderly Caribbeans in Britain" in *Caribbean Families in Britain and the Trans-Atlantic World,* Goulbourne and Chamberlain ed.

Bibliography

Primary Sources

A Official Documents and Reports

THE NATIONAL ARCHIVES, UK

Command Paper 426, Population of the British West India Islands and British Guiana according to the Last Census, 1845.
CO 31/62, Barbados Census 1871.
CO 140/208 Appendix to papers of Legislative Council of Jamaica 1891.
CO 298/47 Deputy Registrar General's Report for Tobago for the year 1890. Papers presented to the Legislative Council of Trinidad, 1891.
CO 31/79. Registrar General's Report, presented to the meeting of the House of Assembly 17 November 1891, Bridgetown, Barbados.
CO 298/122 Vital Statistics. (Report of Registrar General for Trinidad, 1921).
CO 31/107. Documents laid at a Meeting of the House of Assembly, Bridgetown, Barbados 1921.
Census of Jamaica 1943.
CO 31/137 West Indian Census 1946.
Command Paper 479, Select Committee on West India Colonies 1842.
CO 967/118 The West India Royal Commission 1938-39, (1945).

The Stephen Lawrence Inquiry. Report of an Inquiry by Sir William MacPherson of Cluny (London: The Stationery Office, 1999).

Command 8427. *Lord Scarman's Report on the Brixton Disorders*, 1981.

BARBADOS, DEPARTMENT OF ARCHIVES

GH4/52, Colonial Office paper on Position of British West Indians in Central and South American Countries. n.d., but presumably 1933.

B Internet

Educational Experiences and Achievements of Black Boys in London Schools 2000-2003. London Development Agency, 2004. www.lda.gov.uk
National Statistics. Census 2001. www.statistics.gov.uk.
Simmons, Jon, and colleagues. *Crime in England and Wales 2001/2*. www.homeoffice.gov.uk/rds/crimeew1/html.

C. Interviews

Interview material is from *Living Arrangements, Family Structure and Social Change of Caribbeans in Britain* (ESRC award L315253009). Tapes and transcripts deposited at Qualidata Archive, University of Essex. Quotations drawn from the following interviews (accession numbers only). All names in the text are pseudonyms.

JB 007, JB 008, JC 011, JD 012, JD 013, JD 014, JE 016, JE 017, JF 020, JF 021, JF 022, JG 023, JG 025, JH 141, JI 028, JK 030, JK 031, JL 036, JN 049, JN 057, JP 052, JP 061.

BB 056, BF 069, BF123, BG 020, BG 070, BG 091, BG 120, BH 118, BI 075, BK 117.

TA 001, TA 004, TA 015, TA 095, TB 018, TC 029, TC 058, TD 039, TD 053, TE 043, TE 044, TH 051, TH 102, TJ 073, TM 055, TM 098, TP 108, TQ 109, TR 038, TR 097.

Secondary Sources

Books

Agorsah, Kofi E. *Maroon Heritage. Archaeological, Ethnographic and Historical Perspectives*. (Kingston: University of the West Indies, Canoe Press,1994).

A Jamaican Planter. (London:1815).

Alexander, Jacqui M. and C. Talpade Mohanty, eds. *Feminist Genealogies, Colonial Legacies, Democratic Futures*. (London/New York: Routledge 1997)

Al Khalifa Sharif Tayba Hassan. *Resistance and Remembering: History-Telling of the Iraqi Shi'ite Arab Refugee Women and their Families in the Netherlands*. Unpublished PhD thesis. (University of Amsterdam, 2003).

Appadurai, Arjun. *Modernity at Large: Cultural Dimensions of Globalisation*.(Minnesota: University of Minnesota Press, 1996).

Ashplant, Timothy, Dawson Graham, and Roper, Michael, eds. *The Politics of Memory: Commemorating War*. (New Brunswick and London: Transaction Publishers, 2004).

Aymer, Paula. *Uprooted Women: Migrant Domestics in the Caribbean*. (Westport,Conn.: Praeger,1997).

Barber, Karin. *I Could Speak Until Tomorrow: Oriki, Women and the Past in a Yoruba Town*. (Washington D.C., Smithsonian Institution Press, 1991).

Barrow, Christine ed. *Caribbean Portraits. Essays on Gender Ideologies and Identities*. (Kingston: Ian Randle Publishers, 1998).

Barrow, Christine. *Family in the Caribbean. Themes and Perspectives* (Kingston: Ian Randle Publishers, 1996).

Basch, Linda, Nina Glick Schiller, and Cristina Szanton Blanc. *Nations Unbound: Transnational Projects, Post-Colonial Predicaments and Deterritorialized Nation States*. (Langhorne P.A.: Gordon and Breach, 1994).

Beckles, Hilary. *A History of Barbados*. (Cambridge: Cambridge University Press, 1990).

———. *Natural Rebels. A Social History of Enslaved Black Women in Barbados*. (London: Zed Books Ltd., 1989).

Beckles, Hilary, and Verene Shepherd, eds. *Caribbean Freedom. Economy and Society from Emancipation to the Present*. (Kingston: Ian Randle Publishers, 1993).

———, eds. *Caribbean Slave Society and Economy*. (Kingston: Ian Randle Publishers, 1991).

Benjamin, Walter. *One Way Street*. (London: Verso, 1997).

Bertaux, Daniel, and Paul Thompson, eds. *Between Generations. Family Models, Myths and Memories.* International Yearbook of Oral History and Life Stories Volume II, (Oxford: Oxford University Press, 1993).

Besson, Jean. *Martha Brae's Two Histories. European Expansion and Caribbean Culture-Building in Jamaica.* (Chapel Hill and London: University of North Carolina Press 2002).

Bott, Elizabeth. *Family and Social Networks: Roles, Norms and External Relations in Ordinary Urban Families.* (London: Tavistock Publications, 1957).

Bourdieu, Pierre. *The Field of Cultural Production.* (London: Polity Press, 1993).

Boyce-Davis, Carol. *Black Women, Writing and Identity. Migrations of the Subject.* (London and New York: Routledge, 1994).

Brand, Dionne. *Sans Souci and Other Stories.* (Toronto: Women's Press, 1989).

Brathwaite, Edward Kamau. *The Development of Creole Society in Jamaica 1770-1820.* (Oxford: Clarendon Press, 1971).

Brereton, Bridget. *Race Relations in Colonial Trinidad, 1870-1990.* (Cambridge: Cambridge University Press, 1979).

Brereton, Bridget, and Kevin Yelvington, ed. *The Colonial Caribbean in Transition. Essays on Post-emancipation Social and Cultural History.* (Kingston: The Press University of the West Indies, 1999).

Bridges, Edward. *The Annals of Jamaica.* 2 volumes (1828).

Brisbane, Sir Charles. *A Communication from Sir Charles Brisbane, K.C.B., Governor of Saint Vincent, to the House of Assembly of that Colony.* (London:1823).

Brodber, Erna. *Jane and Louisa Will Soon Come Home.* (London: New Beacon, 1980).

Bryceson, Deborah, and Vuorela Ulla, ed. *The Transnational Family. New European Frontiers and Global Networks.* (Oxford: Berg, 2002).

Cassells, P., ed. *The Giddens Reader.* (London: Macmillan, 1993).

Cavarero, Adriana. *Relating Narratives.* (London: Routledge 2000).

Chamberlain, Mary, ed. *Caribbean Migration, Globalised Identities.* (London: Routledge, 1998).

———. *Narratives of Exile and Return.* (London: Macmillan, 1997).

Chamberlain, Mary, and Selma Leydesdorff, guest ed. *Global Networks. A Journal of Transnational Affairs.* Special Issue:"Transnational Families: Memories and Narratives" 4, 3 (2004).

Chamberlain, Mary, and Paul Thompson, ed. *Narrative and Genre.* Routledge Studies in Memory and Narrative. (London: Routledge, 1998).

Chamberlayne, Prue, Joanna Bornat, and Tom Wengraf. *The Turn to Biographical Methods in the Social Sciences.* (London: Routledge, 2000).

Chamoiseau, Pierre. *Texaco.* (London: Granta 1997).

Charbit, Yves. *Famille et Nuptialité dans la Caraïbe.* (Paris: Institut National d'Études Démographiques. Presses Universitaires de France, 1987)

Clarke, Edith. *My Mother who Fathered Me. A Study of the Families in Three Selected Communities of Jamaica.* (Kingston: The Press The University of the West Indies 1999 [1957]).

Cohen, Robin. *Global Diasporas. An Introduction.* (London: UCL Press, 1997).

Comaroff, John, and Jean Comaroff. *Ethnography and the Historical Imagination.* (Boulder: Westview Press, 1992).

Cooper, Carolyn. *Noises in the Blood.* (London: Macmillan, 1993).

Cosslett, Tessa, Celia Lury, and Penny Summerfield. *Feminism and Autobiography: Texts, Theories, Methods.* (London: Routledge 2000).

Dann, Graham. *The Barbadian Male. Sexual Attitudes and Practice.* (London: Macmillan Caribbean, 1987).

Davidoff, Leonore. *World's Between: Historical Perspectives on Gender and Class.* (Cambridge: Polity Press, 1995).

Davidoff, Leonore, Megan Doolittle, Janet Fink, and Katherine Holden. *The Family Story. Blood, Contract and Intimacy 1830-1960.* (London/New York: Longman 1999).

Davin, Anna. *Growing Up Poor.* (London: Rivers Oram Press, 1996).

Dench, Geoffrey. *From Extended Family to State Dependency.* (London: Middlesex University CCS, 1992).

———. *The Place of Men in Changing Family Cultures* (London: Institute of Community Studies, 1996.)

Dollard, John. *Caste and Class in a Southern Town.* (New York: Doubleday Anchor Books 1957 [1937]).

Douglass, Lisa. *The Power of Sentiment: Love, Hierarchy and the Jamaican Power Elite.* (Boulder, CO: Westview Press, 1992).

DuBois, W. E. B. *The Souls of Black Folk.* (New York: Signet, 1995 [1903]).

Fraser, Ronald. *In Search of a Past.* (London: Verso, 1984).

Frazier, Franklin. *The Negro Family in the United States* (Chicago: University of Chicago Press, 1966 [1939]).

Froude, J.A. *The English in the West Indies or the Bowl of Ulysses.* (New York: Charles Scribner and Sons, 1888).

Gates, Henry Louis. *The Signifying Monkey: A Theory of African American Literary Criticism.* (New York: Oxford University Press, 1988).

Geertz, Clifford. *The Interpretation of Cultures.* (New York: Basic Books, 1973).

Gellner, Ernst. *Thought and Change.* (London: Weidenfeld and Nicolson 1964).

Giddens, Anthony, *Modernity and Self-Identity. Self and Society in the Late Modern Age.* (Cambridge: Polity Press 1991).

Gilroy, Paul. *The Black Atlantic. Modernity and Double Consciousness.* (London: Verso, 1993).

Glass, Ruth, *London's Newcomers.* (Cambridge, Mass.: Harvard University Press, 1961).

Glick-Schiller, Nina and Georges Fouron. *Georges Woke Up Laughing: Long Distance Nationalism and the Search for Home.* (Durham: Duke University Press, 2001).

Gorell Barnes, Gillian, Paul Thompson, Gwyn Daniel, and Natasha Burchardt. *Growing Up in Step Families.* (Oxford: Clarendon Press, 1998).

Goulbourne, Harry, ed. *Black Politics in Britain.* (Aldershot: Avebury, 1990).

———. *Caribbean Transnational Experience.* (London: Pluto Press, 2002).

———. *Ethnicity and Nationalism in Post-Imperial Britain.* (Cambridge: Cambridge University Press, 1991).

Goulbourne, Harry, and Mary Chamberlain. *Caribbean Families in Britain and the Trans-Atlantic World.* (London: Macmillan, 2001).

———. *Living Arrangements, Family Structure and Social Change of Caribbeans in Britain.* Final Report, ESRC 1998.

Goveia, Elsa, *Slave Society in the British Leeward Islands at the End of the Eighteenth Century* (New Haven and London: Yale University Press, 1965).

Grele, Ron, *Envelopes of Sound. The Art of Oral History* (Chicago: Precedent Publishing, 1985).

Halbwachs, Maurice, *On Collective Memory* (New York: Harper and Row, 1980).

Hall, Douglas ed., *In Miserable Slavery. Thomas Thistlewood in Jamaica, 1750-86* (London: Macmillan, 1989).

Handler, Jerome and F. Lange, *Plantation Slavery in Barbados: An Archaeological and Historical Investigation* (Cambridge: Cambridge University Press, 1978).

Hannerz, Ulf, *Transnational Connections: Culture, People, Places* (London: Routledge, 1996);.

Henriques, Fernando, *Family and Colour in Jamaica* (London: Eyre and Spottiswoode, 1953).
Henry, Paget, *Caliban's Reason. Introducing Afro-Caribbean Philosophy* (London: Routledge, 2000).
Herskovits, Melville, *The Myth of the Negro Past* (Boston: Beacon Press,1958 [1941]).
Higman, Barry, *Slave Populations of the British Caribbean 1807*-1834 (Kingston: The Press, University of the West Indies, 1995 [1984]).
Higman, Barry, *Slave Population and Economy in Jamaica 1807-1834* (Cambridge: Cambridge University Press 1976).
Hodgkin, Kate and Susannah Radstone eds., *Contested Pasts. The Politics of Memory*, Routledge Studies in Memory and Narrative (London: Routledge, 2003)
Howe, Glenford, and Don Marshall eds., *The Empowering Impulse. The Nationalist Tradition of Barbados* (Kingston: Canoe Press, 2001).
Hulme, Peter, *Colonial Encounters. Europe and the Native Caribbean 1492-1797* (London: Routledge, 1986).
Johnson, Howard ed., *After the Crossing, Immigrants and Minorities in Caribbean Creole Society* (London: Frank Cass, 1988).
Kanhai, Rosanne ed., *Matikor. The Politics of Identity for Indo-Caribbean Women'* (St. Augustine: University of the West Indies, School of Continuing Education, 1999).
Kasinitz, Philip, *Caribbean New York: Black Immigrants and the Politics of Race* (Ithaca: Cornell University Press, 1992).
Kerns, Virginia, *Women and the Ancestors. Black Carib Kinship and Ritual*, (Urbana and Chicago: University of Illinois Press1997 [1983]).
Kincaid, Jamaica, *The Autobiography of My Mother* (London: Vintage, 1996).
Klass, Morton, *East Indians in Trinidad: A Study of Cultural Persistence* (New York: Columbia University Press, 1961).
La Guerre, John, *Calcutta to Caroni. The East Indians of Trinidad* ed. (St. Augustine, The University of the West Indies Extra Mural Studies Unit, 1985).
Lady Nugent's Journal of Her Residence in Jamaica from 1801 to 1805 ed. Philip Wright (Kingston: Institute of Jamaica, 1966).
Lamming George 'Coming, Coming, Coming Home' in George Lamming *Coming, Coming Home. Conversations II* (St. Martin, Caribbean: House of Nehesi Publishers, 2000), 33.
Lamming, George, *In the Castle of My Skin* (London: Longman).
Laurence, Keith O. *A Question of Labour. Indentured Immigration into Trinidad and British Guiana 1875-1917* (Kingston: Ian Randle Publishers, 1994).
Lejeune, Philippe, *On Autobiography* (ed. Paul John Eakin, trans. K.Leary) (Minneapolis: University of Minnesota Press, 1989).
Leo-Rhynie, Elsa *The Jamaican Family: Continuity and Change* (Kingston: Institute of Jamaica, 1993)
Levine, Barry ed., *The Caribbean Exodus* (New York: Praeger,1987).
Levi-Strauss, Claude, *Structural Anthropology* (London: Allen Lane, 1968 [1963]).
Long, Edward, *The History of Jamaica or General Survey of the Antient and Modern State of That Island with Reflections on its Situation, Settlements, Inhabitants, Climate, Products, Commerce, Laws and Government*, Three Volumes, (London, 1774).
Look-Lai, Walton, *Indentured Labor, Caribbean Sugar. Chinese and Indian Migrants to the British West Indies 1838-1918* (Baltimore: Johns Hopkins University Press, 1993).
Marshall, Trevor, Peggy McGeary and Grace Thompson, *Folksongs of Barbados,* (Bridgetown: n.p., n.d).

Marshall, Woodville K., ed., *The Colthurst Journal* (New York: KTO Press, 1977).
McDaniel, Lorna, *Big Drum Ritual of Carriacou. Praisesongs in Rememory of Flight* (Gainesville: University Press of Florida, 1998).
McDonald, Roderick A. ed., *Between Slavery and Freedom. Special Magistrate John Anderson's Journal of St. Vincent during the Apprenticeship* (Kingston: University of the West Indies Press, 2001).
McRae, Susan, ed.,*Changing Britain. Families and Households in the 1990s* (Oxford: Oxford University Press, 1999).
Miller, Barbara *Guilt and Compliance in a Unified Germany. The Stasi Files Unveiled*, (New Brunswick and London: Transaction Publishers, 2004)
Mintz, Sidney and Richard Price, *An Anthropological Approach to the African-American Past, A Caribbean Perspective* (Philadelphia: Institute for the Study of Human Issues, 1976).
Mintz, Sidney, *Caribbean Transformations* (New York, Columbia University Press, 1989 [1974]).
Modood, Tariq, R. Berthoud, J. Lakey, J. Nazroo, P. Smith, S. Virdee, S. Beishon,*Ethnic Minorities in Britain: Diversity and Disadvantage,* (London:Policy Studies Institute, 1997)
Morrissey, Marietta, *Slave Women in the New World. Gender Stratification in the Caribbean* (Kansas: University Press of Kansas,1989).
Moynihan Daniel, *The Moynihan Report: The Negro family, the Case for National Action* (Washington DC: Government and Printing Office, 1965)
Newton, Velma, *The Silver Men. West Indian Labour Migration to Panama 1850-1914* (Kingston, University of the West Indies, Institute of Social and Economic Research, 1987).
Nunley, John W. and Judith Bettelheim eds., *Caribbean Festival Arts* (Seattle and London: St. Louis Art Museum in association with University of Washington Press, 1998).
Ortiz, Fernando, *Cuban Counterpoint. Tobacco and Sugar* (Durham and London: Duke University Press, 1995 [1940])
Passerini, Louisa *Autobiography of a Generation*, tr. Lisa Erdberg (Hanover: University Press of New England, 1996).
Passerini, Louisa, *Fascism in Popular Memory: The Cultural Experience of the Turin Working Class,* tr. Robert Lumley and Jude Bloomfeld (Cambridge: Cambridge University Press, 1987).
Patterson, Orlando, *The Sociology of Slavery* (London: MacGibbon and Kee, 1967).
Peach, Ceri, *The Caribbean in Europe: Contrasting Patterns of Migration and Settlement in Britain, France and the Netherlands,* Research Paper in Ethnic Relations No. 15 (Coventry: Centre for Research in Ethnic Relations, University of Warwick, 1991).
Plummer, Ken, *Documents of Life 2* (London: Sage 2001).
Rapoport R. N., Rapoport, M. P., Fogarty, and R. Rapoport, *Families in Britain* (London: Routledge and Kegan Paul, 1982)
Reddock, Rhodha, *Women and Family in the Caribbean: Historical and Contemporary Considerations: With Speical Reference to Jamaica and Trinidad and Tobago* (St. Augustine: Caricom Secretariat/Women and Development Studies Group/Center for Gender and Development Studies, University of the West Indies, 1994)
Regis, Louis, *The Political Calypso. True Opposition in Trinidad and Tobago 1962-1987* (Kingston: The Press The University of the West Indies, 1999).
Ribbens, Jane *Mothers and their Children* (London: Sage, 1994)
Richardson, Bonham, *Caribbean Migrants. Environment and Human Survival on St. Kitts and Nevis* (Knoxville: University of Tennessee Press, 1983).
Richardson, Bonham, *Panama Money in Barbados 1900-1920* (Knoxville: University of Tennessee Press, 1985).

Ringen, Stein, *Citizens, Families, and Reform* (Oxford: Oxford University Press, 1997).
Roberts, George and Sonja Sinclair, *Women in Jamaica: Patterns of Reproduction and Family* (New York: KTO Press, 1978).
Rodman, Hyman, *Lower Class Families: The Culture of Poverty in Negro Trinidad* (London: Oxford University Press, 1971).
Rohlehr, Gordon, *Calypso and Society in Pre-Independence Trinidad* (Port-of-Spain, Gordon Rohlehr, 1990).
Rousseau, Jean-Jaques, *La Nouvelle Héloise* (Oxford: Woodstock Books, 1989).
Rubenstein, Hymie, *Coping with Poverty: Adaptive Strategies in a Caribbean Village* (Boulder: Westview Press, 1987).
Ryan, Selwyn, *Race and Nationalism in Trinidad and Tobago* (Kingston: University of the West Indies, Institute of Social and Economic Research, 1974).
Samuel, Raphael, *Theatres of Memory*, (London: Verso, 1995).
Schomburgk, Sir Robert, *The History of Barbados* (London,1848).
Schwarz, Bill ed., *West Indian Intellectuals in the Metropolis* (Manchester: Manchester University Press, 2003).
Sells, William, *Remarks on the Condition of the Slaves in the Island of Jamaica*, (London:1823).
Senior, Olive, *Working Miracles. Women's Lives in the English Speaking Caribbean* (London: James Currey/Bloomington and Indianapolis: Indiana University Press, 1991).
Shepherd, Verene, *Maharani's Misery. Narratives of a Passage from India to the Caribbean* (Kingston: University of the West Indies Press, 2002).
Shepherd, Verene, *Transients to Settlers. The Experience of Indians in Jamaica 1845-1950* (Leeds: Peepal Tree Books/Coventry, Centre for Research in Asian Migration, University of Warwick, 1994).
Shepherd, Verene, Bridget Brereton, Barbara Bailey eds., *Engendering History. Caribbean Women in Historical Perspective.* (Kingston: Ian Randle Publishers, 1995).
Shepherd, Verene and Glen L. Richards eds., *Questioning Creole. Creolisation Discourses in Caribbean Culture,* eds. (Kingston: Ian Randle, 2002).
Sheridan, Richard, *Sugar and Slavery. An Economic History of the British West Indies, 1623-1775,* (Kingston: Canoe Press, 1994 [1974]).
Simey, Thomas, *Welfare and Planning in the West Indies* (Oxford: Clarendon, 1946).
Smith, Keithlyn B. and Fernando C.Smith, *To Shoot Hard Labour. The Life and Times of Samuel Smith, an Antiguan workingman 1877-1982* (Scarborough, Ontario: Edan's Publishers, 1986).
Smith, M. G. *The Plural Society in the British West Indies* (Kingston: Sangster's Book Store in Association with University of California Press, 1974 [1965]).
Smith, Raymond T. ed., *Kinship Ideology and Practice in Latin America* (Chapel Hill: University of North Carolina Press, 1984).
Smith, Raymond T., *Kinship and Class in the West Indies. A Genealogical Study of Jamaica and Guyana* (Cambridge: Cambridge University Press, 1988).
Smith, Raymond.T. *The Negro Family in British Guiana* (London: Routledge and Kegan Paul, 1956).
Stockdale, Sir Frank Stockdale, *Development and Welfare in the West Indies 1940-1942* (London: HMSO 1943).
Stockdale, Sir Frank, *Development and Welfare in the West Indies, 1943-44.* (London: HMSO,1945).
Sturge, Joseph and Harvey, Thomas, *The West Indies in 1837* (London: Dawsons of Pall Mall, 1968 [1838])
Sutton, Constance R. and Elsa M. Chaney eds., *Caribbean Life in New York City: Sociocultural Dimensions* (New York: Center for Migration Studies of New York Inc.1994).

Thomas-Hope, Elizabeth, *Explanation in Caribbean Migration* (London: Macmillan 1992).
Tonkin, Elizabeth, *Narrating Our Past. The Social Construction of Oral History* (Cambridge: Cambridge University Press, 1992).
Vail, Leroy and Landeg White, *Power and the Praise Poem: Southern African Voices in History* (Charlottesville: University Press of Virginia/London James Currey,1991).
Vincent, David, *Bread, Knowledge and Freedom. A Study of Nineteenth Century Working Class Autobiography* (London: Methuen, 1981).
Warner Lewis, Maureen, *Guinea's Other Sons. The African Dynamic in Trinidad Culture* (Dover, Mass: The Majority Press, 1991).
Warner Lewis, Maureen, *Trinidad Yoruba. From Mother Tongue toMemory* (Kingston: The Press, University of the West Indies, 1997).
Waters Mary *Black Identities: West Indian Immigrant Dreams and American Realities* (Cambridge, Mass.: Harvard University Press, 2001)
Whorf,Benjamin Lee, *Language, Thought and Reality* (Cambridge, Mass: The M.I.T.Press, 1956)
Williams, Raymond, *The Long Revolution* (London: Penguin 1975 [1961]).
Wilson William Julius, *The Truly Disadvantaged: the Inner City, the Underclass, and Public Policy* (Chicago: Chicago University Press, 1987);
Wilson William Julius, *When work disappears: the Work of the New Urban Poor* (New York: Random House, 1996).
Wright Mills, C., *The Sociological Imagination* (Harmondsworth: Penguin 1970 [1959]).
Young, Michael and Peter Wilmott, *Family and Kinship in East London* (Harmondsworth: Penguin, 1957).

Articles/Chapters

Abernaty Frank "The dynamics of return migration to St. Lucia"in *Caribbean Families in Britain and the Trans-Atlantic World*. Goulbourne and Chamberlain eds. (2001), 170-187
Agrosino, M. "Sexual Politics in the East Indian Family in Trinidad," *Caribbean Studies*, 16:1 (1976): 44-46.
Alexander, Jack, "Love, Race, Slavery and Sexuality in Jamaican Images of the Family" in *Kinship Ideology and Practice in Latin America* ed. Raymond T. Smith, (Chapel Hill: University of North Carolina Press, 1984), 147-180.
Alexander, Jack, "The Role of the Male in the Middle Class Jamaican Family: A Comparative Perspective" *Journal of Comparative Family Studies,* 8,3 (1977):369-389.
Austin-Broos, Diane, "Women and Jamaican Pentecostalism" in *Caribbean Portraits Essays on Gender Ideologies and Identities e*d. Christine Barrow (Kingston: Ian Randle Publishers, 1998),156-176.
Bailey, Wilma "Conflict and Accommodation: Female Gendered Existence in the Inner City of Kingston" Paper presented at Workshop on Family and the Quality of Gender Relations, University of the West Indies, Mona, 1997
Barn, Ravinda, "Caribbean Families and the Child Welfare System in Britain" in *Caribbean Families in Britain and the Atlantic World*. Goulbourne and Chamberlain eds. (2001),204-218.
Barrow, Christine, "Caribbean Masculinity and Family: revisiting 'Marginality' and 'Reputation" in *Caribbean Portraits. Essays on Gender Ideologies and Identities* ed. Christine Barrow (Kingston: Ian Randle Publishers, 1998) 339-360.
Barrow, Jocelyn, "West Indian Families: an Insider's Perspective" in *Families in Britain*, eds. R. N. Rapoport, M. P. Fogarty, and R. Rapoport, (London: Routledge and Kegan Paul, 1982), 220-232.

Baud, Michiel "Families and Migration: Towards an Historical Analysis of Family Networks" *Economic and Social History in the Netherlands*, 5, 1994, 83-107.
Besson, Jean, 'Changing Perceptions of Gender in the Caribbean Region: The Case of the Jamaican Peasantry' in *Caribbean Portraits. Essays on Gender Ideologies and Identities* ed. Christine Barrow (Kingston: Ian Randle Publishers, 1998), 133-155.
Besson, Jean "Family Land and Caribbean Society: Toward an Ethnography of Afro-Caribbean Peasantries" in *Perspectives on Caribbean Regional Identity*, ed. Elizabeth M. Thomas-Hope (Liverpool: Liverpool University Press, 1984), 57-83
Bhugra Dinesh "Migration and schizophrenia" *Acta Psychiatrica Scandanavia* 102 (suppl. 407), 2000, 68-73.
Bhui Kamaldeep, "editorial," *British Medical Journal*,329 (7462), 2004, 363-364.
Branche, Clement "Boys in Conflict: Community, Gender, Identity and Sex" Paper presented at Workshop on Family and the Quality of Gender Relations, University of the West Indies, Mona, 1997.
Brathwaite, Edward Kamau, Introduction to Roger Mais *Brother Man* (London: Heinemann, 1974)v-xxi.
Brereton, Bridget, "Family Strategies, Gender and the Shift to Wage Labour in the British Caribbean" in *The Colonial Caribbean in Transition. Essays on Post-emancipation Social and Cultural History* ed. Bridget Brereton Kevin Yelvington (Kingston: The Press University of the West Indies, 1999), 77-107.
Brodber, Erna, "Afro-Jamaican Women at the turn of the Century," *Social and Economic Studies*, 35:3 (1986):23-50.
Brodber, Rosina Wiltshire, "The Caribbean Transnational Family," paper presented to UNESCO/ISER Eastern Caribbean Sub-regional Seminar, University of the West Indies, Cave Hill, (1988).
Burton, Richard D. E., "Names and Naming in Afro-Caribbean Culture" *New West Indian Guide* 73,1&2, (1999), 35-58
Byng-Hall, John, "The Power of Family Myths' in *The Myths We Live By*, eds. R. Samuel and P. Thompson (London: Routledge 1990), 216-224.
Campbell, Carl, "The East Indian Revolt Against Missionary Education 1929-1939" in *Calcutta to Caroni. The East Indians of Trinidad* ed. John La Guerre (St. Augustine, The University of the West Indies Extra Mural Studies Unit, 1985), 117-134.
Chamberlain, Mary 'Praise songs of the Family: lineage and kinship in the Caribbean Diaspora' *History Workshop Journal* 50, Autumn (2000)114-128.
Chamberlain, Mary "George Lamming" in *West Indian Intellectuals in the Metropolis* ed. Bill Schwarz (Manchester: Manchester University Press, 2003) 175-195.
Chamberlain, Mary and Paul Thompson 1998 "Introduction" in *Narrative and Genre*, Routledge Studies in Memory and Narrative, London: Routledge, 1998), 1-22.
Chamberlain, Mary, "Small Worlds: Childhood and Empire" *Journal of Family History*, 27:2, (2002), 186-200.
Chanfrault-Duchet, Marie-Francoise, "Textualisation of the Self and Gender Identity in the Life Story" in *Feminism and Autobiography. Texts, Theories, Methods* eds. Tess Cosslett, Celia Lury and Penny Summerfield (London/New York: Routledge, 2000), 61-75.
Clark, Gracia, "Mothering, Work and Gender in Urban Asante Ideology and Practice" *American Anthropologist* 101,4, (2000),717-729.
Conway, Denis, "Conceptualising contemporary patterns of Caribbean international mobility," *Caribbean Geography*, 2,3 (1988).
Craig James, Susan, "Intertwining Roots" *Journal of CaribbeanHistory*, 25:2 (1992): 216-228.

Craton, Michael, "Changing Patterns of Slave Families in the British West Indies" in *Caribbean Slave Society and Economy* eds. Hilary Beckles and Verene Shepherd (Kingston: Ian Randle Publishers 1991), 228-249.

Davidoff, Leonore, "Where the Stranger Begins: The Question of Siblings in Historical Analysis," *World's Between: Historical Perspectives on Gender and Class* (Cambridge: Polity Press, 1995), 206-226.

De Albuquerque, Klaus and Sam Ruark, "Men Day Done: Are Women Really Ascendant in the African-Caribbean?" in *Caribbean Portraits. Essays on Gender Ideologies and Identities* ed. Christine Barrow (Kingston: Ian Randle Publishers, 1998),1-13.

Driver, G. "West Indian Families: An Anthropological Perspective" in *Families in Britain*, eds. R. N. Rapoport, M. P. Fogarty, and R. Rapoport, (London: Routledge and Kegan Paul, 1982),205-219.

Eriksen, Thomas Hylland "Indians in New Worlds: Mauritius and Trinidad," *Social and Economic Studies,* 1 (1992) www.caribvoice.org/CaribbeanDocuments/Indians.html .

Foner, Nancy "The Immigrant Family: Cultural Legacies and Cultural Changes" paper prepared for *Becoming American/America Becoming: International Migration to the United States Conference*, Social Science Research Council, Sanibel Island, Florida, January 1996.

Foner, Nancy "West Indians in New York City and London. A Comparative Analysis" in *Caribbean Life in New York City,*Constance Sutton and Elsa Chaney eds. 108-120

Foner, Nancy, "Towards a Comparative Perspective on Caribbean Migration" in *Caribbean Migration. Globalised Identities* ed. Mary Chamberlain (London: Routledge 1998), 47-62.

Forna, Aminatta, "The girl with three mothers" *Independent on Sunday* 8 June 1997.

Gardner, Richard and Podolefsky, Aaron "Some Further Considerations on West Indian Conjugal Patterns" *Ethnology*, 16 (1977), 299-308.

Giddens, Anthony, "Problems of Action and Structure" in Cassells, P (ed) The Giddens Reader, London, Macmillan 1993).

Gopaul Roanna and Morgan Paula *Spousal Violence. Spiralling patterns in Trinidad and Tobago,* proceedings of a Workshop (Kingston: Institute of Social and Economic Research, 1997)

Gordan, Sally W., "I go to 'Tanties': The Economic Significance of Child-Shifting in Antigua, West Indies," *Journal of Comparative Family Studies,* 18, 3 (1987):427-443.

Goulbourne, Harry, "The contribution of West Indian groups to British Politics" in *Black Politics in Britain* ed. Harry Goulbourne (Aldershot: Avebury, 1990),95-114.

Goulbourne, Harry, "The transnational character of Caribbean kinship in Britain" in *Changing Britain. Families and Households in the 1990s,* ed. Susan McRae (Oxford: Oxford University Press, 1999), 176-198.

Goveia, Elsa, "The West Indian Slave Laws of the Eighteenth Century" in *Caribbean Slave Society and Economy,* eds. Hilary Beckles and Verene Shepherd (Kingston: Ian Randle Publishers, 1991), 346-362.

Greenfield, Sidney "Culture-Historical and Structural-Functional Orientations and the Analysis of the West Indian Family" in *The Family in the Caribbean. Proceedings of the first Conference on the Family in the Caribbean* ed. Stanford N. Gerber (Rio Piedras: Institute of Caribbean Studies, 1968),15-27.

Greenfield, Sidney "Dominance, Focality and the Characterization of Domestic Groups: Some Refections on "Matrifocality" in the Caribbean" *The Family in the Caribbean. Proceedings of the Second Conference on the Family in the Caribbean"* ed. Stanford N. Gerber (Rio Piedras: Institute of Caribbean Studies, 1973) 31-49.

Greenfield, Sidney "Barbadians in the Brazilian Amazon," *Luso-Brazilian Review,* 20, 1 (1983), 4-64.

Griffith, Glyne, "Deconstructing nationalism: Henry Swanzy, Caribbean Voices and the development of West Indian literature," *Small Axe* 10, (2001),http://iupjournals.org/smallaxe/sm10.html.

Grosfoguel Ramon "Modes of incorporation: colonial Caribbean migrants in Western Europe and the United States" in *Caribbean Migration. Globalised Identiites*, ed. Mary Chamberlain (London: Routledge, 1998), 36-46

Hall, Catherine, "White Visions, Black Lives: the Free Villages of Jamaica," *History Workshop Journal* 36, (Autumn 1993), 100-132.

Hall, Stuart "Political Belonging in a World of Multiple Identities" in *Conceiving Cosmopolitanism. Theory, Context and Practice* eds. Steven Vertovec and Robin Cohen (Oxford: Oxford University Press, 2002),26-31.

Haraksingh, Kusha R., "Structure, Process and Indian Culture in Trinidad" in *After the Crossing, Immigrants and Minorities in Caribbean Creole Society* ed. Howard Johnson (London: Frank Cass, 1988)113-122.

Hintzen, Percy "Race and Creole Identity in the Caribbean" in *Questioning Creole. Creolisation Discourses in Caribbean Culture*, eds. Verene Shepherd and Glen L. Richards (Kingston: Ian Randle, 2002), 92-110.

Jayawardena, Chandra, "Family Organisation in Plantations in British Guiana" *International Journal of Comparative Sociology* 3 (1962), 43-64.

Johnson, Howard, "Barbadian Migrants in the Putumayo district of the Amazon, 1904-1911" in *Caribbean Migration, Globalised Identities* ed. Mary Chamberlain (London: Routledge, 1998), 177-187.

Kopijn, Yvette, "The Oral History Interview in a Cross-Cultural Setting" in *Narrative and Genre*, eds. M. Chamberlain and P. Thompson, Routledge Studies in Memory and Narrative (London: Routledge, 1998; New Brunswick:Transaction Publishers, 2004), 142-159.

Lazarus-Black, Mindie, "Why Women Take Men to Magistrate's Court: Caribbean Kinship Ideology" *Ethnography*, 30, 2 (1991):119-133.

LeFranc, Elsie, Don Simeon and Gail Wyatt "Family structures and domestic conflict in Jamaica" in *Caribbean Families in Britain and the Transatlantic World*. Goulbourne and Chamberlain eds. 188-203.

Lutz Helma "The legacy of migration: immigrant mothers and daughters and the process of intergenerational transmission" in *Caribbean Migration. Globalised Identiites*, ed. Mary Chamberlain (London: Routledge, 1998), 95-108

Macdonald John Stuart and Leatrice D. Macdonald, "Transformation of African and Indian Family Traditions in the Southern Caribbean" *Comparative Studies in Society and History*, 15 (1973), 171-198.

Mallet Rosemarie, Julian Leff, Dinesh Bhugra, Dong Pang and Jing Hua Zhao "Social Environment, Ethnicity and Schizophrenia: a Case-Control Study" *Social Psychiatry and Psychiatric Epidemiology*, 37:7 (July 2002), 329-335.

Manyoni, Joseph R. "Legitimacy and illegitimacy: misplaced polarities in Caribbean family studies" *Canadian Review of Sociology and Anthropology* 14:4 (1977), 417-427.

Marshall, Woodville K., "'We be wise to many more things: Blacks' Hopes and Expectations of Emancipation" in *Caribbean Freedom. Economy and Society from Emancipation to the Present*. Hilary Beckles and Verene Sheperd eds. (Kingston: Ian Randle Publishers, 1993), 12-20.

Mintz, Sidney, "The Caribbean as a Socio-Cultural Area" *Journal of World History*, 9, 4 (1966).

Mohammed, Patricia "Writing Gender into History. The Negotiation of Gender Relations among Indian Men and Women on Post-indenture Trinidad Society 1917-1947" in *Engendering History. Caribbean Women in Historical Perspective* eds. Verene

Shepherd, Bridget Brereton, Barbara Bailey (Kingston: Ian Randle Publishers, 1995), 20-47.

Mohammed, Patricia, "From Myth to Symbolism: The Definitions of Indian Femininity and Masculinity in Post-Indentureship Trinidad" in *Matikor. The Politics of Identity for Indo-Caribbean Women,* ed. Rosanne Kanhai (St. Augustine: University of the West Indies, School of Continuing Education, 1999), 62-102.

Mohammed, Patricia, "Ram and Sita: The Reconstitution of Gender Identities among Indians in Trinidad through Mythology" in *Caribbean Portraits. Essays on Gender Ideologies and Identities* ed. Christine Barrow (Kingston: Ian Randle Publishers, 1998), 391-413.

Mohammed, Patricia, "The 'Creolisation' of Indian Women In Trinidad" in *Questioning Creole. Creolisation Discourses in Caribbean Culture,* eds. Verene Shepherd and Glen L. Richards (Kingston: Ian Randle, 2002), 130-147.

Morrissey, Marietta, 'Explaining the Caribbean Family: Gender Ideologies and Gender Relations' in *Caribbean Portraits.Essays on Gender Ideologies and Identities* ed. Christine Barrow (Kingston: Ian Randle Publishers, 1998), 78-92.

Morrissey, Marietta "State influences on female-headed family formation in the twentieth century Caribbean" paper presented at 23rd Annual Conference of Association of Caribbean historians, Dominican Republic, March 1991.

Nettleford, Rex, "Implications for Caribbean Development" in John W. Nunley and Judith Bettelheim (eds) *Caribbean Festival Arts* (Seattle and London: St. Louis Art Museum in association with University of Washington Press, 1998), 183-198.

Nevadomsky, Joseph, "Changes in Hindu Institutions in an Alien Environment," *The Eastern Anthropologist,* 3:1 (1980):39-53.

Nevadomsky, Joseph, "Abandoning the Retentionist Model: Family and Marriage Change Among the East Indians in Rural Trinidad" *International Journal of Sociology of the Family,* 10 (1980), 181-198.

Niehoff, Arthur, "The survival of Hindu Institutions in an Alien Environment" *The Eastern Anthropologist,* 12:3 (1959): 171-187.

Olwig, Karen Fog, "Constructing Lives: migration narratives and life stories among Nevisians" in *Caribbean Migration. Globalised Identities* ed. Mary Chamberlain (London: Routledge 1998), 63-80.

Owen, David "Measuring the Caribbean Population of Great Britain" *Working Paper W1/95,* National Ethnic Minority Data Archive, Centre for Research in Ethnic Relations, University of Warwick, October 1995.

Owen, David "The family and household composition of the Caribbean population in Great Britain" *Working Paper W1/96,* National Ethnic Minority Data Archive, Centre for Research in Ethnic Relations, University of Warwick, January 1996.

Owen, David "Marital status and families in the Caribbean and Great Britain compared" *Working Paper W1/98,* National Ethnic Minority Data Archive, Centre for Research in Ethnic Relations, University of Warwick, March 1998.

Owen David "A profile of Caribbean households and families in Britain" in *Caribbean Families in Britain and the Trans-Atlantic World'* ed. Harry Goulbourne and Mary Chamberlain, 64-91.

Owen, David, *A demographic profile of African-Caribbean households and families in Great Britain*, paper presented to a conference on the African-Caribbean family and living arrangements in Britain and the Trans-Atlantic World, Cheltenham & Gloucester CHE, (27-29 March 1998).

Peach Ceri, "Trends in levels of Caribbean segregation 1961-1991" in *Caribbean Migration. Globalised Identities,* ed. Mary Chamberlain, 203-216.

Plaza Dwaine "Strategies and Strategizing. The struggle for upward mobility among university educated black Caribbean-born men in Canada" in *Caribbean Migration, Globalised Identities*, 248-266.

Plaza Dwaine "Migration and adjustment to Canada: pursuing the mobility dream 1990-1998," *Society for Caribbean Studies Annual Conference Papers*, ed. Sandra Courtman, Vol 3, 2002.

Plaza Dwaine, "Aging in Babylon: elderly Caribbeans in Britain" in *Caribbean Families in Britain and the Trans-Atlantic World*, eds. Harry Goulbourne and Mary Chamberlain. 219-233.

Plaza, Dwaine, "Frequent Flyer Grannies," paper presented to the Caribbean Studies Association, (1996).

Portelli Alessandro, "Uchronic Dreams" in Raphael Samuel and Paul Thompson T*he Myths We Live By* (London: Routledge, 1990), 143-160.

Portelli, Alessandro, "Oral History as Genre" in *Narrative and Genre* eds. Mary Chamberlain and Paul Thompson, Routledge Studies in Memory and Narrative (London: Routledge, 1998), 23-45.

Portelli, Alissandro, "The Massacre at the Fosse Ardeatine: history, myth, ritual and symbol" in *Contested Pasts*, eds. Katharine Hodgkin and Susannah Radstone, Routledge Studies in Memory and Narrative (London: Routledge 2003), 29-41.

Portelli, Alissandro, 'What makes oral history different?' in *The Oral History Reader*, ed. R. Perks and A. Thomson (London: Routledge 1998), 63-74.

Portes, Alejandro, Luis E. Guarnizo and Patricia Landolt. "The study of transnationalism: pitfalls and promises of an emergent research field" *Ethnic and Racial Studies* 22, 2, (1999), 217-237.

Powell, Dorian, "Caribbean Women and their response to Familial Experiences," *Social and Economic Studies*, 35:2 (1986), 83-130.

Reddock, Rodha, "Indian Women and Indentureship in Trinidad and Tobago 1845-1917" in *Caribbean Freedom. Economy and Society from Emancipation to the Present eds.* Hilary Beckles and Verene Shepherd (Kingston: Ian Randle Publishers, 1993), 225-237.

Reynolds Tracey "Caribbean fathers in family lives in Britain," in *Caribbean Families in Britain and the Trans-Atlantic World*, eds. Harry Goulbourne and Mary Chamberlain.133-153.

Roberts, George W., "Emigration from the Island of Barbados," *Social and Economic Studies*, 4, 3, (1955).

Robotham, Don, "Transnationalism in the Caribbean: formal and informal," AES distinguished lecture *American Ethnologist* 25,2, (1996),307-321.

Rubenstein, Hymie "Conjugal behavior and parental role flexibility in an Afro-Caribbean village" *Canadian Review of Sociology and Anthropology* 17:4 (1980), 330-337.

Rubenstein, Hymie "Caribbean Family and Household Organization: Some Conceptual Clarifications" *Journal of Comparative Family Studies*, 14:3 (1983), 283-298.

Scott, David "Modernity that Predated the Modern: Sidney Mintz's Caribbean," *History Workshop* 58 (Autumn 2004), 196-215.

Segal A. "The Caribbean Exodus in a Global Context: Comparative Migration Experiences" in *The Caribbean Exodus* ed. B. Levine (New York: Praeger,1987).

Sheller, Mimi, "Quasheba, Mother, Queen: Black Women's Public Leadership and Political Protest in Post-Emancipation Jamaica, 1834-1865," *Slavery and Abolition*, 19,3, (1998), 90-117.

Shepherd, Verene, "Indians, Jamaica and the Emergence of a Modern Migration Culture" in *Caribbean Migration. Globalised Identities* ed. Mary Chamberlain (London: Routledge, 1998), 165-176.

Smith, Raymond T. "The family and the Modern World System: Some Observations from the Caribbean" *Journal of Family History* 3:4 (1978), 337-360.
Soto, Isa Maria, "West Indian Child Fostering: Its Role in Migrant Exchanges" in *Caribbean Life in New York City: Sociocultural Dimensions* eds. Constance R. Sutton and Elsa M. Chaney (New York: Center for Migration Studies of New York Inc.1994), 121-137.
St. Barnard, Godfrey "Demographic characteristics of families and living arrangements in the Commonwealth Caribbean" in *Caribbean Families in Britain and the Transatlantic World* eds. Harry Goulbourne and Mary Chamberlain (London: Macmillan, 2001), 92-116.
St. Bernard, Godfrey, *Demographic Characteristics of Family and Living Arrangements in the Commonwealth African-Caribbean*, paper presented to a conference on the African-Caribbean family and living arrangements in Britain and the Trans-Atlantic World, Cheltenham & Gloucester CHE (27-29 March 1998).
Steedman, Carolyn "Enforced Narratives: stories of another self" in *Feminism and Autobiography* eds. Tessa Cosslett, Celia Lury and Penny Summerfield (London: Routledge 2000), 25-39.
Sunday Express, 13 August 1995,1.
Sutton, Constance "Motherhood is Powerful: Embodied Knowledge from Evolving Field-Based Experiences," *Anthropology and Humanism* 23:2 (1998), 143-4.
Sutton, Constance "Celebrating Ourselves: Keeping Kin Connections Alive. Family Reunions in the Afro-Caribbean Diaspora." Gender and Transnational Families Conference, Amsterdam, May/June (2002.).
Sutton, Constance and Susan Makiesky Barrow "Migration and West Indian Racial and Ethnic Consciousness" in *Caribbean Life in New York City: Sociocultural Dimensions* ed. Constance R. Sutton and Elsa M. Chaney (New York: Center for Migration Studies of New York Inc.,1994).
Sutton, Constance Sutton "Celebrating ourselves:the family reunion rituals of African Caribbean Transnational Families," *Global Networks. A Journal of Transnational Affairs*, 4, 3 (2004),243-259.
Sutton, Constance. Forward to Kerns,*Women and the Ancestors. Black Carib Kinship and Ritual*, (Urbana and Chicago: University of Illinois Press1997 [1983]), ix-xv.
Thompson, Paul and Elaine Bauer, 'Recapturing Distant Caribbean Childhoods and Communities: The Shaping of Memory in the Testimonies of Jamaican Migrants in Britain and North America' paper presented at the *Annual Conference of the Association of Caribbean Historians*, Trinidad, (2001).
Bauer, Elaine and Paul Thompson "'She's always the person with a very global vision': The Gender Dynamics of Migration, Narrative Interpretation and the Case of Jamaican Transnational Families" *Gender and History* 16:2 (2004), 334-375
Thompson, Paul and Elaine Bauer "Recapturing Distant Caribbean Childhoods and Communities: The Shaping of Memory in the Testimonies of Jamaican Migrants in Britain and America" *Oral History* 30:2 (2002) 49-59
Thompson, Paul and Elaine Bauer "Jamaican Transnational Families: Points of Pain and Sources of Resilience" *Wadapagei: A Journal of the Caribbean and its Diaspora* (Summer/Fall 2002), 1-37.
Trotman, David, "Women and Crime in Late Nineteenth Century Trinidad" *Caribbean Quarterly*, 30:3 & 4 (1984),60-72.
Trouillot, Michel-Rolfe, "The Caribbean Region: An Open Frontier in Anthropological Theory," *Annual Review of Anthropology*, 21 (1992), 19-42.
Vertovec, Steven, 'Religion and Ethnic Ideology: the Hindu youth movement in Trinidad, *Ethnic and Racial Studies'*, 13:2 (1990), 225-249.

Vertovec, Steven "Indo-Caribbean Experience in Britain: Overlooked, Miscategorized, Misunderstood" in *Inside Babylon* eds. Winston James and Clive Harris (London: Verso, 1993), 165-178.
Wekker, Gloria "One Finger Does Not Drink Okra Soup: Afro-Surinamese Women and Critical Agency" in *Feminist Genealogies, Colonial Legacies, Democratic Futures*, eds. M. Jacqui Alexander and C. Talpade Mohanty (London/New York: Routledge 1997), 330-352.
Wellings Kaye and Jane Wadsworth, "Family influences on teenage fertility" in *Changing Britain. Families and Households in the 1990s* ed. Susan McRae (Oxford: Oxford University Press, 1999), 319-333.
Whitehead, Tony "Residence, Kinship and Mating as Survival Strategies: A West Indian Example" *Journal of Marriage and the Family*, November (1978), 817-827.
Whylie, Marjorie and Maureen Warner-Lewis, "Characteristics of Maroon Music from Jamaica and Suriname" in *Maroon Heritage. Archaeological, Ethnographic and Historical Perspectives,* ed. E. Kofi Agorsah (Kingston: University of the West Indies, Canoe Press,1994), 139-148.
Wilson, Peter "Reputation and Respectability: A Suggestion for Caribbean Ethnology" *Man* 4, March (1969), 70-84.
Young, Virginia "Household Structure in a West Indian Society" *Social and Economic Studies* 39:3 (1990), 147-177.

Internet

www.statistics.gov.uk/census
www.library.uu.nl/wesp/populstat/Americas/guyanag.htm
www.caribvoice.org/Caribbean Documents/Indians.html

Index

Africa, Southern 51
African(s) 19, 20, 22, 51- 55, 71, 89, 177
Africanism 47
African American 32, 56
African philosophy 9
African-Caribbean community 69, 214, 216, 218
African-Caribbean politics 187
Anansi (Nancy) 51, 59, 159
Ancestors, 24, 120, 127, 137
Anderson, John 22, 23, 54
Antigua 26
Apprenticeship 186
Arya Samaj 189
Aruba 90, 91
Austria 26
Aymer, Paula 92

Bahamas 205
Bangladeshi community 216
Barbados 3, 23, 24, 25, 26, 29, 30, 50, 53, 54, 66, 208
Barber, Karin 51, 59
Barrow, Jocelyn 4
Basch, Linda 92
Bauer, Elaine 92
Bavaria 26
Beckford, George 219
Beckles, Hilary McD. 89
Belgium 26
Belize 57
Benjamin, Walter 48, 154
Besson, Jean 69
Beveridge, William 33
Bhugra, Dinesh 219
Birmingham 83
Bourdieu, Pierre 125
Brand, Dionne 57
Brathwaite, Edward Kamau 46, 55
Brazil 53, 89
Bridges, Rev. George Wilson 20
Brisbane, Sir Charles 23

Britain 6, 12, 13, 30, 69, 94, 95, 170, 190, 216, 218, 221
British Guiana 186
British Rail 107
Brixton riots 1981 4
Brodber, Erna 58, 121, 128, 136, 147
Brodber, Rosina Wiltshire 91
Bryceson, Deborah 91, 93
Burnham, Forbes 217

Calypso 52, 54
Canada 3, 90, 99, 104,107, 110, 218
Canadian Presbyterian 188, 189, 197, 203
Capital
   cultural 84, 215;
   human 124
   symbolic 125, 127
Carriacou 52, 59
Caste 189
   endogamy 189, 190
Cavarera, Adriana 9
Cayman Islands 105
Census:
   1844 West Indies 25, 28
   1871 Barbados 29
   891 Jamaica 29
   1921 Trinidad 29
   1921 Barbados 30
   943 Jamaica 30, 33
   1946 West Indian 30, 31
   1990 Barbados 65
   1991 UK 4, 84
   991 Trinidad and Tobago 207
Chamoiseau, Patrick 59
Chanfrault-Duchet, Marie-Françoise 47
Changing Britain 167
Childhood 141, 142, 163, 168
   childhood memories 142
Child/children
   abuse 148, 216, 217
   child rearing 141-147, 149, 162

child-shifting 119, 123-124, 128, 131-132, 136, 141, 176
child "buying" 178
Chinese 89
Christian(s) 74, 76, 81, 189, 193, 198
Christianity 28, 56, 189, 198, 203
Clark, Gracia 67
Clarke, Edith 34, 35, 69, 81
Cohabitation 23, 25, 32
Colonial authorities 186, 214
Colonial Office 89
Colonial Social Science Research Council 35
Colthurst, John 20, 25
Common-law unions 30
Community 55, 101, 142-143, 217
Communitarian 55, 142, 147, 214
Concubinage 25, 33, 82
Conjugal 35, 57, 168
Conjugal relationships 63
Consanguinity 35, 57, 83, 94, 111
Consanguineal kin 130
Conway, Denis 92
Coventry 83
Craig James, Susan 94, 171
Creole 21, 22, 36, 47, 60, 186, 187, 202, 214
Creole English 46, 54
Creolize/creolization 11, 13, 51, 94, 186, 208, 214- 215
Cuba 89, 99, 169, 172
Cultural template(s) 13, 48, 55, 59, 60
Curaçao 90, 91

Davidoff, Leonore 167, 168
Davidson, Lewis 33
Dialectical 12
Diaspora 60, 163
Dickson, William 22
Discrimination 218, 219
Dollard, John 33
Domestic violence 216, 217
Dominican Republic 89
Douglass, Lisa 36
Driver, G. 4
Drugs 216
DuBois, W.E. 3, 71

Edwards, Bryan 20, 54
Emancipation 25, 26, 27, 28, 36, 53
England 26, 98,133, 157, 178
Erikson, Thomas 187, 208

Europe 110
European(ism) 19, 47, 51, 71, 74, 89, 221
European Romantic tradition 9
Exogamy 23, 219

Family, families 26, 57, 64, 84, 121, 167, 172, 214, 217
    African-Caribbean 3, 4, 11, 14, 64, 120, 123, 124, 126-127, 167, 185, 207, 213 - 214, 216, 219, 220, 221
    and breakdown 5
    Christian 33, 77
    and disadvantage 216
    close[ness] 72, 75, 81-82, 95, 99, 110, 135, 214
    Companionate 33
    deviancy 35
    Disintegrate 33
    dynamic 13, 75, 111
    ethos 13
    extended 51, 190
    ideology 27, 64
    maternal/matrifocal 34, 35, 57
    memory 11, 13, 137, 167
    network(s) 7, 136, 152, 213
    neighbourhood 179
    order 27
    reconstitution 27
    reunion 26, 111
    transnational 93, 107, 109, 111, 169, 171
    values 64, 99, 214
Family as metaphor 6, 101, 126, 142, 167, 174, 203
Family as model 6, 180, 203
Fathers 58, 60, 146-147, 149
    absence 148, 156
    male marginality 34
    paternal involvement 35
    paternal line 128-129
    paternal grandparents 130, 136
    patriarchal 82, 189
Fog Olwig, Karen 92
Foner, Nancy 94
Foot, Sir Hugh 35
Fostering 4
Fouron, George 92
France 26
Frazier, Franklin 32, 33, 34
Frontiering 93

Froude, James A. 28
Garifuna 57
Gates, Henry Louis 56
Geertz, Clifford 7
Gellner, Ernst 45
Gender 36, 82, 149, 168, 189
Gender ideology 27
Genre/s 10, 47, 48, 55, 142
Germany 104, 152
Giddens, Anthony 8, 70, 71
Glick Schiller, Nina 92, 93
Globalization 91, 92, 112
Gorell Barnes, Gillian 157
Goulbourne, Harry 92
Grandfather(s) 14, 129
Grandmother(s) 14, 35, 56, 57, 76, 119-122, 125, 127-132, 137, 219
Grandparent(s) 14, 74, 119-120, 130, 137
Grele, Ron 8
Grenada 53
Guatamala 89
Guyana 217

Halbwachs, Maurice 6
Haraksingh, Kusha 187
Harvey, Thomas 24, 54
Henriques, Fernando 34, 35, 120, 123
Herskovits, Melville 32, 71
Higman, Barry 5, 22
Hindu 29, 176, 189, 190, 195, 197, 198, 203, 205
Honduras 24, 89
Household 34-35, 82, 84, 123, 124, 176
    extended 191, 208
    female headed 4, 69, 124
    patriarchal 188

Identity(ies) 36, 84, 95, 110, 171, 185, 190, 203, 215
Illegitimacy 29, 30, 32, 73
Illegitimate 26
Illegitimate children 25
Immigration Act 90
Indentureship 185, 186
Indentured labourer(s)/servant(s) 186, 188, 189, 203, 214
Independence:
    India 186
    Trinidad 190, 208
    West Indies 35, 36, 216
India 77, 80, 100, 186, 187, 189, 191, 197, 200, 202, 215

Indian(s) 51, 89, 186
Indianism 47
East Indian(s) 29, 176, 177, 185, 187, 188, 190
    East Indian families 190
Indo-Caribbean
    families 14, 185, 191, 214
    community(ies) 186
    identity 207
Indo-Trinidadian 214
Institutional racism 219
Islam 202

Jamaica 3, 22, 23, 29, 36, 53, 110, 217
Jamaican culture 151
Jamaica Welfare Ltd 35
Japan 96, 110
Jews 89

Kerns, Virginia 57
Kin 4, 26, 74, 84, 109, 147, 159, 179, 196, 213- 214, 219;
    fictive 4, 179, 180;
    as metaphor or model 24, 126, 169
Kinship 6, 23, 26, 34, 36, 56, 57, 60, 75, 84, 111, 126, 137, 167, 190
    group 84;
    network(s) 5, 24, 75, 99, 120, 126, 129, 135, 171, 207, 220
    structures 84
    support 130
Kincaid, Jamaica 58
Klass, Morton 190
Kristeva, Julia 58

Lamming, George 6
Language 45- 6, 48- 49
Lawrence, Stephen 219
Lebanese 89
Lefranc, Elsie 148
Leydesdorff, Selma 91
Lewis, Monk 24
Liberia 51
Life story/stories 47
Lineage(s) 5, 6, 22, 56- 60, 72, 73, 83, 94, 111, 121, 127, 213
London 83, 98, 220
London Development Agency 218
Lone parent(ing) 216, 220
Long, Edward 20, 24, 53
Low educational achievement 216

Macpherson Report 218
Makiesky, Susan Barrow 92
Malinowski, Bronislaw 35
Manley, Michael 217
Manley, Norman 35
Maroon communities 53
Marriage 4, 21, 25, 30, 32, 70, 72, 76, 77, 82
   Christian 22, 23, 73
   East Indian 177, 191, 207
   rate 29
Marshall, Woodville 27
Matrifocal/matrifocality 57
McDaniel, Lorna 53, 56, 59, 60
McDonald, Roderick 54
McRae, Susan 92
Memory(ies) 8, 10, 45, 48, 49, 141, 186, 194, 213
   popular 49
   uchronic 49
Metropolitan Police 218, 219
Migration 7, 13, 36, 66, 89, 90- 91, 94, 95, 110-111, 137, 145, 146, 167, 217;
   cultures 91
   networks 50, 170, 213
   return 95
   returning nationals 109, 220
   traditions 91
Mintz, Sidney 19, 37, 51, 67, 96
Missionary(ies) 27, 28, 186, 188
Modood, Tariq 74
Mohammed, Patricia 190, 208
Monserrat 107
Morton, Sarah 188
Moslem 29, 189, 190, 191, 192, 193, 194, 202
Mothers 56
   common law 30
   lone mothers 219, 220
   married 30
   single 30
   single parent 5, 215, 216
   mother headed households 5, 36, 84, 215, 216
   motherhood 59, 67, 76
   co-mothering 176
Moyne, Lord 31, 32
Mozambique 52

Narrative(s) 10, 14, 46, 52, 55, 56, 58, 59, 72, 96, 108, 110, 112, 214

counter narrative 75
cultural narrative 47
personal narrative 47
Nettleford, Rex 53
Nevadomsky, Joseph 190
Nicaragua 89
Nugent, Lady Maria 21

Oral history/histories 10, 47, 48
Owen, David 83

Pakistani community 216
Pan-Caribbean organizations 170
Panama 89, 69, 172
Parang 175
Partner 65, 133, 149
Patriarchal 58, 82
Patrilineal 58
Patterson, Orlando 9, 34
Peach, Ceri 90, 94, 219
Pentecostal church(es) 77
Plummer, Ken 7
Portelli, Alessandro 47, 49
Portes, Alejandro 92
Portuguese 89
Praisesong 51, 52, 55, 56, 59, 60
Price, Richard 67, 96
Prussia 26

Queen Victoria 24

Racism 134, 219
Radcliffe Brown, Alfred 9
Reddock, Rhodha 188
Relativising 93
Remembering 12
Remittances 90, 133, 169, 172, 203, 219;
   cultural 180
Rohlehr, Gordon 52, 54
Robotham, Don 94
Roman Catholic 205
Royal Commission 1945 31
Riots 6, 28, 31
Rousseau, Jean-Jacques 50

St. Bernard, Godfrey 207
St. Christopher 25
St. Lucia 90
St. Vincent 23, 110
Salmon, Jon 5
Samuel, Raphael 50

Sapir, Edward 46
Scarman, Lord 4
Schomburgk, Sir Robert 26
Second World War 90
Select Committee 1842 25, 26, 27
Sells, William 22, 23
Sexual immorality 28,
Sexual morality 70
Sexual relations 21, 23
Sheller, Mimi 28
Siblings 14, 97, 144, 167-168, 169, 171-174, 194
  membership 172
  relationship 167-169, 179
  rivalry 169
  as metaphor 172
Sierra Leone 24
Simey, Thomas 32, 33, 34
Slavery 20, 34, 36, 52, 56, 216
Slaves, 23, 28, 54, 186, 187, 214
  families 22
  marriage 22
  revolt 1816 24
  women 203
Smith, M.G. 36
Smith, Raymond T. 4, 20, 34, 35, 36, 60
Smith, Samuel 26
Social disadvantage 216
Social exclusion 219, 220
Speechify 54
Stockdale, Sir Frank 30, 32, 215
Strauss, Levi 8
"Structure of feeling" 12
Sturge, Joseph 24, 54
Subjectivities 7, 8
Sunday Express 5
Suriname 53
Sutton, Constance 15, 57, 91, 111, 127, 217
Sweden 26
Syrians 89

Szanton Blanc, Christine 92

Tate and Lyle 198
Thistlewood, Thomas 21
Thomas Hope, Elizabeth 92
Thompson, Paul 92
Titmuss, Richard 33
Tonkin, Elizabeth 47, 48, 51
Transnational (ism), 11, 91- 94, 96, 107, 110, 112,
Transnationally 167
Transnational imagination 111
Trinidad (and Tobago) 3, 26, 29, 55, 90, 186-189, 208
Unemployment 216, 217, 219
United Kingdom 90, 102, 219
United States of America (USA) 3, 89, 90, 91, 94, 103,123, 158,172, 176, 216, 218, 219
Vail, Leroy 51, 52
Venezuela 89, 174, 176
Virgin Islands 105
Vuorella, Ulla 91, 93

Warner Lewis, Maureen 46, 53, 71
Waters, Mary 218
Wekker, Gloria 58
West Indies 52, 57, 68, 149
West Indian
  colonies 21
  colonial government 29
  Federation 35
  nationhood 7
  nationalism 163
Welfare Fund 32
White, Landeg 51, 52
Whorf, Benjamin Lee 46
Williams, Raymond 12
Wolverhampton 83

Yoruba 51, 52, 53, 55, 57, 59, 127